A VOICE FOR THE THEATRE

A Voice for the Theatre

HARRY HILL

Concordia University, Montreal

with

Robert Barton, Consulting Editor

University of Oregon

HOLT, RINEHART AND WINSTON

New York   Chicago   San Francisco   Philadelphia
Montreal   Toronto   London   Sydney
Tokyo   Mexico City   Rio de Janeiro   Madrid

To the memory of my Mother and Father

Library of Congress Cataloging in Publication Data

Hill, Harry.
  A Voice for the Theatre.

  Bibliography: p. 259
  Includes index.
  1. Acting. 2. Voice. I. Barton, Robert
II. Title.
PN2061.H54 1985   792/.028   84–15780

ISBN 0-03-063636-1

Copyright ©1985 by CBS College Publishing
Address correspondence to:
383 Madison Avenue
New York, N.Y. 10017
All rights reserved
Printed in the United States of America
Published simultaneously in Canada
5 6 7 8   038   9 8 7 6 5 4 3 2 1

CBS COLLEGE PUBLISHING
Holt, Rinehart and Winston
The Dryden Press
Saunders College Publishing

Preface

A Voice for the Theatre has been written slowly, over years of acting and teaching. It is grounded in the conviction that what young professional and student actors need is a text that addresses the main points of "voice production" while keeping an alert eye and ear on lines actors actually say. The actor's voice is an instrument whose beauty is only truly useful when conveying meaning; this book attempts to combine emotion and intellect in the same way as actors have to do.

This book is for all students of acting. It goes beyond the development of the instrument to the development of a sensitive and technical response to the challenges of acting: What to do when faced with a script—how character can be built from the very shapes of the words, lines, sentences, exclamations and so on, that make up the role. It includes exercises specifically to help projection, agility, and control, all with abundant checklists and advice. So that the student does not feel alone in whatever inadequacies exist in talent or application, I have included interviews with respected professionals from different kinds of theatre (TV, Broadway, repertory, movies) to add to the immediacy of the book and to the learning experience it encourages.

I have taken care in the Introduction to explain exactly how the book may be used at any level of theatre training—as a basic text, a reference text, or even as an "oral interpretation" text. The book is intended to enrich the training received by student actors in theatre schools, colleges, and universities. The book does not concentrate on diaphragm, head tones, or sensitivity groups, but on artistic concentration itself. I hope actors already in the profession will also find its analyses and encouragement helpful.

ACKNOWLEDGMENTS

Without the insistently intelligent critical suggestions of Robert Barton, the book would not have whatever clarity and progressiveness it has, and without those long letters and telephone calls between Montreal and the Drama Department of the University of Oregon in Eugene, I could not have produced a satisfactory offering. The warm-up exercises are Robert Barton's.

Susan Miller of the University of Illinois and Marshall Cassady of San Diego State University also contributed a great deal through perceptive and thorough comments. For clarity and warmth in a research assistant, it would be hard to find anyone better than Fred Enns; it would also be hard to find as quick and sensitive a manuscript typist as Jennifer Cook of the Centaur Theatre in Montreal. Also to be thanked is Richard Thompson of Concordia University, along with Msgr. Russell Breen and Donat Taddeo, Vice-Rector and Dean, for encouragement. John Miller has proofread the book at many stages and Ian Lindsay helped carefully with the index. Anne Boynton-Trigg of Holt, Rinehart and Winston was a steadying hand during the preparation of the final manuscript; also at Holt, Lisa Owens, Jackie Fleischer, and Biodun Iginla (surely the most thoughtful of manuscript editors), have offered calm and thorough advice throughout the production process. From 1979–83 the support of T. G. O'Connor provided the courage without which I could not have written the book.

HARRY HILL

Montreal, 1984

Contents

2. Breath Control, Voice Production, Projection, and Agility

3. Attaining and Preserving an Ear: Inflection, Sound, and Rhythm

4. Comprehending the Script and Absorbing the Lines: Speech Patterns, Focus, and Emphasis

5. Absorbing the Lines: Scene Study and Exercises

6. What Actors Say About Vocal Craft   227

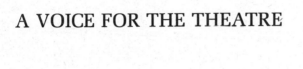

A VOICE FOR THE THEATRE

Introduction

THE VOICE IS A MEMBER
OF A LIVING GROUP

This is a book about the most exciting profession in the world; it is also about how you can play the most beautiful, persuasive, and affecting instrument of all: the human voice. The theatre is a collaborative art, and actors are collaborative people; in fact, they are my favorite people. Actors are vulnerable, cultured, well-read, warm, nervous, disciplined, and magnificently human. Their job is very difficult: They cannot delegate authority, cannot absent themselves from work, and cannot work without collaboration. Acting is a group act.

Actually, actors are group people who have to collaborate with themselves, their roles, and parts of themselves. Body and voice have to move each other with the same harmony that the actor has when moving and speaking with others. These facts make an actor's job both exciting and difficult.

I wrote this book because, as an actor, I have seen many problems young performers have when confronted with an audition, a part, a complicated speech, lines that don't seem to "read" properly, a head cold, inadequate warm-up, fear of projection in a big theatre, character traits, different patterns of speech, verse, scripts translated from another language, pacing and pausing, and the need for inflection. When a director says "This is *boring*, and I don't *believe* it!" what do you do? When you can feel the part inside yourself but people complain that it is not coming across, what do you do? When you have to cry or explode on stage, what do you do when you do not feel like it? This book could really be titled *What To Do with Your Voice?*, but the reason I have called it *A Voice for the Theatre* is to answer the question in that first title. My book is specifically about you as a person of the theatre. Listen to what the great modern classical actor Douglas Campbell says in an interview printed in full at the end of this book:

> An actor needs range. There are a lot of vocal exercises about that don't seem to me to increase an actor's range much. Some training goes off in the psychic research direction: finding your center. That is very good up to a point, you know; it's good for people to have a consciousness of the apparatus that relates to the erotic and that kind of thing . . . but I think you ought to know about singing a song just as well. It's the audience's soul we want to get to, not mine! It's my job to stimulate and keep myself sharpened and perceptive, but not to protect myself, not to protect *my* soul. Speaking is a part of the imagination, and unless you really have the sense of what you're speaking, where you're speaking, and whom you're speaking to, you are not going to be heard, no matter how you produce your voice.

Douglas Campbell has concern for the script and for the audience. If you share this concern you will understand my book and benefit from it, and you will arrive at a point very near the "truth."

Geraldine Page takes the point a stage further and explains most of the reason for my writing this book:

> I want to get the audience involved in what I'm saying rather than with the technique—they shouldn't notice just the technique. It's the difference between (in music) listening to someone play with great technique in order to display it and someone letting themselves be creative. I'm speaking, remember, about artists who *have* technique. Quite a few orchestras now seem to be so preoccupied with technique that they don't realise the beauty of the music. They sometimes play as fast as they can. Actors too. You need to be able to play both fast and slow, "be technical" and "feel," and you don't learn one first. That's the controversy right now in the theatre and in the theatre schools. If you learn to be truthful first but not to be heard, it's terribly hard to learn later to be heard. And if you learn to be heard first of all but don't pay attention to speaking truthfully it's terribly hard to lose that way of speaking later and learn to speak truthfully. Now in some schools they are working on developing both at the same time.

What my book sets out to do is combine truth and technique. The book is about you, your voice, and the theatre you are preparing to use your voice for. I mean not just use it in the theatre but use it *for* the theatre. Hence my choice of *A Voice for the Theatre* as a title. Sometimes you can be bored doing voice exercises, thinking you are going nowhere, slowly. You're unable to apply your voice classes to a performance you suddenly find yourself in, when, wearing a suit of armor, you are required to scream while swinging upside down from a trapeze and then land on your feet and exhort a group of a hundred soldiers to action in a ten-minute speech you deliver while running around the stage on high heels and eating a half dozen bananas. Don't be discouraged. You'll need vocal strength.

Once I played Cocky in *The Roar of the Grease-paint, The Smell of the Crowd*, a part requiring gymnastics, singing, and acting. Act One ends with the great song "Who Can I Turn To?" The choreographer—Walter Burgess—had me hanging by the ankles from high up on a ladder for the final high note of "if you . . . turn . . . away." It was possible to do this mainly because of the varied training I had received as a choirboy and as a young actor. I had been used to seemingly endless hours of discipline, boring, tedious, mind-numbing repetition of phrases and notes. As you use this book, some parts of eventual excellence and expertise will set firmly in your heart and mind; however, your creative urges will be satisfied only by work, work, work.

WORK, WORK, WORK

Morris Carnovsky—a greatly revered American actor most famous for his King Lear—once gave a celebrated lecture to actors; the following is part of the lecture that influenced me so much when I first read it that I can't help sharing it:

> In the twenties, when I first came to New York . . . it was a field day for every sort of exhibitionism, dominated by "stars" who were expected to be exhibitionists par excellence. It was competition not so much of living or cultural values as of showmanship. The lily of truth was often unrecognizable for the gilding that weighed it down. [He goes on to mention names . . .] If the student of acting took these as his models, he was more likely to absorb their foibles and eccentricities than the magnificence of their *idea*. To talk and walk brightly with crisp "stylish" diction in the hectic manner of the day, this was what they'd learned in "school"— that is, by observation, stock, and the threat of losing their job. They

were often pathetically self-conscious about this "technique" of theirs. A very good actor I knew and admired had a singular trick of elongating vowel sounds in the most unlikely places—monosyllables like "if," "as," "but," particularly "but." "B-u-ut," he would say, "Bu-u-ut screw your courage to the sticking point a-a-and we'll not fail," or "i-i-if you be-e-e," etc. I asked him about it once and he answered promptly and with pride, "Why, that's my sostenuto *but!*"

Now, you must not think because I describe these interesting phenomena as quirks that I dismiss them entirely as unworthy of the craft of acting or that I regard a pleasant, fastidious, and crisp manner of speech and presence as a sign of decadence. In our last decade poor Marlon Brando has precipitated upon his head the reputation and credit for having restored the Yahoo to his rightful place in society, but we need not admire him the less for that. All innovators must take their chances. And there is generally a deeper reason for odd behavior, stemming from something that is striving to be said. But the actors of the twenties often seemed to be all dressed up with no place to go.

There was no one around to utter a warning or to say: "Be of good cheer." At last you are about to receive a vessel for your talents. Not a knighthood nor an empty citation, nor a cigar banded with your name. No champagne banquets with speeches to inflate your vanity and encourage you in your worst professional habits. No fan clubs milling about the stage door and shouting your name in the worn, ironic streets. Not these things, but a place where your actor's nature will be understood and used! Through work, through discipline, through struggle, through proper organization, to the end that you will inherit the only thing worth having—namely, your Self.

The way he concludes is wonderful, emphasizing the achievement of finding—through effort—the self. You see, in the theatre, you can only be yourself when you have filtered the cream of experience into yourself. When you read the interviews with actors and actresses at the end of this book, you will find that the actor must not only know his own art but also sharpen his perceptions by appreciating the other arts. If you are young or even middle-aged or old, various roles you are called upon to act in plays are not necessarily those you might have experienced. The offering of experiences is what all the arts are for. The arts formulate experience for us, so that through tragedy, comedy, history, sculpture, color, lines, musical harmony and discord, we can know about and appreciate and even understand most of the richness of human life.

Earlier in his lecture, Morris Carnovsky quoted Stanislavski, the seminal practical theatrical thinker of the last hundred years. Stanislavski was not a mere psychiatrist of the theatre; he was also a superb technician who sought to harmonize truth and beauty in a theatrical whole. He knew that the combination of the knowledge of human nature and disciplined technique produced truth. Listen to what Morris Carnovsky quotes from Stanislavski and how he comments on it:

> On reading [Stanislavski's *My Life in Art*] recently, I was struck again and again by the quantity of things that we already take for granted about ourselves as actors. "But of course!" we say, "how obvious!" It is the case of Columbus' egg—very clear, once it's been demonstrated.
>
> Stanislavski said: "Music helped me to solve many problems that had been racking my brain and it convinced me that an actor should know how to speak . . . isn't it strange that I had to live almost sixty years *before I felt with all my being, it convinced me,* this simple and well-known truth, a truth that most actors do not know?" [Now he goes on to remind us of what the French artist Degas said.] "If you have a hundred thousand francs' worth of skill, spend another five sous to buy more."
>
> Stanislavski said: "The main difference between the art of the actor and all other arts is that other artists may create whenever they are inspired. The stage artist, however, must be the master of his own inspiration and *must know how to call it forth at the time announced on the theatre's posters; this is the chief secret of our art.* Without this, the most perfect technique, the greatest gifts, are powerless."
>
> It's not a general matter of "work to be done," but of concrete tasks, consciously undertaken and mastered by repetition. They are the irreducible minimum of our business. Specific things done, moment to moment. Grasp this, and at once there's a clearing of the decks—all reliance on so-called actors' instinct, inspiration, divine fire, and such-like dangerous fantasies must go. These things . . . are the consequence, not the shapers, of action.

HOW PEOPLE THINK OF THE JOB WE HAVE: THE "SILVER TICKET"

Although actors have sometimes been regarded and treated with contempt by those in other—perhaps more lucrative—professions or more "honest" trades not involving make-believe, they have nevertheless always received approbation based on amazement and gratitude, which sometimes borders, as we all know, on worship and even fetish. Whether they like it or not, actors are a breed apart.

Fifteen years after the Declaration of Independence in the United States, Mozart died, ending a short life of intense production and inspiration. His librettist for *Cosi Fan Tutte* and *Don Giovanni* was Lorenzo Da Ponte, who, before he came to the United States and became involved in the founding of the opera in New York, was financial manager of the King's Theatre in the Haymarket, London (now known simply as the Haymarket Theatre). As a way of raising money for the theatre, which produced operas and concerts as well as legitimate plays, Da Ponte persuaded the owner, William Taylor, to issue long-term admission tickets. The price of the ticket was £150 sterling—tremendous at a time when the average *per capita* income was less than £20 a year.

The respect in which the theatre was held can be seen in the first few lines of the ticket:

This Indenture made the first day of November in the thirty-seventh Year of the Reign of our Sovereign Lord George the Third by the Grace of God of Great Britain France and Ireland King Defender of the Faith and so forth And in the Year of our Lord One thousand seven hundred and ninety six. BETWEEN William Taylor of the Haymarket Westminster Esquire of the one part and Frederick Walsh of Fludyer Street Westminster Esquire of the other part. WHEREAS the said William Taylor for some time past hath been and now is the sole proprietor or owner of the Opera House or Theatre called the Kings Theatre in the Haymarket aforesaid and of the several Messuages Rooms Erections and Buildings adjoining or belonging thereto or held therewith and of the Licence priviledge Scenes Wardrobe Utensils and other things appertaining thereto and used for the performance of Operas and other public Entertainments And of all benefit property and advantage to arise thereby AND WHEREAS the said William Taylor hath contracted and agreed with the said Frederick Walsh for the Sale to him of the Silver Ticket of Admission to the Kings Theatre or Opera House hereinafter mentioned to be hereby granted at or for the price or sum of One hundred and fifty Pounds. NOW THIS INDENTURE WITNESSETH that for and in consideration of the sum of One hundred and fifty pounds of lawful money of Great Britain by the said Frederick Walsh to the said William Taylor in hand well and duly paid at or before the sealing and delivery of these presents (the receipt and payment whereof the said William Taylor doth hereby acknowledge and therefrom and of and from the same and every part thereof doth acquit exonerate release and discharge the said Frederick Walsh his Executors Administrators and Assigns and every of them by these presents) He the said William Taylor HATH given Granted Bargained and sold And by these presents DOTH Give Grant Bargain and sell unto the said Frederick Walsh his Executors Administrators and Assign A Silver Ticket of Admission to the said Opera house or Theatre and premises and doth give and grant to the Bearer thereof to be admitted gratis into any part of the said Theatre of Boxes or other places which now are on from time to time during the continuance of the Term of twenty one years or twenty one Seasons shall be let occupied or taken up by persons who are now or shall become subscribers to the Opera (and the Boxes set apart and reserved for the Use of the excepted) there to be had for and during the term of twenty one Years or twenty one Seasons to be computed from the day of the date thereof and from thence next ensuing and fully to be compleat and ended which said Silver Ticket is already made and engraved in the manner following (that is to say) On the one side "A Crown" in the Centre and round it "Kings Theatre for 21 years from November 1796" Ticket of Admission (TO HAVE AND TO HOLD) the same Ticket with such free licence liberty and priviledge as aforesaid unto the said Frederick Walsh.

IN WITNESS whereof the said parties for these presents have hereunto set their hands and seals the day and year first above written.

The care that certain members of the eighteenth-century audience took to enjoy their experience in the theatre to the fullest can be seen in many publications of the period, none perhaps more fascinating and complicated than Joshua Steele's *An Essay Towards Establishing the Melody and Measure of Speech, to be Expressed and Perpetuated by Peculiar Symbols*, printed in 1775. Steele tried to record accurately the delivery of the most famous actor of all, David Garrick, at a time long before mechanical reproduction was possible. The following is what he says about Garrick's return to the role of Hamlet.

Since writing the foregoing treatise, I have heard Mr. Garrick in the character of Hamlet; and the principal differences that I can remember, between his manner, and what I have marked in the treatise, are as follows:

In the first place, that speech or soliloque, which I (for want of better judgment) have noted in the stile of a ranting actor, swelled with *forte* and softened with *piano*, he delivered with little or no distinction of *piano* and *forte*, but nearly uniform; something below the ordinary force, or, as a musician would say, *sotto voce*, or *sempre poco piano*.

Secondly, as to measure, the first line thus:

To be — or not to be — that is the question.

Thirdly, as to accent and quantity thus:

To die, — to sleep, — no more.

As Steele says, people took great care to "perpetuate" the beauties and qualities of what they had seen in the theatre. Theatre was, and still is, the most ephemeral of all the arts, despite the increase in recordings and, of course, movies and videotapes. The acerbic theatre critic Kenneth Tynan was very good at this type of "written recording," and *Curtains*[1]— the anthology of his newspaper reviews for *The Observer* (for which he wrote in the fifties and sixties)—makes entertaining and enlightening reading. One of the most faithful and enthusiastic playgoers was the English critic William Hazlitt (1778–1830), who wrote the following almost moving piece about actors:[2]

> Players are "the abstract and brief chroniclers of the time"; the motley representatives of human nature. They are the only honest hypocrites. Their life is a voluntary dream; a studied madness... The Stage is an epitome, a bettered likeness of the world, with the dull part left out ... How many fine gentlemen do we owe to the Stage! How many romantic lovers are mere Romeos in masquerade! How many soft bosoms have heaved with Juliet's sighs! ... Whenever there is a play-house, the world will go on not amiss ...
>
> If the stage is useful as a school of instruction, it is no less so as a source of amusement. It is a source of the greatest enjoyment at the time, and a never-failing fund of agreeable reflections afterwards. The merits of a new play, or of a new actor, are always among the first topics of polite conversation ...

Most of us were born with the voices we have, which seldom change much; they can improve, and they can deteriorate, but they are our instruments, and it is our pleasure and our duty to play them well. This book contains suggestions and exercises for playing the voice. The book does not tell you how to *produce* your voice but how to *play* it. I can see little sense in creating a beautiful instrument if the inability to read the music prevents its use; there is no virtue in an instrument without a melody to play on it. I assume that young actors know that their art demands sharpness, intelligence, and imagination, and that the other arts like music, painting, sculpture, and writing are essential areas of exploration for those who seek to go on the stage. From my experience, I know that actors must read, know good music, and appreciate the fine arts in order to experience the culture and perform well the plays that express it. Therefore, this is not an instrument book, but a voice book—a book about intelligent acting.

[1]Kenneth Tynan, *Curtains*, London: Longmans, 1960.
[2]William Hazlitt, in *The Examiner*, January 5, 1817. ("Round Table" in *Hazlitt, On Theatre*, New York: Hill & Wang, 1957).

Singing is the best vocal training for an actor; it sharpens the sense of pitch, forces attention on rhythm, increases awareness of tempo, and calls for accuracy and clarity. I would encourage readers training for a career in professional or educational theatre to join a choir, get a part in a musical, sing in the shower, learn to play an instrument, and study harmony and theory, even composition. The reader with some knowledge of music will profit greatly from my book.

All actors must read a great deal; good books expand vocabulary, make us aware of nuances, introduce us to shades of character and characterization, subtleties of dialogue, processes of thought, ranges of emotion, and the possibilities of the imagination. We live in a time when print seems to be slowly going out of style and when audiences as well as actors often make do with less than they might want— assuming they are truly capable of wanting it—because they are not as alive to words as they were even twenty years ago. Actors are in a position of power and influence as they always have been, and most good actors today will tell us that the more they know about life and the more actively they use their intelligence, the more permanently useful and rich their performances are likely to be.

As an actor, you are highly thought of. You have to work to earn and keep your audience's love, regard, and pleasure, and to make a lot of people happy.

HOW TO USE THIS BOOK

This book is not necessarily a "Hill Method" or "Hill System." For training in pure instrument you might read Kristin Linklater's *Freeing the Natural Voice* or Cecily Berry's *Voice and the Actor*. Arthur Lessac's *The Use and Training of the Human Voice* is also marvelously useful, especially when in the presence of Lessac himself and at his workshops. The best use of my book is as a textbook in class; another way to use it is in a theatre group or drama society; but the book can also be read by you alone, provided you have a friend or partner with whom to share the exercises. The book is not about monologues and the single actor. When I give exercises on single passages, the assumption is that an audience and other characters are present.

You begin with physical well-being and a clear mind, proceed through the stages of relaxation, vocal warm-up, breathing, voice placement, alignment, and projection, then go on to problems and challenges presented by scripts that call for variety of inflection, agility, focus, emphasis, pause, and subtlety. This procedure is not simply "oral interpretation" but playing your instrument according to the script, a process that constitutes the larger part of the book. I have dealt mostly with speech patterns because I believe they are what truly interest actors.

Sometimes you will find nondramatic examples. I have deliberately included two poems and four prose passages so that you can—for exercises in sentence structure and diction—be freed from concerns of character and concentrate on matters of sound and sense. These exercises are as important as studying scenes because they study words. As many fine performers assert, it does good to get out of a play for a while and deal with other art forms.

Terms used in vocal training as well as terms of theatrical and literary criticism used in this book are explained in the Glossary.

At the end of most sections, you will find a Scene Study List, which summarizes the main points raised in the section and points you toward your own scene work and study.

So A Voice for the Theatre is written out of a concern for words and inflections as the theatre's means of conveying a playwright's truth. Have fun with the book. Give yourself to its discipline. Listen to the sounds it provides. Develop a voice and an ear. Become an actor.

1

Relaxation—Physical and Vocal Well-Being

**STAGE FRIGHT IS A KILLER
BUT IT CAN BE HELPED**

I am a fat man. I am also a nervous person who suffers terribly from stage fright. Even worse than that is the torture I can go through when doing something as semiprivate as shooting a dialogue in a movie. Once, while walking through a rehearsal with Jane Seymour and Omar Sharif in a forgettable film called *Oh Heavenly Dog*, I nearly fainted. Why? The studio was extremely hot, and there were crowds milling about and muttering; I did not feel at anything like a physical peak. The call was for six in the morning and the previous night's shoot had gone on until eight. Jane Seymour, John Stride, Margaret Courtney, and Omar Sharif are rather famous people. I felt they were judging me, and this feeling is the primary cause of stage fright, which is silly. Stage fright shows lack of confidence; it paralyses; it can produce palpitations, vomiting, and worse. One consolation is that the greatest performers also suffer from stage fright. Read Sir Laurence Olivier's *Confessions of an Actor* and you will learn about the five years of torment he endured *on stage* not so very long ago at the height of his world renown. The other consolation is that the condition can be alleviated by careful physical work at relaxation.

THE BODY AND THE VOICE

It is true to say that when the body is well, the voice stands a better chance. For the actor, both need to be relaxed, and this is something I did not know early on. I was always in such a hurry to get at the final effect that I would learn lines quickly (known in the profession as "being a quick study"), get to the bottom of my character, and largely forget about myself and what I was doing to myself. Because I had had many years of vocal training as a member of a choir and later as an amateur soloist, I never did harm to my voice. But my poor body! The tension began hours before rehearsal or performance and continued during it; this produced good performances, as directors and reviewers were sometimes in the habit of saying. But the sacrifice! How stupid I was. Nobody told me, and I did not know. The tension began to show itself in the voice after a while. There were hesitations, splutters, stutters, constrictions, and breathlessness. Now I have reduced the pain and uselessness of this tension. I am still afraid. But I am afraid within a context of relaxation.

RELAXATION EXERCISES FOR THE BODY

The following exercises take a little bit of learning, but their particular marvel is that they can also be done *in the imagination*.

The steps are fairly simple, and the whole procedure takes twenty minutes to learn. After you have tried them a few times, you will understand that to be able to induce the kind of relaxation they encourage it is necessary to do only the first few stages, thus taking up no more than five minutes of your valuable preperformance time; one cannot think about one's role when doing relaxation exercises, so I recommend that you do them at least an hour and a half before any performance. The exercises cannot increase concentration, although they are, as you will see, very concentrated physically.

You should do the first few sessions of these exercises with a friend, teacher, partner, or fellow student—depending on whether you are using this book by yourself or as part of a course—who can slowly read the following instructions. Obviously reading them silently by yourself will interfere with their purpose.

Location: An area as quiet as possible where you will not be disturbed. There should be no music playing, and no conversation other than the low voice of your partner. The lighting should be very low and *not* fluorescent. Ideally you should be on a large bed or couch where you can stretch out your whole body. If this is not possible, lie on the floor with something comfortable—not a high pillow—under your head. Preparation: (1) Take some long, deep breaths. (2) Feel yourself in contact with the surface you are lying on and concentrate on that feeling. Try to feel as "heavy" as you can. (3) Close your eyes and be prepared to follow the instructions completely, since that very desire will relax the mind and focus it for the duration of the exercises.

THE EXERCISES—STAGE ONE

Scalp and Brow

Raise your eyebrows as far as they will go, even until you feel great tension and discomfort. Be aware of them almost meeting the hairline, creating a cold or metallic feeling across your brow and into your scalp. Hold this position, focusing on the uncomfortable tension. Hold it for a count of ten. Release the tension. Lower your eyebrows to where they normally are. Breathe deeply and be aware of the pleasant tingle in the areas you have just relaxed as the blood circulation is restored and the tensed muscles relax. Take another long deep breath.

Eyes and Nose

Wrinkle up your nose until you think you may be pushing it up into your eyes, and at the same time lower your eyebrows as far as they will go. Your eyes will be tightly shut. Focus on the tension you have created in the upper cheeks, the bridge of the nose, eyelids, eyeballs, and eyebrows. Increase this tension. Hold it for the count of ten. Release the tension. Breathe deeply, and be aware of the tingle in those areas as circulation is restored and the muscles relax. Take a long breath.

Chin, Jaw, Lips

By pressing your upper lip into your lower and the lower into the upper, purse your lips together until they tremble. You can feel your chin, your jaw, and the upper muscles of your neck quite sore and tense. Hold for a count of ten. Release the tension you have created; breathe and feel the pleasant tingle of relaxation and circulation.

Arms, Hands, and Chest

Raise your arms to at least a 45° angle. Clench your fists tightly, then tighter. Feel the horseshoe shape of tension from the left hand, through your shoulders and along your right arm to your right hand. Concentrate on the discomfort. You may find yourself holding your breath unwillingly. Try to breathe, but do not let the tension go until you have counted ten. Release. Let your arms drop to your sides. Focus on the tingling of the circulation and the relaxation in those areas. Breathe deeply.

Neck and Shoulders

Firmly press your head into the pillow on the right side until you feel great tension in the muscle on the left of your neck. Focus on this tension. Hold for a count of ten. Release. Feel the release. Breathe. Firmly press the left of your face into the pillow until you feel tension in the muscles of the right of your neck. Hold—release—feel release— breathe. You may find that you have been yawning quite a bit. Good.

Torso, Stomach, etc.

Tense your stomach muscles so that you are prepared for someone to hit you. Tense them harder. Push your stomach up and out until your back leaves the surface you are lying on. Hold—release—feel—release—breathe. Feel the warmth as circulation returns to your torso. Tense the stomach the other way, holding it *in*. You may experience some difficulty breathing. Try to breath, but do not lose the tension. Hold—release—feel the warm relaxation—breathe.

Hips and Thighs

Tighten your buttocks together. Knock your knees together and hold them there. Try to raise your pelvis. Hold the tension, and focus on the discomfort in the thighs. Hold—release—focus on the warmth of the release—breathe deeply.

Calves and Feet

Turn up your toes as if they were trying to reach your eyebrows and turn them toward your head until you feel the strain in the ankles and the calves, possibly proceeding up past your knees. Hold—release—focus on the warmth of the release—breathe deeply. Lie still for about a minute. Feel the tension go away down your legs, across your left foot, and out through your left toes; then feel it across your right foot and out through your right toes.

STAGE TWO

The first stage of the relaxation exercise worked simply and physically to restore circulation where it had been constricted and to bring relief to muscles where they had been tensed. In this second stage, you will be repeating the *same* exercises in Stage One, but *only in your imagination,* using the influence of the mind over the body. You will find this procedure amazingly effective. What you will be doing is lying in the same position, and repeating the exercises with a friend or partner or teacher who is reading the instructions to you in a calm and reassuring voice. The more deeply you let these things happen in your mind, the more you will find your body behaving, *inside itself,* as it did before—a kind of hypnosis. As an actor, you will be able to achieve this.

STAGE THREE—CONCLUSION

After the exercises in Stage Two, do not rise. Imagine the tension draining from your fingertips and toes. Run over the exercises quickly now in your head, spending a few seconds in each area, feeling the strain come and go and the muscles tensing and relaxing. You will feel heavy and even sleepy. Very slowly, turn over on one side, keeping your eyes closed; then open them slowly. Sit up slowly. Rise slowly. You will feel light and thoroughly relaxed.

Further Uses and Benefits

As I said before, you will soon be able to produce the effect of these exercises without actually doing them physically—a useful accomplishment at a busy rehearsal or even in any tense situation. This state of mastery, however, will be acquired only after many physical enactments of all the stages. I find, in fact, that when confronted with a problematical situation involving tension, I have only to raise my eyebrows, and the good breathing starts by itself. Or rather, I control my breathing, and therefore I am unlikely to react inappropriately to whatever the situation is, and would certainly not experience the whole of the terrifying anxiety that seems to grip artists even more than so-called ordinary people.

It is perfectly possible to perform some of these relaxing exercises in front of people without their knowing you are doing them. Seated at a table, for instance, the best four exercises (neck and shoulders, torso and stomach, hips and thighs, calves and feet), with obvious slight adaptations, can be performed with benefit. You may find, of course, that you have been sitting with your feet curled around the legs of your chair or table—itself a sign of tension that needs release. When you are driving or riding in a car, the facial and chest exercises can be performed as long as your companions do not mind the scrunched-up face. While waiting in the wings for an entrance, or sometimes when weary during the hours of rehearsal when you are merely on call—these are good times to relax if you know how, and now you do. Let me explain some more details of these exercises.

The exercises should be done as outlined *twice a day for a few weeks,* and this will help them become second nature. Then, when you are thoroughly used to these exercises, you can begin to do them only in your imagination; or perhaps exercise only the knees and the face, and your breathing will become regular and deep. However, to keep your relaxing reflexes in shape, I would suggest going back to the complete set and lying down whenever you have the time and the need.

Some performers feel no need at all for special exercises to speed, focus, or maintain that beautifully enjoyable balance of relaxation and concentration that constitutes one of the most physically and psychologically satisfying states of the creative being. Some performers need, in fact, to be in a particular state of nervousness without which they feel their performances will lack the accustomed energy and spark. In my experience there are very few performers who use any preparation other than their own forms of magic and superstition. Let me tell you about some of these forms, although of course, in a way, this is breaking trade secrets. I have known actors and actresses who prepare in the following number of ways:

1. Carry a bent nail.
2. Make the sign of the cross three times, twice in the dressing room and once in the wings before going on stage.
3. Say *merde* to other cast members.
4. Arrive at the theatre at exactly the same time every night.
5. Arrive at the theatre as soon as it is opened.
6. Arrive at the theatre fifteen minutes before going on stage.
7. Apply makeup in the same order every night.
8. Try a different makeup every night.
9. Go over lines.
10. Forget about the play, particularly not going over lines.
11. Have a weak drink.
12. Have a strong drink.
13. Have no alcohol.
14. Take a drug.
15. Take no drugs.
16. Read a book.
17. Read the play.
18. Have sex.
19. Abstain from sex.
20. Apply makeup in the nude.
21. Have a massage.
22. Sit quietly.
23. Find someone to chat with.
24. Take a number of steps from dressing room to stage every night, having measured and counted them.
25. Go for a walk, either on the stage or along whatever corridors there are.
26. Never go near the stage until curtain-up.
27. Spend considerable time on stage before curtain-up, checking properties or just enjoying the smell and the chatter of the audience.
28. Check out the audience through a peephole.
29. Avoid hearing or smelling the audience until curtain-up.
30. Get makeup over as soon as possible, since it is impossible to relax during that process. (This often happens to actors who have makeup artists—these days more obviously in film than in the theatre.)
31. Be alone.
32. Be with others.
33. Chalk a secret notation on the dressing-room mirror.

34. Say some favorite lines from the play out loud, or say them softly.

35. Do some tongue twisters.

36. Yawn a lot.

37. Meditate.

38. Do the relaxation exercises from Chapter 1.

39. Jump up and down.

40. Shower, shave, etc.

41. Use the toilet.

42. Avoid using the toilet until at least after the first act.

43. Chew gum.

44. Chew candies.

45. Wait until the five-minute call before completing costume.

46. Apply makeup in costume.

47. Pray.

48. Hum.

49. Sing.

50. Arrange things on the dressing table in a regular way.

51. Recall effects, successes, failures from the night before.

52. Get good and nervous, knowing the nervousness always vanishes on stage.

53. Eat.

54. Don't eat.

55. Stare at yourself in the mirror for a long time.

56. Always carry a bent nail.

These fifty-six varieties of preparation can, of course, be combined. My point is to show you how many things there are to do, and how many of them utterly oppose the others. There are actors—and very good ones indeed—who, like Sir in Ronald Harwood's magnificent theatrical play *The Dresser,* would ask "What play is it tonight?," while there are others who would think about it from the moment of waking. One of these latter is John Colicos, who played Sir in *The Dresser* as his comeback to the legitimate stage after many years of success and enjoyment in films and television. During the run of that play at the Citadel Theatre in Edmonton, Canada, in 1982, he lived, breathed, ate, and drank the play and his part. We do not know which of the fifty-six varieties of preparation and relaxation of the body and voice Colicos used before performances, but it is proper and likely that he needs only his own magic, as he is already such a strong man with a voice of great power and versatility.

In the early seventies Sir Laurence Olivier was interviewed by Dick Cavett on television, and during the conversation—presented nationwide—the great man admitted to the help he got from "a tiny pill, just a tiny yellow pill." It was a standard 5 mg tranquilizer tablet. Sir Ralph Richardson was once asked to take part in a relaxing improvisation during rehearsals for a stage play directed by someone from a school of theatre different from his; he very politely declined and returned to the rehearsal stage when the improvisation was over and people were ready to get on with the rehearsal. During a rehearsal at Stratford, Ontario's Shakespeare Festival, an actress, together with the rest of the cast that was generally uptight and nervous about doing such a stylish play as *The Importance of Being Earnest*, was at one point encouraged to be a bat. "I will *not* be a bat!!" she yelled, and left the stage until the flapping had ceased. Of course, these last two examples are of performers who are not used to what they have both called "the tyranny of directors."

In what follows you will find another kind of physical warm-up that is not so much relaxation as it is exercise and concentration on the total body.

PHYSICAL WARM-UP

Begin lying on the floor on your back, eyes closed, legs uncrossed, body loose and comfortable.

Here and Now (3 Stages)

1. Let responsibilities borne from past and expected in future fall out of focus so you are only in this room at this moment.

2. Record small physical sensations that focus your attention on your present state.

3. Select a word that sounds good to you and that represents a state of relaxed readiness. Repeat it silently and continuously without effort.

Prune

Tense each area of the body, cumulatively working from the face down through the toes. As more areas are tightened, be certain other areas of body remain loose and relaxed; once the entire body is tensed, pull up toward your center so that torso is lifted off ground and body is supported only by back of head, shoulder blades, and heels. Release fully and let sense of confines of gravity disappear.

Alignment

Allow spine to stretch out along the floor with sensation of head easing out of torso in one direction as tailbone moves in opposite direction. Feel vertebrae separating like an accordion, as if air whirls around each one. Simultaneously feel shoulders and floating ribs spreading out across the floor. Move to standing position, maintaining sensation of long spine, with head floating above body like a balloon and feet planted firmly so that you feel very tall but not as if you are working at it.

Head Rolls

Drop head forward into chest, keeping torso erect. Move head in a full, wide circle to the right on a count of 8, then to the left. Repeat. Do same movement to count of 4, then 2. Avoid engaging shoulders in action. Allow circle to be as wide as possible.

Puppet

Drop entire body forward like a rag doll so that hands almost brush floor and head and torso are quite limp. Legs may be slightly bent. Test looseness by swinging arms and head apelike back and forth. Imagine a string connected to your tailbone pulling upward and similar strings attached to each vertebra all the way up into the back of your skull. Allow yourself to rise very slowly, untensing slightly with each tug of each imaginary string.

Sun (11 Stages)

    1. Hands clasped, body tall.
    2. Salute to sun, body open in X figure with arms leaning back, face upward.
    3. Legs together, hands grasping ankles, full stretch along backs of legs.
    4. Hands on floor, one leg extended behind torso, other leg bent, stretch on extended side.
    5. Body in upside-down V with behind in the air.

6. Move down as if to do a push-up but, at last instant, curve torso into cobra position so body makes a C curve with toes and head pointing toward wall behind you.

7. Repeat 5.

8. Repeat 4, with stretch on other side of body.

9. Curl body into smallest possible position, with head over knees and arms wrapped around lower legs.

10. Repeat 2.

11. Repeat 1.

Reaches (5 Stages)

Perform movements as stretches, not bounces. On counts 2 and 3, aim to stretch slightly farther than on count 1. Keep feet planted firmly about two feet apart throughout.

1. Attempt to touch ceiling above you 1, 2, 3.

2. Reach for wall behind you 1, 2, 3.

3. Grasp backs of thighs and lean way back 1, 2, 3.

4. Extend arms behind you and clasp hands. Bend forward with clasped hands reaching for ceiling 1, 2, 3.

5. Keep hands clasped and move to standing position. Reach for ceiling with both head and hands simultaneously.

Lung Vacuum

Collapse upper body as in *Puppet*, simultaneously blowing out air vigorously. In rag-doll position, continue to blow out air in short, powerful spurts until you feel completely emptied of air. Stand. Secure footing. Hold air out until you simply must inhale, then allow it to sweep in, feeling it pour almost to the ends of your fingertips and toes. Particularly register its presence in the small of your back. Repeat at your own rate.

Lion

Stretch your face into Kabuki lion expression, bug-eyed, open in all directions, with tongue extended and lowered. Imagine executing a silent scream. From this extreme position, allow all facial muscles to collapse slowly, including jaw, which should drop open. Allow chin to move back and forth, eyes to fall half shut, and any other face/throat area relaxation that feels appropriate to you. Move into a chewing motion, which becomes very powerful and then fades away.

Swings (10 Counts)

This is a highly rhythmic exercise unlike the others. You should lead with the body part noted, but make a commitment to each movement with the total body as well. Knees dip with each count.

 —and 1: *right* arm swings across front of torso while *left* swings behind
 —and 2: *left* across front while *right* swings behind
 —and 3: arms out front
 —and 4: arms move in full circle, moving forward, up, and back, and around and forward
 —and 5: arms reverse circle, moving down, back, up, around, and down
 —and 6: arms touch the floor
 —and 7: arms reach for the ceiling
 —and 8: arms drop behind torso, completing a half circle
 —and 9: *right* shoulder moves in a large circle
 —and 10: *left* shoulder moves in a large circle

Here and Now

Repeat the first exercise.

2

Breath Control, Voice Production, Projection, and Agility

I think it's fair to say that very few actors produce their voices freely . . .

(Fiona Reid, Canadian actress)

Breathing is the most natural process: We did not learn how to breathe. We do not know of any other bodily function over which we have so little general control. Like our heartbeats, our breathing is a survival mechanism that begins with the diaphragm, worked by unconscious muscles that fill and empty our spongelike sacs called lungs, which in turn allow us to pass air through the larynx to produce the voice.

In this book I have decided to avoid emphasis on *one* way of producing the voice. Instead of physiological explanations, I will outline the principles of breathing and resonance, occasionally summarize what some of the main pointers are from those teachers whose fine voice work has met with international approval, and provide you with exercises to try alone as well as to supplement whatever voice production work you are already doing with teachers or coaches. Readers who are not taking voice classes will learn the rudiments from these pages and profitably go from there, *provided* they remember that in the theatre *no theory is of help without practice.*

THE SPEECH MECHANISM

The Lungs

"When we are born, we cry that we are come / To this great stage of fools" (*King Lear*). If we did not breathe, we would not so much be out of breath as out of life because our blood would have no oxygen, which the brain especially needs to give its orders to the functioning parts of our miraculous and complicated body. Breathing is the only way our blood absorbs oxygen from the air, and the lungs are not so much bags as sponges, continually supplying oxygen and removing carbon dioxide, continually being filled and emptied. Lungs are controlled both by chest muscles acting in tandem with atmospheric pressure and by the important diaphragm muscles.

The Diaphragm

The diaphragm, a set of muscles and sinews, separates the abdomen from the chest cavity in which the lungs are situated. The diaphragm itself does not move the rest, but the muscles attaching it to the abdomen. The diaphragm constantly moves up and down to alter the size of the chest cavity.

The Rib Cage

The ribs—we all know what they look like—prevent the walls of the chest cavity from collapsing onto the lungs and the heart. When the ribs are drawn in, the size of the chest cavity is reduced, and air is expelled from the lungs. In reverse, atmospheric pressure forces air *into* the lungs. The diaphragm is working at the same time, so there is a supporting role played by each of the parts.

Diaphragmatic Breathing

There is no mystery to diaphragmatic breathing, which happens naturally when the body needs more oxygen—after strenuous exercise, for example. What happens in both parts of the breathing process just described—the ribs and their cage, and the diaphragm muscles—is that some muscles raise the ribs a bit, while others flatten and lower the diaphragm; the chest is being expanded both downward and sideways while, simultaneously, the muscles on the abdomen loosen and allow the abdomen to expand outward enough to compensate for the downward force of the diaphragm; then, for the expulsion of breath from the lungs, opposite muscles lower the rib cage and force the diaphragm up into its relaxed position, high and arched, while the abdominal muscles contract (to hold the digestive organs against the raised diaphragm).

Of course, most of us do not breathe that forcefully because most of us avoid using the diaphragm muscles, which are low down, and we seldom think about them except in moments of stress or perhaps when gasping for breath after exercise. Instead, we use the muscles of the shoulders and upper chest, usually raising the upper chest and shoulders when exhaling. In fact, we can see each other's shoulders rising and falling. On stage this is distracting to the audience and not helpful in producing a natural and agile voice. What happens in this "normal," shallow breathing is that we are using our muscles to inhale and not using them at all to exhale. The exhaled breath is, therefore, what we call *unsupported*. (Exercises in Diaphragmatic Breathing are given later in this chapter.)

The Soft Palate

The inhaled and exhaled air passes through the bronchial tubes (attached like branches to the lungs), the windpipe (or trachea), the throat (or pharynx), and the nasal cavities. Around the nose and throat, however, the air passages are shared with the eating and drinking mechanism, and two valves help separate the two functions: the soft palate and the larynx. The soft palate is that thin, soft membrane at the back of the roof of the mouth with the uvula—the small, conical, fleshy mass of tissue suspended from the center of the soft palate right above the back of the tongue.

You can raise the back of the soft palate, making contact with the back wall of the throat and shutting off the nasal cavities from the mouth and the throat. This is swallowing; no food or drink can go up into the nose when we are swallowing properly. Sometimes, of course, we forget, and fizzy drinks and scrap can get into the nose, especially when we eat too much or when we are in haste.

The Larynx

We sometimes loosely call the larynx the voice box. The larynx has two folds known as the vocal cords, and the opening between them is called the glottis.

HOW WE SPEAK

Speech is the only real use of exhaled breath; we cause the vocal cords to vibrate by forcing air energy out through the closed glottis. The muscular power used in this process is called breath support. Our voices and what they sound like are influenced greatly by the breath support, which should be strong, sustained, and controlled. Obviously, how "strongly" we speak depends on how strongly we are using the muscles we use to exhale.

Equally evident is that how *long* we talk depends on how much air we take in and how carefully we exhale it. The easiest way to achieve a greater capacity for breath is, of course, to breathe with our diaphragm.

HOW WE CONTROL HOW WE SPEAK

The vocal cords vary from person to person; do not think of them as cords, for they are rather folds, as I have said. Resonators are cavities in the throat, mouth, nose, chest, and so on.

As Fiona Reid and Douglas Campbell say in the interviews at the end of this book, there are many methods of voice control. If your teacher is using the Berry, Linklater, or Lessac methods, then you are in good hands. What follows is a series of vocal warm-ups you can do to limber up the areas of muscle use and resonance.

VOCAL WARM-UP

(If done with Physical Warm-up, insert between Lion and Swings— pages 21–22.)

Relaxation

1. Slowly release all muscles of face/throat area, allowing jaw to hang loose.

2. Open and close mouth several times (controlled move followed by release move), allowing the opening to get slightly larger each time. Test for a two-finger opening. (From now on, allow mouth to open and close throughout sequence without making any effort unless exercises call for it.)

3. Yawn with the entire body participating.

4. Raise shoulders and drop them three times, each time with less actual movement, more relaxation.

5. Incline head to right and left in gentle rocking motion, feeling soothing sensation in throat area with each move.

6. Nod head back and forward as if slowly agreeing. Allow head to fall as far back as it goes toward your front.

7. Tense back of head pulling in toward back of neck; release and savor (remember) feeling.

8. Same as #7 for front of neck: pull chin toward neck, tense, tighten, release, and slowly return to neutral position.

Breath

9. Breathe in through nose, taking time to record and separate sensations of:
—air passing through upper chest without causing expansion in that area
—spreading of lower floating ribs to fullest
—lowering and flattening of diaphragm
—lodging of air comfortably in small of back.

10. Sigh out in exhalation, recording reversal of process in #9. Repeat inhalation/exhalation process.

11. Yawn again with entire body, allowing sound to escape on exhalation; stand firmly, concentrating on state of standing alignment and easy breathing.

Rooting Sound

12. Plant feet firmly and imagine voice planted partly in tailbone, partly in facial mask, with roots passing down your legs into ground below.

13. Reach down (in mind) for sound on inhale and begin hum on exhale.

14. Work hum up and down register (like sound roller coaster) with "roots" grabbing the inside of earth more and more firmly. Record sensation of vibrating sound along front of torso during resonation.

15. Establish full, rich sound with each of sounds below, establish basic sound, allow full volume, pull in until sound disappears: (a) er; (b) ah; (c) ay; (d) i

Exercising Lips

16. Fish—isolate and expand lips as if moving through water.
Horse—non-plose B sound with maximum lip vibration.
Motor boat—VVVVVVV sound, starting slowly, changing gears, dying out.

17. Repeat following sequence with maximum lip effort but all else totally relaxed:
    a. *Pepepe Pepepe Pepepe Pah*
    b. *Bebebe Bebebe Bebebe Bah*
    c. *Mememe Mememe Mememe Mah*
    d. *Mah Maw Moo Mow*
    e. *Pah Paw Poo Pow*
    f. *Bah Baw Boo Bow*

Teeth

18. Fly—Zzzzzz sound varying pitch and volume: Snake—Sssss sound varying intensity.

19. *Zezeze zezeze zezeze zah*
    Sesese sesese sesese sah

Tongue Tip

20. Cat Lap—lap at milk in all different directions and distances as rapidly as possible.

21. *Lalala lalala lalala lah*
    a. *lah lay lee li*
    b. *tah tay tee ti*
    c. *dah day dee di*
    d. *nah nay nee ni*
    e. *lear tear dear near*
    f. *lair tair dair nair*

Back Tongue and Soft Palate

22. Jungle heart beat—ng sound repeated ten times followed by breathing in through mouth and sighing out.

23. a. *kekeke kekeke kekeke kah*
    b. *gegege gegege gegege gah*
    c. *kaaaaaah gaaaaaah kaaaaaah gaaaaaah*

24. With a partner, reading each others' lips, starting very slowly and precisely, then increasing tempo more without increasing tension or volume or pitch:

> *The tip of the tongue*
> *The roof of the mouth*
> *The lips and the teeth*

25. Repeat total body yawn.

Summary

1. Face release
2. Jaw drop
3. Body yawn
4. Shoulder drops
5. Head inclines
6. Head nods
7. Head pull backs
8. Head chin pull
9. Recorded breathing: inhalation
10. Recorded exhale
11. Body yawn and alignment
12. Rooting
13. Hum
14. Roller coaster
15. Resonated sounds
16. Fish, horse, motorboat
17. Lip sequence (p, b, m)
18. Fly, snake
19. Teeth sequence
20. Cat lap
21. Tongue lip sequence (l, t, d, n)
22. Jungle beat
23. Tongue back sequence (k, g)

24. Tongue twisters
25. Body yawn

PROJECTION

It is not merely the voice that is to be "thrown out" to the audience, but the entire characterization involving the whole body and its spiritual state. Many writers on the subject admit that it is largely a question of will power.

How does the actor project, and with what precise qualities of will power? Of course, there must be adequate relaxation, with the sort of rib-cage-raised breathing already described; it must be possible to throw forward vowels as well as consonants; and there must be something there to throw forward. As far as the voice is concerned, there must be breath enough to allow a more open cavity in the throat. But how is all this to be done?

I have tried the following methods not only with myself when adjusting to new theatres and acting areas but also with theatre students. I have found the methods satisfactory as a practical means of inducing the power of the will necessary to project not only the voice but also the self. Not surprisingly, the methods are in stages.

The most desirable effect for the audience occurs where the actor seems to be *near*, where there is an intimacy. Mr. and Mrs. Smith in Q 23 and 24 would want the actor to be acting *for them* to the extent that the actor is *not feeling for them* but *making them feel*; they have come to the theatre for a physical presence that would produce a spiritual sensation made up of the thought and feeling not frequently possible for them in their daily lives.

STAGE 1

Have someone—friend, partner, or teacher—act as an audience for you. Choose a sentence or two (for instance, "I have come here to project these thoughts and words to you, and I want you to be close to them") and say them into the earlobe of your "audience."

The people in your audience will, of course, experience a tingling in the earlobe, because you have tickled it with your breath and the surface of your lips. Maybe the people's spines tingled a bit. The reaction, however weak or strong, has been almost purely physical; you were too close for comfort.

STAGE 2

Now, aiming once again for the lobe so as not to blow into the aural cavity, say the sentence(s) once more, from an inch away. What you are doing here is attempting to produce the same tingling effect on the skin without using any more pressure. Focus on the lobe and concentrate on willing the sound and intention into it.

STAGE 3

Now repeat the process in Stage 1 from a foot away, several times, until your audience says that the sensation is as strong as the first one.

STAGE 4

Now put a physical distance between yourself and your audience, but *will yourself to feel as if they are as close as in Stage 1*. Make this "distance" about six feet. Focus very hard on sending a physical sensation to the ears of your listener. Note that you are doing this without the aid of eye contact. You are probably also using some of the articulations suggested elsewhere in this book and are finding yourself feeling your own sounds more than usual: Take care not to indulge them too much or your audience will be aware of sound and not sense. Only when your audience has indicated that the desired closeness has been achieved should you move on to the next stage.

STAGE 5

This stage is difficult, of course. Your audience is now a room's length away from you, but keep them close. Using the same interior "pressure" you discovered you were exerting in Stages 1–5, will yourself out to the other side of the room. You may possibly find yourself opening the mouth more; your posture will almost certainly be good, and you will be experiencing a heightened form of relaxation and will be feeling as if you are extending your whole self *without exaggeration, distortion, increase in volume, or tension of the larynx.* When your audience appears to be satisfied with the closeness of effect, you can proceed to the final stage: the stage.

STAGE 6

If you are able to practice this phase on a stage with a front curtain, all the better. Close the curtain. Repeat Stages 1–5. In 1, your lips will touch the upstage surface of the curtain material. Step back from the curtain more at each stage, until you can, for Stage 6, arrange to have the curtain opened. You have been filling the curtain material with your thoughts, words, and feelings until it is full of them; now, the curtain opens, the energies you have filled it with are floating out over the stalls in the theatre and as far as the recesses of whatever balconies and galleries and back seats and exits there are. On the vibrations and wills of your first six deliveries, project your seventh, imbuing the backs of the empty theatre seats with them. Have someone sit three-quarters back in the theatre; project your sentence.

If there are balconies or even galleries in the theatre in which you are fortunate enough to be doing these exercises, all the better. If you *"will"* Stage 6 into further stages that include an audience above eye level, you will naturally (or by craft, rather) have to adjust your physical posture; in doing this, never strain. Exercise the will, remembering the success of the first six stages.

HOW DO I RECOGNIZE STRAIN?

It is all very well for me to say "never strain." How do you know when you are straining? Ask yourself the following questions:

1. Do I feel in control? (If not, you are either straining or not projecting.)
2. Do I feel constriction in the throat?
3. Am I leaning forward to reach out?
4. Am I on the tips of my toes with the effort?
5. Do I find myself using my hands and not my voice to reach out?

If you answer "yes" to any of questions 2–5, you are probably straining. If you are unable to answer these questions, you need to do the exercises frequently. You will be glad you did! You will find, too, that your partner or teacher will be able to answer questions 3, 4, and 5. The whole point, as you know by now, is to appear to be making no effort at all. But it is an effort to learn projection. That is the reason for the next exercises on pages 37–40.

CLOSENESS OF EFFECT

You may say, of course, that you are seldom likely to be in a position to act in a very large theatre without the aid of some form of sound amplification system. Let us talk about that now.

Some of you may have seen *Agnes of God* by John Pielmeier, which, when I saw it, was played by Elizabeth Ashley, Geraldine Page, and Amanda Plummer at The Music Box Theatre in New York. For the first few minutes of the play, before the entrance of Geraldine Page, I thought that Elizabeth Ashley was wearing a body microphone. Unlike most of that audience, this was my first encounter with her work and I had not even seen her on television talk shows. From my seat in the center of the twelfth row of the orchestra, the actress sounded as if she were speaking from row eleven. Hence, my assumption about the body microphone. Her footsteps on the wooden set were not obtrusive, so it certainly could not have been a floor microphone. There was, in fact, no microphone at all in the production; while The Music Box Theatre is not large by any means, the *closeness of effect* created by these three actresses (Page and Plummer were equally well projected, in my view) was gratifyingly good. What if they were in a bigger theatre? How would they go about enlarging their voices without exaggerating their performances?

Laurence Olivier is both a stage and a film actor, and in the past few years has been wonderfully effective also on television in *Brideshead Revisited* and *King Lear*. In 1965, at the height of his world renown, he was persuaded to have his amazing performance of Othello committed to film for the world to see—actually a film of the stage production, although with the essential (and, as it turns out, crucially mistaken) difference that the camera was "on stage" for much of the action so that the audience was given the chance to view the play from the proximity normally permitted only to the other actors. Frank Finlay, whose performance of Iago had already been very subtle and malevolently quiet, may be said to have stolen the show from Olivier and his Desdemona, Maggie Smith. Why? The film was shot almost immediately after the closing of the production, and Finlay's performance needed only the lowering of the voice; whereas Olivier—who after months of vocal training and physical gymnastics as well had to lower his voice by a near octave and alter his gait to suit the noble Moor he wished to portray—could never be expected to readjust his creation in so short a time. What the audience saw in the film was Olivier acting; what they had seen in the theatre was Othello being. So transfixed were many members of the audience at the Old

Vic Theatre that it brought back to older memories the famous night when Sir Johnston Forbes-Robertson had played the part,[1] and a gentleman in the front row of the Dress Circle had called out when the actor approached Desdemona to strangle her, "leave her alone, you big black brute!", leapt down into the orchestra stalls, ran up onto the stage, and tried to prevent play and murder from taking their natural course. *From fifty feet away,* Olivier was Othello, black, large, noble, deep-voiced and red-lipped. From the six-foot focus of the camera, however, Olivier's eyes rolled, his mouth was grotesquely open, lower lip hanging by makeup and technique, and his voice downright strange. Olivier was creating the role before our eyes. Let me explain by quoting Arthur Koestler, from *The Act of Creation:*

> . . . if illusion offers escape it is escape of a particular kind, sharply distinguished from other distractions such as playing tennis or bingo. It teaches us to live on two planes at once. Children and primitive audiences who, forgetting the present, completely accept the reality of the events on the stage, are experiencing not an aesthetic thrill, but a kind of hypnotic trance; and addiction to it may lead to various degrees of estrangement from reality. The aesthetic experience depends on that delicate balance arising from the presence of *both* matrices in the mind; on perceiving the hero as Laurence Olivier and Prince Hamlet of Denmark at one and the same time; on the lightning oscillations of attention from one to the other, like sparks between charged electrodes. It is this precarious suspension of awareness between the two planes which facilitate the continuous flux of emotion from the Now and Here to the remoter worlds of Then and There, and the cathartic effects resulting from it. For when interest is deflected from the self it will attach itself to something else; when the levels of self-assertion tension falls, the self-transcending impulses become almost automatically dominant. Thus the creation of illusion is in itself of cathartic value—even if the product, judged by more sophisticated standards, is of cheap quality; for it helps the subject to actualize his potential of self-transcending emotions thwarted by the dreary routines of existence. Liberated from his frustrations and anxieties, man can turn into a rather nice and dreamy creature; when he changes into a dark suit and sits in a theatre, he at once shows himself capable of taking a strong and entirely unselfish interest in the destinies of the personae on the stage. He participates in their hopes and sufferings; his frustrated cravings for communion find their primeval outlet in the magic of identification.

Unhappily, in the film of *Othello,* what Koestler calls the "lightning oscillations" were not so swift nor so frequent. The problem here is—

[1] Lyric Theatre, 1902

to reduce it to the utmost simplicity—that the actor could not adapt his projection, either of face, body, or voice. We must, as actors, remember that too much projection is as harmful as too little. What Olivier could have done if he had had the time was work on adapting his characterization for the medium of film. But there was not time. You can learn from this example, however, by remembering that the theatre is a group act and that it is therefore necessary to be in harmony of projection with the other players. You must know that performances do vary from night to night and that there is a lot of give and take. Olivier's problem on the film set of *Othello* is something for you to think about. His face was just too big.

HOW DO WE ENLARGE WITHOUT EXAGGERATION?

Some of you may well know by instinct or have known by experience what I am talking about here: the joy of providing an audience of thousands with intimate vocal contact without the aid of a microphone. It will not hurt to think about this experience in someone else's terms, and you can discuss it with people who have not yet had it. The joy, of course, is the satisfaction of having imprinted oneself on an extraordinarily large group of other people, and of a job well done. You might remember Stanislavski's statement in my Introduction: "The main difference between the art of the actor and all other arts is that other artists may create whenever they are inspired. The stage artist, however, must be the master of his own inspiration and *must know how to call it forth* at the time announced on the theatre's posters; this is the chief secret of our art. Without this, the most perfect technique, the greatest gifts, are powerless." He would surely have agreed that another "chief secret of our art" is the ability to make an audience think we are not even raising our voices, let alone shouting, when we are closely heard.

I am sure you will have noticed that I have not yet answered my question and yours, "How do we enlarge without exaggeration?" The moment has come, and here goes: Your understanding and appreciation of what is coming depends heavily on your already trying Stages 1–6 and having adequate feedback about your success.

Let me repeat the questions to ask yourself and your teacher or partner, while adding one.

> Am I in control?
> Do I feel constriction in the throat? Do I sound as if I do?

Am I leaning forward to reach out?
Am I on the tips of my toes with the effort?
Am I using my hands instead of my voice to reach out?
Does my face show the effort?

HOW DO I DO IT?

Let me list the answers to these questions in point form and then enlarge on them without exaggerating.

1. All acting is by its very nature an exaggeration to begin with. We have to magnify this original exaggeration without changing the original, rather like a photographic enlargement.

2. This process of enlargement involves extra careful use of the body to avoid the unnaturalness of mime while using it to create the illusion of naturalness: a process in which the voice cannot be used independently of a special bodily state as well.

3. The special bodily state of many actors and actresses is best described, perhaps, by performers themselves.

Now let me explain each point as carefully as I can.

1. It goes without saying that acting is exaggeration but—like Stanislavski's point about inspiration having to be called forth at the time announced on the theatre poster—this is often left unsaid in our search for naturalness. Remember that Stanislavski also said the famous line: "To act you have to *be*, but to be you have to *act*."

Consider an ordinary photographic print of a shot you took on vacation, perhaps, and that you have it back from the lab. There it is, about 3″ × 2″, maybe glossy, maybe matte, maybe color, maybe monochrome. You see the photo only because it has been printed from a negative on film to a positive on paper. Well and good. You order an enlargement for several reasons: You would like the photo to be more visible, and you want to appreciate its details without having to peer through a magnifying glass; you want to frame it and let more people see what you know as a pretty nice original and would rather not hand around from person to person. What you are doing is preserving the tone, color, and quality of the original for a wider audience, even if only you constitute that audience. You will frequently find that you have to crop the photo to make it good as an enlargement and fit the dimensions of the paper you have selected for it. In doing so, you are slightly altering the original while remaining true to its basic intention and integrity. Doing this, you might find yourself obliged by the form of the paper, its size and shape, to omit peripheral details such as the unfocused bits around the edges. In fact, you may be improving upon the original, just as in acting we are to a certain extent improving upon life as it is mundanely and routinely lived. I am going through the same process right now in writing these lines on my typewriter in my den: What I am writing here is marginally better than what I said at the dinner table a half hour ago, and, as a matter of fact, is a refinement of an energetic conversation over coffee. When I write I am speaking to a larger audience. But to return to the photograph: Let us bear in mind that acting is *not* photography. It is true that Shakespeare made Hamlet say "to hold, as 'twere, a mirror up to nature" when he was speaking to the players about putting on *The Mousetrap* for Claudius to catch the rat; this is not a definition of acting, nor is it meant to be. Hamlet knows well that because it focuses, acting is a much more telescopic art than mere reflection.

2. *How can we use the voice and body in such a way as to "enlarge" them?* Let us assume that, to begin with, you are not the actor of a character in a play but a maker of speeches. You are in a huge auditorium with an audience of three or four thousand; its acoustics are, let us say for the moment, perfect, and so is your audience: They do not cough, they do not rustle; they merely, slowly, quietly—as though with one will—breathe. But the people in the audience are not of one will, or at least not beyond the basic fact that they have all come to hear you talk. Your subject is a quiet one, and you have decided that it would be utterly inappropriate to shout, although you have also decided that you must win them over completely and that in the communion of four thousand separate entities and you there will be a splendid unity achieved by your talent and their persuaded acquiescence.

For the important exercise in projection to a mass audience, I have chosen something unusual: an extract from a California attorney's argument for zero population growth,[2] from *Newsweek* Magazine, not from a play. It may well be a statement you feel strongly about; at any rate, its argument, right or wrong, is hard to ignore. I have chosen the argument for this exercise especially since, as you

[2]Johnson C. Montgomery, "The Island of Plenty," copyright 1974 by *Newsweek*, Inc.

will see, it is very hard to project some of the words because of their peculiar combinations of consonants. Here it is:

> The problem is not that there is too little food. The problem is that there are too many people—many too many. It is not that the children should never have been born. It is simply that we have mindlessly tried to cram too many of us into too short a time span. Four billion humans are fine—but they should have been spread over several hundred years.
>
> But the billions are already here. What should we do about them? Should we send food, knowing that each child saved in Southeast Asia, India, or Africa will probably live to reproduce and thereby bring more people into the world to live even more miserably? Should we eat the last tuna fish, the last ear of corn and utterly destroy the garden? That is what we have been doing for a long time and all the misguided efforts have merely increased the number who go to bed hungry each night. There have never been more miserable, deprived people in the world than there are right now.

For a solo speaker in front of a large crowd, there are many difficulties in this excerpt, and they begin with the first sentence.

How in heaven's name do we project *not* and *food*?; we can if we sing them and if we shout. But both are short words with (as they are generally pronounced) short vowels. Johnson Montgomery is obviously not a playwright, nor a speaker without microphones. But let us criticize him no more. We have decided to take this part of his speech and work with it to the best of our ability.

Adopt the final stance you used in Stage 6 of the rudimentary projection exercises. Breathe slowly, properly, and well (see the beginning of this chapter if you think you can use a reminder). Take in every part of the auditorium with your eyes, even if you are under lights and cannot see much at all. Be sure you are "monarch of all you survey"[3] and that you are enjoying the feeling of control before you start to speak. Remember that you are going to have to breathe more often. Your neck should feel longer than it is, and your jaw should be prepared to drop lower while your head is held higher, but none of this is to *appear* to be exaggerated. Make it more a matter of thought than of fact, and remember that you are being depended on not to lose any intensity just because things are obviously going to be a shade "louder." Any tension is going to spoil things, so be sure to

---

[3]"I am monarch of all I survey/My right there is none to dispute . . ." William Cowper (1731–1800), *Verses Supposed to be Written by Alexander Selkirk.*

have done the relaxation exercises, or at least the beginning ones, before trying this exercise. *If you become tense you will simply turn up your volume control switch, and that is not what is wanted at all.* You want to reproduce your original, and you have worked on it thoroughly and know that it is good.

Having adopted a relaxed but controlling posture, taken in the four thousand people with your eyes ("embraced them" as some actors say), and imagining with all your strength of will that each one of the four thousand is close to you, is sitting near yet far, say silently to yourself the sentence from the first six stages, "I have come here to project these thoughts and words to you and I want you to be close to them." Say the first sentence of your Montgomery speech.

What has happened to the *not* and the *food?* Maybe nothing. Try it again, then. You will then find that you have had to put in an unusual pause, perhaps, after *not,* in order for its *t* to sound over the receptive spaces. Did you make *food* comprehensible? Did it sound like—could it have been—*foot* instead? If it did, you need to do the exercises for agility and control immediately before trying this one again.

What happened if you succeeded in projecting this line of your speech was probably a pleasant pressure in the diaphragm as you pronounced the words *not* and *food*. The other thing that happened was most likely that you found it necessary to insert pauses. To use an old term, you *pointed* the sentence; you focused on certain elements of it, not in place of the others but more than the others; the only reason you did this was to make those elements heard and felt, however unimportant they are to the general tenor of the speech. Another interesting, even essential, matter to have noticed is that because *there* contains a wide vowel that needs a naturally open mouth anyway, that word was disproportionately louder than the rest; the word *problem* may also have been louder, particularly its first syllable. You noticed that you had to control your output even more than usual. But you enjoyed this big sense of control, of course, because it is another of the greatest joys of the profession.

In cropping your photograph to make an adequately visible and audible enlargement, no significant details were omitted, the significance of nothing has been changed, and the whole has been enlarged.

Find the solutions to the various problems presented after this point. The word *too* needs "pushing," and the three *many's* need to be reduced because they are so easy to do, as they are wide open sounds. The challenging bits for the exercise of speaking reasonably to a crowd of four thousand are as follows: *simply; too short; should;*

hundred; but; should; should; food; each; bring; into; live; miserably; should (but by this point you will know what to do with this word); *tuna fish; ear; utterly destroy; garden* (be careful with this last syllable!); *what we have been doing;* the conclusion should be relatively easy by now.

What were the problems you had with those words? Were you able to provide intensity and volume on all of them? Make a list of sounds that did not come across as perfectly as others, and practice them especially hard. You will find help in the section on Agility.

3. *What is the special bodily state that needs to be experienced in this "final stage" projection?* Most good performers know when they have achieved this state, which is rather like riding a horse. Some people have compared the state to flying with the feet on the ground, and some have even sounded visionary and likened it to that combination of delicious tension, control, and lightness that sometimes accompanies starvation or fasting or even drug trips. What separates this state from all these comparisons and what makes it work in art and in the theatre is that the emotions and the intellect control the body. I first experienced the state on stage when I was twenty, in a solo number in a musical revue, although I had had feelings like it in nontheatrical situations from an early age. The English poet Wordsworth regretted that such experiences dwindle in frequency as we get older and, in *Lines Composed a Few Miles above Tintern Abbey,* described them in this way:

> That blessed mood,
> In which the burthen of the mystery,
> In which the heavy and the weary weight
> Of all this unintelligible world,
> Is lightened:—that serene and blessed mood,
> In which the affections gently lead us on,—
> Until, the breath of this corporeal frame
> And even the motion of our human blood
> Almost suspended, we are laid asleep
> In body, and become a living soul:
> While with an eye made quiet by the power
> Of harmony, and the deep power of joy,
> We see into the life of things.

(lines 37–49)

On the stage, when you are projecting, when all the elements of your performance are in harmony with yourself or with others, the bodily state and the power and insight that accompany it can be described no better than in Wordsworth's lines.

However, to reach the state of your art where such a joy is possible, you need to have a range of expression. And before you can have a range of expression, you need to have a wide vocal range. How can you achieve this? By work. Read the next section on Agility. You can start on the road toward range by developing a limber mouth. But first, let us use the lines just quoted as a projection exercise.

The lines are fairly easy to project because of the preponderance of wide vowels; your mouth will be in the best position for sending out sound. Here are the problems as I see them after trying the projection a few times in a large space with an audience.

The first four lines have only one word that needs extra attention: *weight*. The final *t* can get lost in the heaviness of the words that precede it. *Lightened* is difficult. The *d* can be expelled with a hint of vowel after it, perhaps, a sort of *d(uh)*; remember that it is safer to do this than to rely on the audience following you up to this point. Why should they hear only *lighten*? The word is, after all, *lightened*, and that is what they should hear. Use the technique you are developing to make sure that the ending of the word is clear from far off.

The only other difficulty in the piece is the *f* of *life*. From afar, this can sound like *lie* or *liventhings*. Many directors have said to me, as I also say to actors if I am directing, "What? I beg your pardon? What did you say? What was that?" If your audience has to wait a word or two to clarify the sound of what you say, they lose the joy of working at the meaning. And it is important to bear in mind that the audience is the judge of meaning.

Now . . . some vowels.

PURITY OF THREE VOWELS *AH, EH,* AND *EE*

"Purity" of vowels is not important in theatre speech, but it is vital in the training of actors. How can this be true? Let me explain.

Purity of vowels used to be sought after. In fact, purity within standard North American stage diction and British stage diction was a *sine qua non* of the employable actor. This was a nineteenth-century concern, and in Britain it died out with the advent of the "Angry Young Men" school in the fifties and the arrival on the international theatrical scene of such actors as Albert Finney and Tom Courtenay, whose regional accents were perfectly acceptable and that in some measure actually contributed to their success. Audiences do not crave them now, although of course, they are still to be found in the voices of John Gielgud, Ralph Richardson, and Gregory Peck as well as in hosts of other so-called "old school" actors.

So, why are pure vowels useful for the actor in training? Pure vowels are like the scales in piano exercises: You have to know them before you can play the piano. There are other good reasons for the practice of perfecting these sounds: It loosens the facial muscles; it makes you conscious of what your lips are doing when they stretch; above all, it increases projection and aids resonance when done frequently. As a relaxer of the face and jaw, this practice is also part of your vocal warm-up.

What are pure vowels? First of all, here are three: *ah, eh,* and *ee.*

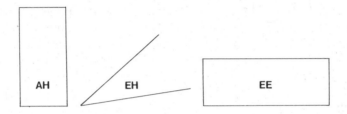

What those shapes on the page represent are the approximate shapes your mouth should be in when pronouncing the three vowels.

1. Think of the *ah* as an upright rectangle. Open your mouth as *vertically* as you can, as if the doctor were examining your tonsils. When the sound comes out, ask your partner, friend, or teacher if it is really a straight, upright, vertical, purely unadulterated, undiphthongized *ah.* There are very few words that use this vowel these days without sounding pretentious or affected, so do not put words into this exercise. This vowel is seldom found in *father* or *bath* and is not found in *mat* or *cat,* with the exception of regionalisms.

2. Think of *eh* as much flatter than *ah.* Your mouth cannot form the shape given in the illustration, but the sound certainly can if you will it. Think of that sideways triangle, and a sound at a 45-degree angle will be produced after some work.

3. The *ee* is a good stretcher of the facial muscles. Smile the broadest smile that you can, from ear to ear, and feel the tension in the jaw and neck as well as in the cheeks.

4. Do the three vowels slowly, beginning with *ah: ah/eh/ee.*

5. Do them faster, joining them so that *ah-eh-ee* becomes *ahehee.*

6. Do them in reverse until you get *eeehah.*

7. Now be able to do them forward and backward frequently at speed, getting *aheheeehah*.

8. Put a rhythm to this to help you to maintain the purity of each of the three joined sounds. This rhythm would help nicely: AHeh-EEehAHehEEehAHehEEehAH. You are focusing on *ee* this way and doing the exercise three times and coming to rest on the *ah* you began with as in *one* two *three* four *one* two *three* four *one* two *three* four *one*.

TWO MORE VOWELS

o and *oo:* These, too, can be "pure." And for the purposes of these exercises that are an essential part of my vocal warm-up, the vowels must be pure.

1. Think of *o* as a pure circle that your mouth can form by being a perfect tube. Do not allow yourself to produce a diphthong of any kind, and be sure to have someone listening to you doing this sound.

2. Think of *oo* as a small tube through which insufficient air can pass to produce an *o*. Purse your lips as tightly as you can until there is only a tiny round hole to let the sound out. You will find a straining in the throat, of course. This is natural, unharmful, and not to be worried about at all.

3. Stretching your cheeks, do *oo-o-oo-o-oo-o-oo* to the rhythm of *a-one and a-two and a-three and a-four*.

4. Now return to your *ah* and *eh* and *ee,* and do it ten times as in *aheheeehah*.

5. Now, for a complete warm-up, join the *o* and the *oo* to the *ahehee* in the following way, and you will have a wonderful exercise for agility, relaxation, and even resonance: *ah-eh-ee-oo-o-aw-ah*. You see that I have added an *aw* here to provide a transition into *ah*. Learn the whole chain, as it is an essential part of the vocal warm-up you should do several times while limbering up yourself for a rehearsal or a performance.

EXERCISES FOR AGILITY AND CONTROL

It is clear that a pianist cannot play well a technically easy piece such as *Claire de Lune* until he can also play things more challenging. It is commonly accepted, also, that the difficult sports that provide most pleasure are those in which the players and competitors have succeeded in making great strain and effort appear simple. The daring young man on the flying trapeze is admired because he flies through the air with the greatest of ease. Such performances arouse a great deal more than admiration: They arouse the spectator to something that can approach ennoblement; this joy brings what Wordsworth called "elevated thoughts"; it is possible to function more fully as a human being when one observes something magnificently done.

Slow speech requires considerably more control of breath and phrasing than quick speech, just as slow locomotion on stage takes more straining of the muscles than does a rapid walk. This principle of execution is perhaps what makes *Claire de Lune* so tricky. One of the difficulties is, simply, the possibility of mere lack of speed. The audience that says, "How slowly that was said!" has not received the pleasure of the audience that says, "That was splendid—and so slow!" Because fewer new sounds are being uttered, those heard are given much more critical attention, and the spectator has time to relish them. Without self-indulgence, the actor must relish them too.

Some of the sounds produced by the following exercises will not be attractive at all. But work on them, preferably in a group.

Plosives

Plosive is the noun and adjective given to the act and nature of the sound produced when air is expelled from the lips in a sudden and explosive burst, soft or loud, generally on the letters *p* and *b*, and usually voiced. These letters have the most force when followed by *l*, and the least when by *r* or on their own.

A. **pl** (with a note on labial *l*): *Planning to plop in the public pool?*

1. When you say these words, you will hear that the volume and force of **pl**anning to **pl**op are probably quite different from *public pool*. The task here is to even out the words until they are of equal force, first by strengthening the weaker and then vice versa.

Rehearse the first three words first, making sure the final *p* of *plop* is forceful and of the same quality as the *p* of *planning* and *plop*. You will find diaphragmatic pressure is necessary because offstage very few people have to care about final consonants.

Once you are used to "forcing" the final *p*, rehearse the three words as rapidly as possible until the three plosives are of equal strength, and the phrase can be said quickly and smoothly: *planning to plop planning to plop planning to plop planning to plop.* You will notice, of course, the "uh" needed between plo*p* and *p*lanning; practice will quieten it, and must. (In large-stage theatres such "uh' "s are *de rigueur*, particularly in singing, and are not to be reduced in such circumstances.)

Now reassemble the sentence, and you will likely find that your *p* in **p**u*blic* and **p**oo*l* is better controlled.

2. Given the force of these plosives, it is obvious that the final *l* of *pool* is weak. Some actors have the bad habit of voicing this consonant to the extent that it is literally sung. This extra push is necessary only in lines like the one we are looking at here, where the noises that surround or precede the *l* are very strong either in themselves or from accumulation. *Give the extra push by not releasing the tongue from the teeth until the l has been voiced a fraction of a second longer than usual. No real push is called for at all, simply a longer note.* (You can try to imitate the bad habit I have described by increasing the volume, and you will no doubt find it a distasteful practice.)

3. So far Exercise A has stimulated control, and it is also a useful line for plosive agility. Utter the line without voicing it. Rapidly and loudly, until the lips are numb and you must rest them. Begin again, and rehearse it until you can "say" it while holding the breath. Because of the elocution of the plosives, the line should be audible to someone who is looking at your mouth. Be careful of *public* since there is no *l* after the *p* to force the lips forward into a more hollow explosion.

B. **bl:** very similar to *pl,* of course, but a deeper sound. The lips are farther forward and the mouth cavity is larger. *Blame Blake's bulbs* will be the treacherous phrase for *bl*; it has an annoying reversal in *bulbs*. Little agility is achieved in this exercise, but you will have a feeling of well-being when you get it right.

C. **p** (with a note on the final dental *d*): There is an old rhyme for *p*, easy to execute and worth doing properly:

Peter Piper picked a peck of pickled pepper;
A peck of pickled pepper Peter Piper picked;
If Peter Piper picked a peck of pickled pepper,
Where's the peck of pickled pepper Peter Piper picked?

(Peter Piper's Practical Principles of Plain and Perfect Pronunciation, 1819)

In fact, this verse is more useful for the two *d* sounds it contains: the *t* of picke*d* and the *d* of pickle*d*, the latter being difficult to present audibly at speed. This *d* must be focused and slightly separated from the preceding *l* for it to be heard at all. You may notice that your first read-through brought the *d* out as *pickle-pepper,* and that is one reason the rhyme has been included here: The *d* is the obstacle in an otherwise simple process. As in A3, it is fruitful to practice this rhyme voiced and unvoiced, increasing speed until the delivery becomes an interesting and metrical popping rattle and a good exercise for the lower jaw.

Tonguing the *S* Sibilant

Those seeking help with pronounced sibilants (the "hissy *s*" that is the bane of many a director's life) will not find a cure in the following exercises but may well be so encouraged by the resulting sound that they look for help elsewhere.

1. Beginning with the most challenging tongue twister of them all as far as sibilants are concerned can improve the results on the later exercises: *The sixth sick sheik's sixth sheep's sick.* The most frustrating stumbling blocks in this sentence are the transition in the *sheik's sixth* and *sixth sheep's.* Focus on those in your first slow reading. You will discover that the physical posture is of great help. One way to achieve the most productive attitude of neck and chest (since pronunciation of this sentence calls for some activity of the diaphragm and chest muscles) is to place oneself in a mental attitude of calm control, a relaxed firmness rather akin to what is needed when driving a car and, more especially, a horse: when the back cannot slouch. In fact, it is difficult to say this sentence when seated with the back resting on the back of a chair. It is better to sit forward or stand up. *Sheik's/sixth* has to be treated in much the same way as the *d* in Exercise C.

After perfecting this sentence, the tongue should be so coordinated that *She sells sea shells on the sea shore* should appear as child's play.

2. *Sister Susie's sewing shirts for sailors* will also be easy now; its only difficulty is the temptation of the tongue to say *shewing sirts,* the same error in concentration that has been found for over a century in the party-game tongue twister *Not a ship in sight* (*not* "Not a sip in shite"). If you voice the *s* and make it thereby into a *z,* the sentence's obstacle all but vanishes: Try to discover the reason for this.

3. In *The Taming of the Shrew,* Petruchio enters and says to Baptista:

> Sir, my business asketh haste.

Many actors take this line slowly and deliberately, an interpretation wholly consonant with the text and with a man making himself clear while in a hurry. As in most of these lines, concentration is the only way to ensure that your technique will not fail you. (One of the world's five most celebrated actors let his mouth utter, in *King Lear*, a surprising salutation: "Ye sen-fucked bogs," for "fen-sucked bogs.")

Exercise for General Tongue and Lip Dexterity

The following sentence is a great restorer of the spirit, enlivener of the mouth, and enlarger of self-esteem when flawlessly vocalized at least twenty times while moving and while attempting to concentrate on other things as well, such as applying makeup, tying shoelaces, going to the bathroom, checking personal properties and other magic preparations and warm-ups before the performance or rehearsal:

She stood on the balcony inexplicably mimicking him hiccuping, amicably welcoming him in.

More Exercises for Difficult Sounds

The following passages and speeches are examples of prose requiring dexterity of delivery. After each there are comments and questions, and the main purpose of each extract is indicated.

GASTON So your son had no friend. That's a pity. I mean it's a pity if we find that I'm your son. There must be nothing more comforting, when you've become a man, than to see your childhood mirrored in the eyes of a small boy of once upon a time. Yes, a pitch. For I'd rather hoped that I'd regain my memory through this imagined friend. It would be a perfectly natural thing for one person to do for another.

A. This extract is from Anouilh's *Traveller Without Luggage* (*Voyageur Sans Bagages*), translated into English by John Whiting in 1959—a quite poised speech. The following are the difficulties as I see them:

1. Moving from *d-th* in *find that* . . .
2. Getting the *p,d,* and *th* sufficiently strong in *rather hoped that* . . .
3. The *d* again. This time try to get it forward in *imagined friend.*

B. Try the enjoyment of getting *perfectly natural* perfectly natural while pronouncing every phoneme fully and quickly.

Gentle Dentals

ANTHONY   That were somewhat out of our purpose, cousin, sith (as I have told you before) the man were not then in sorrow and tribulation, whereof our matter speaketh, but in perilous merry mortal tantation. So that is we should, beside our own matter that we have in hand, enter into that too, we might make a longer work between both than we could well finish this day.

A. Thomas More, in "The Second Book of Comfort" from his *A Dialogue of Comfort* (1534), is not creating rapid speech, but it will be good practice for the actor to imagine a situation where this argumentative character, Anthony, is in some haste to make his point.

B. In fact, to read the first phrase slowly requires more concentration than would a rapid reading. Try that too, being as gentle as possible (but still audible and crisp) on the *t*'s of *that, somewhat,* and *out.*

Perilous merry moral tantation is a wonderful exercise for getting the mouth into various shapes very quickly. But begin slowly, in order to discover exactly what stretching of your jaws and cheeks is necessary to produce these vowels fully. Do it often, and add it to your list of phrases and sounds for your vocal warm-ups.

Vowel Transition

> Gallant and gay, in Cliveden's proud alcove
> The bower of wanton Shrewsbury and love.

A. From Pope's *Moral Essays,* Ep. iii, to Lord Bathurst, this couplet encourages a rhythmical pronunication of *Shrewsbury.*

B. The main reason for the inclusion of this couplet is the agile change necessary from the vowel of *bower* to that of *wanton.* The couplet is worth repeating many times.

Vowel Transition and Transfer of Dental to Plosive

> Ring out wild bells, to the wild sky.

A. From Tennyson's *In Memoriam* (cvi), these words are celebrated for their vowel series, which expands to the end of the phrase. The change of vowel is not easy.

B. More useful still to the actor seeking dental and labial agility particularly is the transfer to the *d* to the *b* in *wild bells* at speed.

n to *w* Transfer

A. Though wisdom cannot be gotten for gold, still less can it be gotten without it. Gold, or the value of what is equivalent to gold, lies at the root of wisdom, and enters so largely into the very essence of the Holy Ghost that "no gold, no Holy Ghost" may pass as an axiom.

Samuel Butler (1835–1902) was not a quick speaker, and his prose is often as slow as his speech. However, in this passage from "Cash and Credit, Modern Simony" in his *Note Books*, there are repeated g sounds and repetitions of the words *gold*. Try the passage quickly without making it a *tour de force* of any kind.

The first sentence is especially troublesome for its transfer of *n* to *w* in *gotten without* and *n* to *f* in *gotten for*.

B. It cannot in the opinion of His Majesty's Government be classified as slavery in the extreme acceptance of the word without some risk of terminological inexactitude.

This sentence from Winston Churchill's Speech to the House of Commons on February 22, 1906, has, of course, no effect without the understated relishing of its last five words.

Transfer of the Voiced *th* to *d*

I have a rendezvous with Death
At some disputed barricade

(Alan Seeger, 1888–1916)

These lines from a poem of World War I are, if the actor thinks strongly about the statement they contain, excellent practice for the living: the need for care of the *th* of *with* (which is preferably voiced), and the transfer from *d* to *b* in *disputed barricade*.

The Very Long Word

COSTARD   O! they have lived long on the alms-basket of words. I marvel thy master hath not eaten thee for a word; for thou art not so long by the head as honorificabilitudinitatibus: thou art easier swallowed than a flap-dragon.

There is a multitude of opportunities for agility in this speech from Act IV, Scene iii, of *Love's Labour's Lost*—the crispness of *alms-bas-*

ket, the elegance of the alliteration on *lived long* and *marvel thy master*. The coined Latin word is more edible and enjoyable to pronounce than the *supercalifragilisticexpialidoshus* of Mary Poppins. The word is not as long, however, as the just possible German word for "the wife of the representative of the fire insurance company manager": *die Feuerversicherungsgesellschaftsdirektorsstellvertetersgemahlin.*

Quick Change of Pace

These are begot in the ventricle of memory, nourished in the womb of pia mater, and delivered upon the mellowing of occasion.

(Love's Labour's Lost, III, i)

This is a fool-proof exercise for concentration while warming up before rehearsal or performance because the tripping consonants of the first phrase are warmed and "softened" by the second and utterly changed (although in a poised way by because of the *d*'s of *delivered*) by the *m*, *l*, and *ng* of *mellowing* and the low-voiced *zh* of *occasion*. (This last *zh* was not pronounced that way in Shakespeare's day, so we can draw no conclusions about phonetic trickery in that word. This exercise is not interpreting the speech but using it as vocal medicine.)

The Common *d* to *n* Transfer, Using the Base of the Tongue

Keats provides, in *Endymion*, Bk. i, a sentence giving the actor the chance to focus the *d* before the *n*. It is difficult to voice the *d* properly and land on the *n*, but the sense of accomplishment produced with success is appreciated much by the base of the tongue:

> Never, I aver,
> Since Ariadne was a vintager

Exercise for the Reduction of *d*

As in the exercise for Quick Change of Pace, this exercise is good for a tightening of vocal concentration and control before professional activity. It will keep up the dexterity, but it is intended to avoid overelocuted speech. Just as in *and to* (it is irritating to hear an actor give too much value to the *d*, resulting in something like "andhuhto"), the quietude of the following line from the Second Collect in the

Service of Evensong in the English *Book of Common Prayer* would be disturbed by a voiced vowel between *accord* and *to*.

. . . with one accord to make our common supplications unto thee.

ng to *st* and *th* to *h*

> For Age, with stealing steps,
> Hath clawed me with this clutch

(Thomas, Lord Vaux, 1510–1556, *The Aged Lover Renounceth Love—a Ditty*)

At speed, transfer from *with* to *stealing* is difficult if one is to pronounce the *th* at all. The object here is to utter the *th* confidently while making it quite distinct from the *st* so that one hears both sounds at equal intensity.

sh to *s* and Preserving the Force of *m*

> The tigerish Spring was in each vein,
> The glittering wind of Spring, my mane.

(Edith Sitwell, 1958, *La Bella Bona Roba*)

It is tricky to maintain volume on the *m* of *mane*, given the greater length of the *n* in normal delivery of this word and particularly given the great force of the *Spr* that precedes it.

To Avoid Confusion of *th* and *s*

The following line, from *The Merchant of Venice*, V, i, is not as difficult as the *sixth sheik's sheep* we saw on page 46.

> This night methinks is but the daylight sick.

Subtlety of *d* to *d*

The transfer of *d* to *d* in a line like the following is easy with a pause between the two words:

> Damned disinheriting countenance.

(Sheridan, *The School for Scandal*, IV, i)

At speed, however, we either have the intrusive *uh* between the *d*'s or lose the final *d* of *damned* altogether unless we take care to lose enough power on it to make the following *d* stronger.

b and *m* Confusion (Caused by an *l*)

As is obvious from tongue twisters that present these two sounds, they are both produced from the same lip position and can become confused. The following line from Book I, Canto I, stanza ii, of Spenser's *The Faerie Queene*, said ten times rapidly, encourages concentration. It is possibly the *l*, also so near the front of the mouth, that creates the problem here.

A bold bad man.

A PRELIMINARY LIST OF PHRASES FOR YOUR VOCAL WARM-UP

Planning to plop in the public pool?
Blame Blake's bulbs.
Peter Piper picked a peck of pickled pepper;
A peck of pickled pepper Peter Piper picked;
If Peter Piper picked a peck of pickled pepper,
Where's the peck of pickled pepper Peter Piper picked?
The sixth sick sheik's sixth sheep's sick.
Sister Susie's sewing shirts for sailors.
My business asketh haste.
Gallant and gay, in Cliveden's proud alcove
The bower of wanton Shrewsbury and love.
Ring out, wild bells, to the wild sky.
Though wisdom cannot be gotten for gold, still less can it be gotten
    without it.
Without some risk of terminological inexactitude.
I have a rendezvous with Death
At some disputed barricade.
The Alms-basket lived long to marvel thy master with
    honorificabilitudinitatibus.
These are begot in the ventricle of memory, nourished in the womb
    of pia mater, and delivered upon the mellowing of occasion.
The mellowing of occasion.
Never, I aver,

Since Ariadne was a vintager.
With one accord to make our common supplications unto thee.
Hath clawed me with his clutch.
The night methinks is but the daylight sick.
Damned disinheriting countenance.
A bold bad man.
She stood on the balcony, inexplicably mimicking him hiccuping,
    amicably welcoming him in.

There, quite a few phrases to go on with. Memorize them, get used to them, and you'll find yourself developing not only an agile face and mouth but also a new posture. Remember *never to put the energy into the facial expression* when you are doing these warm-up exercises. There is a rich feeling of control that comes from making them appear easy even to yourself. Form into sentences those words that are only phrases. Compose some sentences yourself too.

You are ready, now that you know something about the breath and projection and have worked at making your mouth agile, to proceed to meaning. In the English language, meaning cannot exist in speech without inflection, which is what the next chapter is about.

3

Attaining and Preserving an Ear: Inflection, Sound, and Rhythm

Present-day performances of Shakespeare and other playwrights of poetic drama follow twentieth-century methods, and it is no longer necessary to train as a chorister to be employed as a classical actor. Just as the choric and declamatory techniques of Greece and Rome were superseded by the more relaxed but nonetheless formal delivery of the Elizabethans in England and later by the crisp lines of the Comédie Française in France, so modern vocal acting has been greatly influenced by William Gillette's school of "the illusion of the first time" and calls less on the musicality of speech. However, the stage leaders who have created what amounts to a new naturalism may be generally observed to have a fine vocal craft that works to form the impression of spontaneity and naturalness, and they can be heard— through natural talent, practice, and application—to work the voice with care.

The following exercises should be done with a group or with at least two other people who can compare meanings for you and for each other.

EXERCISE I—INFLECTION, SOUND, AND RHYTHM

A. Because it concentrates the attention on vowels requiring elementary breath control in addition to its present use, this first exercise involves the line from Macbeth "Hang out our banners on the outward wall" (eight words hammered into voice students for over a century now). One evening, Stanislavki performed over twenty-five interpretations of the simple phrase "Good Evening," receiving applause of understanding with each variation. This exercise will develop a facility of inflection.

Study the sentence as set out on this staff, and decide on an exact subtext of sense: (each space on the stave represents one note, a musical third away from the next).

hang		ners on		wall
	out		the	ward
	our			
		ban-		out-

Questions

1. Is the sentence a question or a statement, as inflected?
2. Is the question in response to something someone else has said?
3. Is the speaker in agreement with whoever said it first?

The stresses are obviously "Hang out the *banners* on the *outward* wall?"

B. So far we are playing the interpreter/spectator, wringing meaning out of a certain inflection. Create now the following meaning and render it in notation:

You have told me to hang out the banners. I am familiar with our banners. I *always* hang up the banners. Banner-hanging is what I do best. I have never hung them up on the outward wall before, and respectfully question your judgment in telling me to do this.

As you did that, you realized that the first five syllables of the sentence rested on one probably quite high note. In English speech, familiarity, habit, and custom of this kind almost invariably produce a *melody coming to rest on a lower note than where it started* or *remaining on one* (which is what happens here, where the habit, the custom, the familiarity are in response to a command).

hang out our banners on		wall?
	the	ward
	out-	

Now, this by no means implies that stress always equals lowering of pitch. In this particular question, however, and given the precise subtext of B, this notation is the only one possible to give a clear reading of the intent. The *only* "character" to the speaker is response to command and doubting question. No other attitude is present. Return now to A and B of this exercise, and make your meanings clear and distinct from one another. It is important, remember, to do these exercises with a friend, teacher, or partner so that they can confirm your own inflections.

Changing the Tune with a New Attitude

C. Render the following meaning in notation. It is an extension of 1B, involving careful attention to the rise and fall of your own speech. Remember you are not being asked to "act" but plainly to record the shifting notes created in speech by attitude. Whatever your normal and usual speech pattern, the result will be the same unless you still have a very noticeable regional or national accent with the concomitant peculiarities. *Do not allow pauses here,* as they bespeak attitude, and will confuse the exercise.

Oh, there you go again, telling me to hang out our banners on the outward wall. OK.

hang out our		outward
	banners on the	wall

This would be made impudent if the highest notes were higher, the lowest ones staying where they were:

hang out our		outward
	banners on the	wall!

It may safely be inferred from examples A, B, and C that the note, that is to say pitch, betokens the subtext. And to the question "The note of what?" we answer, "The note of the phoneme." A phoneme is a unit of sound. Just as the most common kind of Chinese spoken in Hong Kong has *um goi* for the sounds representing *thank you,* the words do not mean "thank you" unless pitched right, the *um* low and the *goi* a few notes higher. In the following example, D, we shall revert to the procedure of A, but be sure to master A, B, and C first.

Deciding on a Subtext and Exercising It

D. Study the sentence as set out on the staff, trying it with the voice and deciding on an exact subtext: (: represents a pause)

	ners :	
	on the outward	
hang out our ban-		wall

Questions

1. Does the first half sound like a question? It is deceptively interrogative, but could only be a question if *hang up our* were a few notes higher than *ban-*. We should realize that not all upward inflections are queries, as we shall see further in the dipthongs of Exercise 2. The first phrase is in fact an acquiescence uttered in straightforward tone of acceptance rather like—but more actively so than in—B.

2. The coming-to-rest on the low note of *wall* concludes the attitude of custom prepared in the first phrase before the pause. What is the effect of the pause? What does it do to what preceded it? The matter of pausing is dealt with later in this chapter.

3. While *avoiding any change of note during vowels,* decide on one or more of the following subtexts for the sentence, and present it to other students for notation and discussion. Be sure to write your intentions on the staff and deliver the result slowly with *no change in facial expression.*

EXERCISE 2—CONTROL AND CONCENTRATION

Throughout this chapter, we are dealing with small units of meaning presented with the voice alone, divorced from the usefulness of the face and eyes. The coordination and control effected by careful performance of the exercises will be gratifying. Occasionally, the frustration encountered in the difficulty of keeping the eyebrows level, for instance, will be similar to learning to twiddle the thumbs in reverse or raising one seldom singled finger while the rest are still. Perseverance will surmount such creative crises. In this sense, Exercise 1 is harder than those that succeed it.

In Exercise 1 there was call for immense control because no changes of note were given during the pronunication of the vowels. Let us now ornament the meaning of A, keeping its principal intent intact, and slide down the staff on *hang*, thus:

a.

ha-

ners

ng out our ban-

Consider that, and now slide *up* the staff instead, thus:

b.

ng out our banners

ha

Questions

1. What is the main distinction in meaning between the two?
2. What other phrases can you think of that inflect the first verb as in a?
3. We could hear that a. makes *hang* sound like a resigned command, possibly from a subordinate, to even lesser mortals. The phrase can also be a question of disbelief—see 4c.
4. While on this exercise, nourish your agility by sliding the *a* in *hang* rapidly up and down, followed by the *ng* only. Then to develop vocal concentration, switch to an alternating pattern. Staffs for this useful exercise are given in the following:

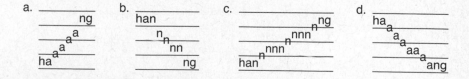

5. What is the effect of sliding down on *wall*?

```
                          wa
    the outward       a
                        a
                          a
                          l
```

The tone is of realization and understanding.

6. While taking care not to move facial muscles except as necessary for the production of the sound, decide on one or more of the following subtexts for the sentence, and present it to others for notation and discussion. Be sure to write your intentions on the staff and deliver the result slowly, *changing the note on the vowels only,* if possible.

a. We are not accustomed to hanging up the banners, but we think it is a reasonable thing to do if only we could do it properly; what is more, you suggest the outward walls as the best place for them. Of course! How right you are! Hanging them there is much easier than elsewhere. Great! As I was speaking, I saw the sense of this plan.

b. I can imagine hanging some things on the outward walls, but certainly not banners. To suggest the outward walls, what is more, is thoughtless and foolhardy. You must be mad.

c. You mean to hang them as opposed to simply wave them? And on the walls rather than the doorposts, window ledges, and trees?

a. _____   b. _____   c. _____
   _____   _____   _____
   _____   _____   _____
   _____   _____   _____

E. After discussing the fruits of your research into basic vowel inflection, Exercise 2 concludes with a deliberately meaningless interpretation of the line to encourage rapid note changes. The line should be learned by heart and repeated several times at increasingly high speeds.

Rapid Note Change Exercise

```
hang      our                 out-      wall

                  banners

      out                 on the    ward
```

Why should anyone be asked to do this exercise? Of what possible relevance is it to your training as an actor? Let me tell you. If you can do the exercise quickly, you have learned agility of inflection, something that many actors crave to do but cannot because their mouths and minds have become lazy with habit, which you don't want to happen. And by far one of the best ways to avoid that is to do this kind of "meaningless" exercise until you're nearly in a frenzy of madness and boredom. *Then* comes what some people call the "creative crisis," when you think there's no use going on and nothing makes much sense and suddenly, out of the blue (but not really, it's out of practice and application and discipline), you've *got it!*

What Can You Do Now?

You can continue doing exercises. The following phrases are for substitution and use for further exercises in inflection. You *might* go mad if you said "Hang up the banners on the outward wall" for more than a few days, and I wouldn't want that to happen.

> I accordingly applied to my old friend Hume.
> I must have slept pretty well.
> In like manner when the pistols were loading.
> At his meals a book lay by his side.
> Always reading terrible epics.
> Will your baby tell us anything about preexistence, Madam?
> She spoke with an air of deep disappointment.
> How provokingly close are those newborn rabbits!
> Aubrey de Vere was quite right.
> A man of singularly vague and dreamy habits.
> Here lies one whose name is writ in hot water.
> His heart was not in business at all.
> The Siddharta spent the night with dancers and wine.
> Don't be mad at my dad like that!

I think you should make up your own now. I've run out of phrases. But keep on doing the exercise, as fast as you can, changing the notes. You are developing an important technique.

Why is this technique important? Emergencies happen in performance, and you need to be able not only to think quickly but also to act quickly. Change the pace. Change your inflection to accommodate a mistake or a new idea a fellow actor has come up with in the inspiration of the moment. This facility with inflection and agility with change are both excellently comfortable things to fall back on in moments of stress.

Well, you haven't been looking at the meaning of anything very interesting so far. Read on, and you'll find some of the richest sounds in the English language.

EXERCISE 3—DIVING IN AT THE DEEP END: SOME RICH SOUNDS

A phoneme is the smallest unit of sound and a morpheme the smallest unit of meaning, as in the phonemes *ph/o/n/e/me* and the morphemes *phon/eme*. It is more vital for the actor to be aware of phonemes and the audience of morphemes, as the two processes combine into the uttered meaning. This exercise is not intended to encourage the "beautiful speech" that characterized some of the weak British acting of the forties and fifties which, in the films of the period, can still be heard more than seen. Since Burbage, then to Garrick and on to Olivier and Gielgud, the critical spectator has struck a balance between praising and deploring intense and full vocal delivery (which often becomes an eccentricity), particularly when heard at close range. There is, however, little doubt that mere *clarity* of speech is not enough in acting. Actors unaware of the *texture* and *noise* of the sounds they utter are simply not interesting enough to be saying the lines of Miller, Williams, O'Neill, Shaw, Shakespeare, and Wilde. A phonetic innocence is necessary: a heart willing to open itself to the multifarious possibilties of sounds issuing from human beings.

Just as the plain act of opening a door on stage can be split up into at least five component parts, so words can be profitably opened to reveal what makes them give forth the richest, most useful meaning. Let me tell you what I mean.

You're on stage and you have to open a door and go out through it. Let us assume that you are utterly neutral about the door and that so far no great emotional shake-up has happened in the scene. You still must "establish a relationship" with the door, or your audience won't believe your action. You must see it, focus your body on it, move toward it. Then . . . look, it's closed and has a handle that can open it. You establish a relationship with the handle. You see it, focus your hand on it, touch it, hold it, turn it, and open the door. These are eight actions for the acting of one act. That's what acting is, and it's the same with words: They have component parts that have sounds. You will remember that we can call these parts phonemes, that is, units of sound that in themselves do not necessarily carry the complete meaning.

There was a time when almost all plays were written in verse. Later in this book there will be opportunities to work on parts of plays from the repertoire of the poetic drama. But first, it is important to look at a poem. I have deliberately chosen one that seems at first sight to be very difficult, one that works mainly through sound and rhythm. Actors are not unintelligent, and in a book on the care and use of the voice, it would be insulting to omit consideration of complex poetry. In the following explication of Hopkins' sonnet *The Windhover*, I shall incorporate the points that might normally be made about elocution in a categorical and methodical way. There are two excellent recorded performances of this poem available by Richard Burton and Cyril Cusack (both on Caedmon Records) that will illustrate my main points well.

I caught this morning morning's minion, king-
    dom of daylight's dauphin, dapple-dawn-drawn Falcon, in his riding
    Of the rolling underneath him steady air, and striding
High there, how he rung upon the rein of a wimpling wing
5   In his ecstasy! then off, off forth on swing,
    As a skate's heel sweeps smooth on a bow-bend: the hurl
      and gliding
    Rebuffed the big wind. My heart in hiding
10 Stirred for a bird,—the achieve of, the mastery of the thing!

Brute beauty and valor and act, oh, air, pride, plume, here
    Buckle! AND the fire that breaks from thee even, a billion
Times told lovelier, more dangerous, O my chevalier!
15   No wonder of it: sheer plod makes plough down sillion
Shine, and blue-bleak embers, ah my dear,
    Fall, gall themselves, and gash gold-vermilion.

More than most poets, Hopkins was an actor/interpreter who, as he explained in his letters, sought to convey the essence of feeling at the very moment of vision. He called this process "inscape" and his metered way of presenting it "instress." That is to say, he sought to make a reader/listener observe the feelings until they were felt as he felt them himself: a high aim indeed, and the exact literary counterpart of the actor's desire to induce "empathy" in the spectator.

Line 1—*Caught*
I caught this morning is the first indication that here everything there is to pronounce is to be pronounced. *Caught,* with the sharpness

of its initial *c* and bright finality of its closing *t*, evokes the speed with which Hopkins captured his picture, and the permanence of its power. It can be readily shown that no synonym will suffice—*captured* contains neither the ambiguity and richness nor the phonetic intensity of *caught,* with its near coldness standing in fine contrast to the hum the mouth produces on *morning.*

Lines 1–2 *m, n, ng*

That the bird is at once the favorite servant of the morning and is indeed a dauphin, almost a king in fact, is felt roundly in the satisfying hums and deep nasalities of *morning's minion,* which is reinforced in retrospect, as it were, by the repetition of *morning.* So, not only has Hopkins caught the morning's minion this morning as opposed to yesterday evening or any other time, but he has also caught a being that is almost called "morning morning's minion." And the being is almost a king, as the hesitating linger on the first syllable of kingdom indicates. If the voice dwells on the nasal of *king* long enough, the listener begins to enter more deeply into the state of feeling by following the same *process of thought* as the poet (admittedly complex and full of many turns). The poet was the first person to absorb the experience and is making the listener experience it in the same way as the playwright first absorbs the experience (imaginatively in most cases, of course), and the actor is making the spectator absorb it by *observing and feeling* the actor experiencing it. Hopkins' mind— and ours—changes or enriches its thought by now making the falcon the dauphin of the kingdom of daylight.

Line 2—*d*

The excess of *d* in this line should not be exaggerated but uttered; the result is far from explosive. Rather, the *d-d-d-d-d* is a kind of stutter of the soul, a hesitancy of the imagination brought on by the wonder of the sight of the free-flying bird drawn to, drawn (etched) against or on, the dappled skies of the dawn. It is plain that the quasi-paraphrase I have just given is not even a subtext for the concept presented in the poem because the line as written is a mirror image not only of what the poet sees but also of how he feels about what he sees. What the poet sees *is in the phonetic shape of his reactions,* and when it is spoken with careful elocution of the upward short *a* in *dapple,* gentle *d's* and attention to the rhyming vowels or assonance of *dawn-drawn* with their irresistible pulling motion, the oral reader has *become the character and his state,* just as in good acting, and the listener is invited to join.

Line 3—Lingering on *Riding*

In his riding is very interesting indeed. Hopkins is giving the fullest "stage directions" at any poet's command. Where O'Neill and Shaw and Albee provide the following kinds of help with delivery,

EPIFANIA   (*Her teeth on edge*) You hear this, Mr. Sagamore!

                                                (Bernard Shaw, *The Millionairess*)

DIANE ANTHONY   (*With a suffering bewilderment*) Why am I afraid to dance, I who love music, and rhythm, and grace, and song, and laughter?

                                                (Eugene O'Neill, *The Great God Brown*)

MARTHA   Are you kidding? We've got guests.

GEORGE   (*Disbelieving*) We've got what?

                                                (Edward Albee, *Who's Afraid of Virginia Woolf?*)

poetic dramatists and poets work only with the shape of the line and the contours of its sound. Hopkins is using the convenient ending of a line of verse (at which all readers of poetry pause for an extremely brief moment) to create in the voice alone the sensation of the falcon riding the air effortlessly as a prince would a horse. Again, with careful elocution, the voice will give birth to a living thing if it lingers momentarily on the *ng* of *riding* before proceeding to line 3.

Line 3—Sounding Like the Experience

I hope that by the time you have reached this line with me you will have decided that what in this poem seemed at first merely eccentric and strange—the coined words, the flouting of conventional grammar and grammatical sense—is the writer's only way of expressing the "inscape" of the experience. *Of the rolling underneath him steady air* is no doubt a most individual expression of something like "the steady air which rolls underneath him"; however, as written, the latter phrase cannot possibly convey the sense of weight below and lightness above given in the line. The reader is forced to pronounce *rolling underneath him steady* as if the words were one long adjective; the reader is forced to sound like the man who first experienced it, or rather, sound as he felt when he experienced it while at the same time sounding like the experience felt. The actor's voice is made to sound like the feel of the air to the falcon and like the sensation of Hopkins' wonder in beholding the experience. The reading is *rollingunderneathhimsteady air.* (Many poets of the twentieth century have considered this device satisfying, one of the most popular examples occurring in e. e. cummings' *In Just Spring* with his *eddieandbill came running,* which gives at once the sense of the childhood inseparability of Eddie and Bill, their breathlessness, and the willful rush of the poem's assumed speaker.)

Line 3—A Transition

Striding receives the same treatment as *riding.* Note, however, how much more strength the falcon has with his control of the rolling air. It would be inadequate not to give full value to the *r* after the powerful *st* of *striding.*

Line 4—Alike Sounds

If not written in carefully, rhyme and assonance could be intruders in spoken prose, but they have a central purpose in verse. For instance, if a character in a play is made to say, *How many cows are brown now?,* we may assume either that the character knows he is rhyming and has a purpose in doing so or that the playwright did not notice and did not hear the oddity of the effect. (In Alan Ayckbourn's *Bedroom Farce,* Trevor bids goodnight to Kate, having repeatedly called her Kath, with the line, "You're really great, Kate." This is a different matter. It should be obvious to the audience but not to Trevor that the rhyme makes the statement slightly comic, because the speaker is not conscious of the effect he is creating.)

In this line from *The Windhover, high* is assonant with *striding.* As one pronounces these widest of vowels formed by the diphthong *ah-ee,* the very height of the scene is suggested by the sound one makes. The continuity of the action is reinforced, too, by the slight pause after *striding* caused by the technique of line-ending that we just discussed.

Line 4—The Agreement of Alliteration

Anglo-Saxon alliterative verse provided models for Hopkins to experiment with his ideas about the "instress" of "inscape." In almost all extant Anglo-Saxon literature, the ubiquitous patterns of alliteration appear to be present for the sake of form adjunct to meaning. However, the actor with aural sensitivity (otherwise more simply known as good hearing) will note the brilliant reason for the *r r w w* pattern of *rung upon the rein of a wimpling wing* in this line. Quite apart from the fact that *rung* reminds us of *hung,* that there is likely a pun in *rein* on *reign*, and that the *h* of *how* has alliterated harmoniously with the *h* in *high*, we should observe that although the bird is in control of the air and itself, it is also completely in harmony with the air. Alliteration in verse and prose frequently has the effect of indicating agreement between the words involved that share the same initial letter. For more on this important phonetic and stylistic point, see the sections on *Hamlet* and *King Lear*. Meanwhile, rehearse these particular alliterations until you sense the continuity and harmony.

Line 5—Sibilants

In his ecstasy! Here the mouth is enjoined to utter noises of an altogether different quality from anything else in the poem so far except *striding*. The phrase contains the first hard sibilants, concentrated in a cluster in the bright, loud whisper of *ecstacy*, and it is a great first climax, full of life and joy. Of course, the phrase's effect reaches the listener subliminally, but the poet was as aware of its technique as surely as the reader and actor must be.

Line 5—The Glottal Stop

Then off, off forth on swing is our first encounter with the glottal stop. The glottal stop is more common to German and the Scandinavian languages than to English, and it is avoided in French. Whereas the railroad official may say in English, "Everybody out!" and slide from *everybody* to *out* with a half-pronounced consonant *y*, his German equivalent will stop between his two words *"Alle aussteigen!"* to obtain a forceful beginning to the second. In English this glottal stop is so occasional that it is highly noticeable when it does occur. (However, some dialects, that of Glasgow especially, are so fraught with glottal stops that they sound like Low German.) In this line the glottal pause between the two *off*'s is a muscular and phonetic representation of the bird's change in movement.

Practice the glottal stop in class. You can start in the following way. Open your mouth widely and growl quietly, vibrating the vocal cords just enough to produce a sound. Now say "uh-uh" and you'll notice a sensation in the glottis between the two utterances; that is a glottal stop. Now say "All out." Don't join the *l* to the *o*, but separate them as you separate them as you separated "uh-uh" before. You'll probably sound a bit German. Now say the "Off, off" from line 5 of *The Windhover*. You can do it. You've mastered the glottal stop. Try it with your partner or teacher and make sure you all understand the same thing.

Line 5

We should note that in a satisfactory elocution of this poem, there must be no hint of an indefinite article *a* before *swing*, since the falcon is not on the swing but the beginning of a swinging motion. Here we have an instance of the necessity for caring enunciation, where the interpreter becomes a technical medium through which the writer is making a rather special statement. This is not to say that the actor loses the "character" (in this case poem/poet) in favor of the position of machine and voice only, but that at moments like this the writer and the interpreter are entering into a kind of presentation relationship where it is being made clear that *what is being said is being said in the only possible way and the individuality of that way is being acknowledged.*

Line 6

The sibilants and sudden plosives of *As a skate's heel sweeps smooth on a bow-bend* provide a challenging task in rhythm and emphasis that repays an innocent approach in which the actor is laid open to the phonetic changes. The line is uncommon in that it contains so many spondees; it scans:

$$\cup \ \cup \ / \quad / \quad / \quad / \ \cup \ \cup \ / \quad /$$

As a skate's heel sweeps smooth on a bow bend.

There are very few lines in the literature of any language that so carefully and so well represent in sounds the sensation specified in the image as here of a skate's heel taking the beginning of a turn. The contrast between the *s* of skate and the *b* of the turn should be nourished by conscious vocal attention and not exaggerated. *Everything is already there on the page, awaiting the knowledgeable voice.* (See Chapter 4 on absorbing the lines.)

Line 6

The hurl and gliding: the distinction between the *ur* of *hurl* and the *li* of *gliding* requires attention. Hopkins was Welsh, whose language and accent call for "pure" vowels. *Hurl* is rounded and enclosed; *gliding* is open and wide. This contrast is preparation for the meeting of bird and wind in the next line.

Line 7

Rebuffed and *big wind* provide, to put it succinctly, the harmony of opposition. That is, the *b*'s of *rebuffed* and *big* sing a song of strength, not victory, and of action, not the rest of defeat. The bird's power does indeed rebuff the force of nature, but to a creative end. Again here as before, the alliteration is producing a picture and a feeling of harmony and agreement. Following this strong, even loud climax is a masterstroke to which the voice need only respond.

Line 7

My heart in hiding. This phrase, continuing the alliterative pattern (*b b h h*), is the first mention, after the opening *I caught*, of the poet's presence, and of course, the aspirates make it hushed. The phrase is in tune with *hurl and gliding.* The meaning is also rich: My heart is in hiding, and in the process of hiding it stirred; even a hidden heart, one locked away from the world as Hopkins' was, does stir with the joy of physical being, the ecstasy of flight. No matter how much his Jesuit training had emphasized the things of the spirit over those of the flesh, his heart is still as much a part of nature as the bird he envies and admires, although his heart is now merely a watcher of life. The sensitive ear will mark the resemblances of *hurl and gliding* to *heart and hiding.*

Line 8

A new assonance appears, and a new noise in the poem. The vowel *ir* in *stirred for a bird* has not appeared before—sufficient evidence of a new attitude and of a springing of the soul in appreciation of what before had been only perceived. If the voice includes the final dentals of *stirred* and *bird* with a soft emphasis, the preparation for the great major first climax (and climax of the octave of the sonnet) is complete.

Line 8

The writing of a verb as a noun is a shade easier than its elocution; *achieve* is strictly a verb, and *achievement* is a noun. *Achievement* is a conclusive concept, however; there is little possibility of development in the same vein after something has been achieved. *Achieve* is a transitive verb; it seeks an object. *Achieve* as a noun contains the activity of the verb and is richer than the finality of its conventional grammatical noun *achievement.* The actor/reader aware of this will necessarily enjoy the rush of active noise to be propelled in the *ch* of *achieve,* readying the listener for the rich hummed *m* of *mastery* that echoes the deep nasalities of line 1.

Line 8

The mastery of the thing! With its colloquial remembrance of statements such as "Look at the poor little thing!" and "Just the thing," this phrase nonetheless brings us close to Hopkins' ideas about what he translated from Duns Scotus' *haeccietas* as "thisness." *The* and *thing* do not alliterate since the first is voiced and the second unvoiced; as it happens, this is fortunate. The voiced *th* is low and, as anyone who tries it aloud will hear, serves as a springboard from which to plunge vocally into *thing.* This last, reverberating nasal hum is a natural climax to the preparatory *ng*'s of all the line-endings of the octave of the sonnet, *king-*, *riding*, *striding*, *wing*, *swing*, *gliding*, and *hiding*. It is, and the voice can make it so, at once the weakest word and the strongest sound idea of the first eight lines.

We have spent some pages on only eight lines of only one poem and not once mentioned the techniques of elocution. The omission is the method of this exercise in elocution. It is not possible to study the uses of sounds without immediate reference to a meaning.

Line 9

By now it should be plain that the *b b p p* alliterative sequence of *Brute beauty* and *pride plume* takes a rest in the aspirated *h* of *here. Here* is another springboard, if you like, into the force of *Buckle* in the next line. (To think of those noises in this poem as living in "lines" may be misleading insofar as it implies a linearity of experience. Such an implication is not intended.)

Line 10

Hopkins' *AND* is infamous; it can mean "yet," "because of this," "despite this," and it can act as a connective of the most definite kind. Pronounced fully, with a good *n* at its center, the word conveys the intended feeling of inevitability.

Line 10

Richard Burton's reading tries to make this sonnet much richer and fuller of sound than it is and succeeds in making masculine what is in fact a striving after virility rather than the achievement of it. Hopkins spoke of "the naked thew and sinew of the English language," and Burton seems to embody that idea. However, in the contrast between *billion* and *Times told lovelier*, we have a special rendering of something androgynous at least and effeminate at most. There is a rush of enthusiasm of the *b* of *billion* that is augmented by the urgent alliteration of *t*'s in *Times told*. This is followed by an amazing musical play on *m* and *n* in preparation for the final, unprecedented climax.

Lines 10–14

You will note the *m* in *more* and the *n* in *dangerous* and how they impel the pitch downward in readiness for the bowed and hushed explosion of the conclusion. There are still, too, echoes of the *ch* of *achieve* sounded in line 8 to be heard in the *g* of *dangerous*, the *ch(sh)* of *chevalier,* and the *sh*'s of *sheer* and *Shine.* These echoes end with *Shine* and the sound is not uttered again until the magnificent obeisance of *gash.* The *m* and *n* pattern in lines 12, 13, and 14 (*n m n n n m m m m n*) is stunningly executed and deserves conscious utterance. No audience in the world could know that there are five *m*'s and five *n*'s in these final three lines of the sonnet nor understand that this numerical equality is a major factor in the ineffable harmony produced; but the actor should know. The oral reader must also be aware that *gash,* containing as it does the wide vowel *a* (such an uplifting change from the *aw* sounds of *Fall* and *gall*), is an active pause in the *mn* pattern before it concludes the poem in the liturgical *mn* of *vermilion.*

The ending of this poem has been compared to the effect of a medieval altarpiece. The poem's ending certainly offers some of the richest, deepest, most satisfying sounds to be found in the English language.

The exercise just given in the form of an *explication de texte*[1] should demonstrate that a phoneme[1] uttered without a grasp of the morpheme[1] directing it is a poor thing indeed. Weaker still and dispensible is the morpheme uttered in performance without an actor's sure grip on its phonemes. Talking is thought walking; unsounded, it is sitting still and helping no one.

EXERCISE 4—THE INVOLUNTARY FALLING CADENCE

Possibly the most prevalent fault in the inflection of an actor with an untrained ear is the habit of ending almost all phrases on a downward slide. This habit is most often caused by the trauma of transferring the written page to the independent voice.

The following exercises are all drawn from *The Third National Reader,* published in New York in 1867. Why have I drawn these

[1]See the glossary.

examples from such a dusty old volume? For one thing, the examples are straightforward; for another, they establish a link with our oral past. I found the book in an old emporium in Essex, in upstate New York, and was intrigued to find that the modern actor's concerns with problems of inflection were concerns over a hundred years ago. I thought you might like to join the ghosts of poor young schoolchildren who, in 1867, got these exercises in cadence drilled into them day after day in log-cabin schools as well as in the traditional ivy halls of universities. The book's authors, Richard Green Parker and J. Madison Watson, use \ to indicate a downward slide and / for a rising one. For example, words that are used to affirm or command anything, or to ask a question which can be answered by *yes* or *no*, usually require the *rising* inflection, as,

              /   /   /

I have not been long away. If the war must go on, did he say he

      /

would come?

Thoughts that are not sincere or earnest, but are used in mockery or jest, usually require the circumflex (⌣ or ⌢) [a larger slide, producing a slight wave of the voice: Ed]:

          ⌣   ⌢   ⌣

For my own part, I shall be glad to learn of these wise boys.

Here, follow Parker and Watson's "Exercises in Inflections." It will be fruitful to note differences between the accepted inflection of 1867 and those current today.

             \   /

1. I want a pen. It is not a book I want.

             \   / \   /

2. This book is yours, not mine: red, not brown.

         \   / \   /

3. I said good, not bad: happy, not miserable.

      /   /

4. O James! O my brother! how art thou fallen.

        /   /   \

5. Thanks to the gods! my child has done his duty.

         /   /

6. Do men gather grapes from thorns, or figs from thistles?

    \

7. Sínk or swìm, lív́e or dìe: I give my hand and heart to this
vote.

8. Hath a dŏg money? Is it possible a cŭr can lend three thousand
dóllạrs?

A moment's thought will show how much more interesting and alive
a rising inflection is in cases where a falling inflection produces sense
nonetheless. A few of these exercises call for further study, for instance numbers 4 and 6.

4. O James! O my brother! how art thou fallen!

```
            James!              brother!      how          fall-
O                      O my                    art thou       en!
```

A more obvious but much less controlled and interesting way of
delivering this is the one most people would think of first:

```
O J a               O my br o              how art thou fa ,
   a ames!             o o                              I I
                           ther!                           en!
```

In the first of these two inflections of the kind, there is a vocal excitement created by the rising—hardly even slid—inflections on the
first two phrases, whereas in the second staff we can hear a regularity
of inflection that amounts to an almost literal monotony.

Study the following two renderings of number 6. One is Parker
and Madison's, the other mine. Neither is superior to the other, but
each has an individuality of tone and attitude.

```
              grapes        thorns            thistles?
Do men gather          from        or figs from
```

```
                         o orns,      figs           les?
Do men gather grapes from tho        or        from thist-
```

While it is true that an artificially forced rising inflection is more
jarring to the listener than the boredom of a barrage of falling inflec-

tions, a greater truth resides in the fact that variety is prerequisite to performance. Of course, the other extreme of constantly going up is equally annoying.

EXERCISE 5—REVIEW OF EXERCISES 1, 2, 3, AND 4

The first three main exercises of this chapter developed your techniques of self-examination and showed you some ways of "troubleshooting" problems. The fourth opened and sensitized your ears. I hope you will always be able to read your scripts slowly and carefully, feeling their sounds as well as their meaning. Now you're more on your own; but I would still recommend that you do the exercises in a group, especially if you have difficulty with them. In any case, it is always more fruitful in an art like acting to have constant feedback on your progress and your ideas.

What follows is an exercise that is not a scene from a play or a poem but rather a piece of acted prose. I say "acted" because Edgar Allan Poe, in the following passage, is playing the part of the storyteller, the person to whom the dreadful events happened. As you know, all acting is storytelling.

Making use of the techniques of self-examination described in Exercises 1, 2, 3, and 4, rehearse the following opening paragraph of *The Fall of the House of Usher*. You might wish to consult the notes that follow it and compare them with your own.

THE FALL OF THE HOUSE OF USHER
Edgar Allan Poe

During the whole of a dull, dark, and soundless day in the autumn of the year, when the clouds hung oppressively low in the heavens, I had been passing alone, on horseback, through a singularly dreary tract of country, and at length found myself, as the shades of evening drew on,
5 within view of the melancholy House of Usher. I know not how it was, but, with the first glimpse of the building, a sense of insufferable gloom pervaded my spirit. I say insufferable; for the feeling was unrelieved by any of that half-pleasurable, because poetic, sentiment with which the mind usually receives even the sternest natural images of the desolate
10 or terrible. I looked upon the scene before me—upon a mere house, and the simple landscape features of the domain, upon the bleak walls, upon the vacant eye-like windows, upon a few rank sedges, and upon a few white trunks of decayed trees, with an utter depression of soul

which I can compare to no earthly sensation more properly than to the
after-dream of the reveller upon opium, the bitter lapse into everyday
life, the hideous dropping off of the veil. There was an iciness, a sinking,
a sickening of the heart, an unredeemed dreariness of thought which
no goading of the imagination could torture into aught of the sublime.
What was it, I paused to think, what was it that so unnerved me in the
contemplation of the House of Usher? It was a mystery all insoluble; nor
could I grapple with the shadowy fancies that crowded upon me as I
pondered. I was forced to fall back upon the unsatisfactory conclusion
that while beyond doubt there are combinations of very simple natural
objects which have the power of thus affecting us, still the analysis of
this power lies among considerations beyond our depth. It was possible, I reflected, that a mere different arrangement of the particulars of
the scene, of the details of the picture, would be sufficient to modify,
or perhaps to annihilate, its capacity for sorrowful impression; and, acting upon this idea, I reined my horse to the precipitous brink of a black
and lurid tarn that lay in unruffled lustre by the dwelling, and gazed
down, but with a shudder even more thrilling than before, upon the
remodelled and inverted images of the gray sedge, and the ghastly
tree-stems, and the vacant and eye-like windows.

(The following notes are not as comprehensive as those on *The
Windhover*. It will be helpful to refer back to the exercises on that
poem and discover the techniques common to Hopkins and Poe.)

Line 1—Alliteration
What purposes can be served by delivering the alliteration of
During, dull, dark and *day?*

Line 2—Try Missing Something Out to Determine the Use of It
Be courageous enough to use the technique of excision and substitution. Much can be learned about the rhythm of this line by omitting
oppressively and hearing that this adverb slows down the sentence:
Without it, the rhythm would be quite regular and the pace ongoing,
as in:

ᵕ   ᵕ   /   ᵕ   / ᵕ   ᵕ / (ᵕ)
when the clouds hung low in the heavens.

As written, the effect is a great deal heavier:

ᵕ   ᵕ   /   /   ᵕ   / ᵕ   ᵕ / ᵕ   ᵕ / (ᵕ)
when the clouds hung oppressively low in the heavens

The clause also takes much longer to say because it has five strong beats rather than the three in our "wrong" version, which excludes *oppressively.*

Line 3—Commas
It is worth noting that, like many dramatists constructing prose who pay attention to how it is going to be finally delivered, the short-story writer Poe is providing useful pauses with his commas. Grammatically, no commas are strictly necessary after *alone* and before *through,* and their addition underlines the subordinate nature of the descriptive phrase *on horseback,* giving it more emphasis than otherwise. Furthermore, the comma helps to establish the ponderous rhythm the passage will maintain.

Line 4—Polysyllabic Words
The *singularly* before *dreary* is similar in effect to the *oppressively* in line 2. What follows it is worse: Whereas *low* in line 2 is monosyllabic, the repeated *ee* and *i* vowels of *singularly* and *dreary,* combined with the two syllables in the latter word, have an expandingly deadening effect.

Line 5—A Periodic Sentence
The first sentence of this story is *periodic,* which is to say that its main point, literally its object, is kept back until the final phrase, and all preceding phrases and clauses are a suspenseful preparation for it. *Oppressively, singularly,* not to mention *soundless,* have all succeeded in "holding back" the nouns they qualify; it is therefore appropriate that the first and eventual mention of the House of Usher is put off just a second more by its adjective *melancholy.*

It is often said wisely that good writing has little need of the burden of apparently unnecessary descriptive adjectives and adverbs. In this story, however, the adjectives and adverbs are very much a part of the rhythm that creates the feeling of desolate anxiety.

Line 6—Another Glottal Stop
A glottal stop on the u of Usher might be a good idea. Why?

Line 7—A Pattern of Rhythm
Insufferable gloom maintains the rhythm and style of *oppressively low, singularly dreary,* and *melancholy House.*

We can hear from the phrases and moments I have noted that the author is creating a mode of speech for his narrative character, in whom habits of vocabulary, rhythm, and emphasis are quickly distinguishable from those of anyone else: This is called a speech pattern; it is essential to drama, indispensable in the theatre, and treated more fully in the next chapter, by which time you will be more used to the method.

Lines 9 and 10—How Cold Sounds "Frighten" Warm Ones

There is a coldness here that should be perceptible to the listener; it is created largely in the crisp dentals of *desolate* or *terrible* that follow the dentals warmed by *n* and *m* in the preceding *sternest natural images.*

Lines 13 and 14—More Cold Consonants

Windows are a sign of life; they are for seeing through. The common apprehension that in the wrong circumstances, the windows of a house are otherworldly and menacing is chillingly conveyed in the cold consonants of *vacant eye-like windows;* however natural and welcoming the *windows* may be by association and sound, it is set in a pattern of less than human rigidity by the *c*, *t*, and *k* before it.

Eye-like is a fine opportunity for a glottal stop. Indeed, it is unavoidable unless one wants the wrong effect *vacan tielike windows.*

Line 15—A Special Rhythm

The phrase *with an utter depression of soul* is the nadir of the sentence, indeed of the whole passage so far. This effect has been rhythmically prepared by the preceding repetitions.

> ⏑ / ⏑ ⏑ ⏑ / ⏑ / ⏑ ⏑ ⏑ ⏑ / / ⏑
> I looked upon the scene before me—upon the mere house, and
> ⏑ / ⏑ / ⏑ / ⏑ ⏑ ⏑ ⏑ / ⏑ ⏑ ⏑ /
> the simple landscape features of the domain, upon the bleak
> / ⏑ ⏑ ⏑ / ⏑ / / / ⏑ ⏑ ⏑ ⏑ / / / ⏑
> walls, upon the vacant eye-like windows, upon a few rank sedges,
> ⏑ ⏑ ⏑ ⏑ / / / ⏑ ⏑ / /
> and upon a few white trunks of decayed trees,
> ⏑ ⏑ / ⏑ ⏑ / ⏑ ⏑ /
> with an utter depression of soul

Upon is repeated almost irresistibly six times. As we can see in the scansion, the word is unemphatic but is, however, a device of emphasis: So short, it emphasizes anything that follows it. This simple prepositional phrase gives this part of the long sentence its weight and its thrust. Feel the beat of these lines. Until *with an utter depression of soul* there is no regularity of meter that can comfort the speaker or the listener. Instead, with the strong beats being so close together in a generally spondaic pattern, there is a drum beat of irremediable insistence:

ᴗ/ᴗᴗ/ᴗ/ᴗ—ᴗᴗ//, ᴗᴗ/ᴗ/ᴗ/ᴗᴗᴗ/, ᴗᴗ/ᴗ/ᴗ/ᴗᴗᴗ/, ᴗᴗᴗ/ᴗ///ᴗ, ᴗᴗᴗ///ᴗ, ᴗᴗᴗᴗ///ᴗᴗ//, ᴗᴗ/ᴗᴗ/ᴗᴗ/

By tapping out the beats on a desk a few times, one can discover that the strong ones become much stronger as the lines progress, culminating in the inescapable regularity of the last ᴗᴗ/ᴗᴗ/ᴗᴗ/.

Here again, as we saw in our discussion of *The Windhover*, the interpreter is the writer and performer, a new creator, and the satisfaction of the listener depends on receptivity to the qualities and values of the sounds and rhythms given in the writing.

Lines 15–18—The Relentless Rhythm

As conclusive as the break in the sentence sounds on *depression of soul*, the sentence is obviously not over yet. In fact, there is not even a comma. The sentence is as relentless as the feeling that oppresses the character. The rhythm quickens hopelessly, as does the comparison it formalizes, and comes to rest at a level lower than what we had thought of as the lowest point. The voice is forced downward by the triple pressure of the qualifying phrases and is forced even to shudder on the aspirate on *hideous,* a sound uttered only once before in the piece—in *House of Usher.* How toxic the hangover of *everyday life* is made to sound in such surroundings! We must also note the tormenting finality of the concluding rhythm of the sentence:

ᴗ / ᴗ ᴗ / ᴗ / ᴗ ᴗ /
the hideous dropping off of the veil.

Lines 19 and 20—The Sibilants

The rhythms established, the mood sunken, hopes buried, the description moves irrevocably into its second phase. Repeated sibilants in *iciness, sinking,* and *sickening* precede one of the character's most individual vocal traits, the /ᴗ//ᴗᴗᴗ/ of *unredeemed dreariness of thought.*

Lines 21–33—Rapid Voice Change

Now there is an attempt of the mind to "grapple with the shadowy fancies" that constitute impediment to thought. The speech becomes as logical and "undescriptive" as it can. Just as biofeedback tries to strike off unhelpful moods and thoughts and replace them with positive physical sensations leading to an improvement in the general condition, so this passage tries to remove the scene's effect by looking at it both physically and mentally from a different angle. The moment this decision is put into action—"acting upon this idea"— the speech becomes first hesitant, then thick, then as cold as the renewed horror of the vision before the character.

Lines 33–38—Rhythm Echoing Sense

As in *The Windhover*, where the motion of the falcon is so accurately represented in sound and rhythm, the reining of the horse to the precipice is turned into a sensation of the muscles and mouth that reproduces in speech both the image and feeling of the action. Feel the pulling back caused by the unstressed syllables amid the strong stresses of the *reined, horse, cip,* and *brink*:

$$\smallsmile \; / \quad \smallsmile \; / \quad \smallsmile \; \smallsmile \; \smallsmile / \smallsmile \smallsmile \quad /$$
I reined my horse to the precipitous brink.

The perceptive listener will have the pleasure (and terror) of sensing the horse and rider stop before the danger and possible destruction of the precipice and will then be forced to view the destructive and destroyed sight seen from its edge, the calm strong threat of the regular beat:

$$\smallsmile \smallsmile \; / \; \smallsmile \; / \smallsmile \; /$$
of a black and lurid tarn (3 stresses)

$$\smallsmile \smallsmile \smallsmile \; / \; / \smallsmile \; / \; \smallsmile$$
that lay in unruffled lustre (3 stresses)[2]

Lines 35–38

We can see that the narrator is impelled, by what he sees from the precipice of the tarn, to revert to the periodic sentence structure

---

[2]This phrase can, of course, be scanned differently; there are still three stresses, however:

$$\smallsmile \; / \smallsmile \; / \; \smallsmile \smallsmile \; / \; \smallsmile \qquad \smallsmile \; / \smallsmile \smallsmile \; / \smallsmile \; / \; \smallsmile$$
that lay in unruffled lustre (or even: that lay in unruffled lustre).

with which he began this opening paragraph of his tale. At least, he leads us to believe so. The sentence is in fact completed grammatically by *gazed down*, and what follows is, as it was to him when he first experienced it, a frightened repetition of what he saw first of all.

I hope you enjoyed the interior mechanisms of that classically terrifying passage. The following is a checklist of questions you can take to other passages as well as to play speeches.

CHECKLIST FOR SCENE AND SPEECH STUDY

This list is only preliminary and will be augmented by things discussed in chapters 4 and 5. Meanwhile, you should get used to asking yourself the following questions of every scene or speech you study and rehearse. By being true to your character you will become true to yourself.

1. First, your short physical and vocal warm-up.

Raise eyebrows, tense, release
Scrunch eyes and nose, tense, release
Purse lips, tense, release
Turn head left, tense, release
Turn head right, tense, release
Raise head, tense, release
Lower head, tense, release
Raise arms, clench fists, tense, release
Pull stomach in, tense, release (repeat)
Push stomach out, tense, release (repeat)
Tighten buttocks, push out pelvis, tense, release
Press knees together, tense, release
Raise toes, tense, release
Yawn
Stressing the *h*, repeat me-hay, me-hay, me-hay
Stressing the *m*, repeat a-hum-a, a-hum-a, a-hum-a
Loosen your jaws with *ah-eh-ee-oo-o-aw-ah* ten times
Maintain your range by doing *ah*, starting high, ending low, slowly
    getting higher and lower

For your lips and tongue and jaw, do:

> Planning to plop in the public pool?
> Blame Blake's bulbs.
> Damned disinheriting countenance!

Finally, for the relaxation that only agility and concentration can produce:

The sixth sick sheik's sixth sheep's sick

concluding with:

She stood on the balcony, inexplicably mimicking him hiccuping, amicably welcoming him in.

2. Checklist
Ask yourself the following questions of your part in the scene:

a. *Falling cadence:* am I ever going down when going up might be better?

b. Do any *d* sounds need emphasizing or unfocusing?

c. Are there any *m* or *n* or *mn* sounds that aren't coming over as strongly as the vowels around them?

e. Are my *ng* sounds being heard? Should I focus on them?

f. Any sibilants sounding hissy? What can I do?

g. Am I giving a glottal stop where it isn't needed? Are there places where one might mean something to my character?

h. Are my plosives clear? Are there any that signal something about my character and the character's mood or feeling?

i. Any polysyllabic words that the character uses for an interesting reason? (Remember, *all* reasons for speech in good plays are interesting!)

j. Any sentences that keep the main point back until the end (periodic sentences)? How can I use them to create my character through my voice?

k. Any repeated patterns of rhythm in my character's lines? What do they say about my character?

l. Any rapid changes of thought or rhythm? Should I change the pace? Is a change of pace perhaps unavoidable?

m. Any sounds in my lines that might be intended to sound like the experience my character has lived or is living through?

n. Are there any phrases the value of which I cannot see? (Omit them and discover the reason for their presence!)

Once you give your lines the test of these questions, you will see how your lines make up your character. Once you are able to answer at least eight of them, you will be thoroughly ready to go on to Exercise 6, which tells you more about rhythm and how it creates character relationships.

NOTES ON MARKINGS USED IN THE BOOK; AND AN EXERCISE IN SCANSION

Basic Scansion

∪ denotes a weak, unstressed syllable in prose or poetry, and / a stress, as in:

    / ∪ / ∪ / / /   / ∪ ∪∪   / ∪ / ∪
    ∪ denotes a weak, unstressed syllable in prose or poetry
    ∪   /∪ /
    and / a stress.

It takes little practice to perfect one's ability to scan lines at sight. We should remember that these markings indicate only one person's way of saying the line.

Lines Scanned with Pauses

A normal, brief pause is represented by : and a longer one by : :
A standard delivery of the line above could be:

    ∪:∪ / ∪ / :/ /   / ∪ ∪∪   / ∪ / ∪:
    ∪ denotes a weak, unstressed syllable in prose or poetry,
    ∪   /∪ /
    and / a stress.

Without resorting to terms of musical notations, this system of ∪, / , : , and :: can give a useful accurate rendering of the rhythm of an utterance.

Upward and Downward Inflection

The marks / and \ , and also ⌒ and ∪ are used and described in this chapter. These marks are drawn from *The Third National Reader* of 1867, and they begin on page 71.

    The staffs used as indications of inflection in chapters 3 and 4, each line of which is separated from the next by an internal of approximately three notes (a musical third) are self-explanatory:

```
                                    higher
                          gets
                  note
the
```

Exercises in Scansion

```
    /   ∪ / ∪ ∪   /  :/ ∪∪∪   / ∪ / ∪
```
Scan the following lines, indicating normal pauses:

a. How frequently in the extraordinary history of mankind do we

find speech the ruler of action.

b. That is true, in that that and this are always in this place.

c. The inseparable corollary.

d. Hello, why are you here?

The following scansions may differ in emphasis from yours. You might find it useful to consider them.

a.　//∪∪∪∪∪∪/∪∪∪/∪∪∪∪/∪∪∪/∪/∪∪/∪.

b.　/∪/:∪∪/∪/∪/∪∪//.

c.　∪∪/∪∪∪∪/∪∪ (try ∪//∪∪∪∪/∪∪).

d.　∪/::/∪∪/ (try //::/∪// and ∪/:∪∪∪/).

EXERCISE 6—THE SO-CALLED "STRONG AND WEAK ENDINGS" IN RHYTHM

In drama, prose, and poetry (even in letters, memos, and telephone conversations that are the stuff of which some parts of some drama are made), there are strong and weak endings to phrases and sentences. These endings began to be called "strong" and "weak" mainly in the poetic criticism of the nineteenth century. The actor should be aware of these endings, so that they can contribute to the richness of performance.

Briefly, then, a *strong ending* occurs when a line or phrase ends on a *single beat or stress*. All the following have strong endings:

> ˘ / / /
> I'll bring her too.
>
> ˘   / ˘ /   /
> But what about me?
>
> / ˘ ˘ / ˘ ˘ / ˘   / ˘ ˘   /
> That is the end of the meeting, ladies and gents.

All the following have *weak endings* because each end on an un-stressed syllable:

> ˘ /   / / ˘
> I'll bring her also.
>
> ˘ / ˘ / / ˘
> But what about Mary?
>
> / ˘ ˘ / ˘ ˘ / ˘ / ˘ ˘   / ˘ ˘
> That is the end of the meeting, ladies and gentlemen.

Here, let us look at a few lines from Harold Pinter's *The Caretaker*.[3] Those who have not read nor seen the play need only know (since this extract is early on in the play) that Davies is a tramp or hobo and Aston an unemployed clerk to whose house Davies has come in search of shelter. They are speaking about the furniture.

DAVIES   Must be worth a few bob, this . . . put it all together. (*Pause*)

ASTON   There's a good bit of it, all right.

DAVIES   You sleep here, do you?

ASTON   Yes.

DAVIES   What, in that?

ASTON   Yes.

DAVIES   Yes, see, you'd be well out of the draught there.

[3]Harold Pinter, *The Caretaker* (London: Methuen, 1962), p. 11.

ASTON   You don't get much wind.

DAVIES   You'd be well out of it. It's different when you're kipping out.

ASTON   Would be.

DAVIES   Nothing but the wind then. (*Pause*)

ASTON   Yes, when the wind gets up it . . . (*Pause*)

DAVIES   Yes . . .

ASTON   Mmnn . . . (*Pause*)

This interchange from Act I of *The Caretaker* takes no more than thirty seconds to act and is not as significant as many other moments in the play. I have chosen the interchange because it is representative and ordinary in that it shows the playwright at work and is an example of the attention actors must pay to rhythm in order to convey the playwright's intent.

Examine the dialogue now almost solely from the point of view of the strong and weak endings:

  /   (/ᴗ)
Must be worth a few bob, this

An attempt at a strong ending. The intruder in the household is trying to assert himself.

    ᴗ / ᴗ
put it all together

He doesn't make it. The rising inflection necessary on *together* decreases the strength further.

    /   ᴗ ᴗ
There's enough of it.

A weak ending on two unstressed syllables, this phrase indicates Davies' possibly grudging admiration. Undoubtedly the rise and fall of it bespeaks something other than an attitude of ownership.

          / ᴗ ᴗ
There's a good bit of it,
(/)(/)
all right.

Aston's reply is very interesting rhythmically. It begins in triumph with the focus on *bit* and with two rather weak major stresses.

                  /   ∪ ∪
You sleep here, do you?

As befits a question from one homeless man to one sheltered (albeit mentally weak and confused), this is a weak ending.

       /
Yes.

Probably neutral, but certainly not a weak ending. One stress.

       /   ∪   /
What, in that?

Davies suddenly has the upper hand. The bed is not magnificent; the blankets and sheets have not been washed for a long time. His attitude to this results in a strong ending.

       /
Yes.

One stress, neither strong nor weak, is all Aston can give to his reply.

     /   /   ∪   ∪   /   /
Yes, well, you'd be well out
∪   ∪   /   /
of the draught there.

Davies' response begins with a sort of echo, in half-mockery of Aston. If you try it, the rhythm of his response (//∪∪//∪∪//) is so accommodating as well as satirical as to remove any promise of power the three double spondees might have had.

       ∪   /   ∪   /   /
You don't get much wind.

Although the language of this remark is apologetic and explanatory, its strong ending makes the actor assert his comforts, however weakly.

             /   /   ∪ ∪
You'd be well out of it.
It's different when you're
      /   ∪   /
kipping out.

The feeling of power that comes from giving advice is well rendered here and is a gift to the actor. Having tried advice with "you'd be well out of it" and found that the ending is weak, Davies' voice attempts a strong ending with a statement about his own experience. He succeeds, and it is not a victory.

/   ᴜ
Would be.

         /   /
Nothing but wind then.

Misinterpreting the irony of Aston's "Would be," Davies continues into an even stronger rhythm. The interest of *his* experience has won the rhythmic argument for the moment. There is a pause.

   /   ᴜ   ᴜ / ᴜ
Yes, when the wind gets
 / ᴜ
up it . . .

Aston cannot recover his mastery of his voice's strong ending. There is another pause, during which one of the things happening to audience and actor (although in different ways, one unconscious and the other conscious) is preparation for the upper hand in the subtle contest.

Yes . . .

This is the first opportunity in this piece of dialogue for Davies to indulge in the mediocre strength of the one-stress line. Moreover, it is the first such instance in the play.

Mmmnn . . .

Aston neither wins nor loses, of course.

All plays and all speeches contain material of this kind—so obvious once one knows what is going on. Of course, some actors are able to work without conscious attention to this material; they are fortunate to have that particular talent of instinctive response to the rhythms of the playwright. One such actor is Donald Pleasence, who played Davies at the Duchess Theatre at the premiere in London of *The Caretaker* in 1960. The critics and the public were so astonished at the naturalism of his performance that an excerpt from the play was televised *as a curiosity*. Many could not believe that the actor was not improvising, so completely akin to everyday speech and cadence was his delivery.

A passage from any dramatic work—or any poem or piece of crafted prose—would suffice to demonstrate the necessity of the actor's response to the rhythms of the lines to be uttered in character.

CONCLUSIONS TO CHAPTER 3

You can see from the preceding discussion of a poem, a prose passage, and a remarkable piece of dialogue from a remarkable play that words change their meanings with change of order in the sentence. As Elder Olson writes in *The Elements of Drama: Character*:

> By their words shall ye know them: each speech of Hamlet's is not merely a communication of meaning but a verbal act selected from a great many other acts that might have been possible, a "choice" therefore that reveals the nature of the chooser, an act performed with a certain style that discloses the nature of the performer.

Robert Corrigan writes in *Comedy—A Critical Anthology* (which I recommend as a superb collection of plays for actors to study):

> All of the materials available to the dramatist, whether they be from his own experience, from history, or from the accrued traditions of the drama itself are, in fact, neutral. It is only by the playwright's shaping of them that they take on meaning—a meaning which may be tragic, comic, melodramatic, farcical, or what have you. Not to understand this fact is to blur the crucial distinctions which exist between art and life.

To expand on his latter point, which I find especially interesting (and the actors and actresses I have interviewed for this book share my interest), let me quote the distinguished author and examiner of the creative process, Arthur Koestler:

> The spectator knows, in one compartment of his mind, that the people on the stage are actors, whose names are familiar to him; and he knows that they are "acting" for the express purpose of creating an illusion in him, the spectator. Yet in another compartment of his mind he experiences fear, hope, pity, accompanied by palpitations, arrested breathing, or tears—all induced by events which he knows to be pure make-believe.

This is quite unlike the main point of Brecht's *Verfremdunseffekt* ("alienation effect"), but here is a remark about the conventional stage in his *On The Experimental Theatre*:

Human beings go to the theatre in order to be swept away, captivated, impressed, uplifted, horrified, moved, kept in suspense, released, diverted, set free, set going, transplanted from their own time, and supplied with illusions. All of this goes so much without saying that the art of the theatre is candidly defined as having the power to release, sweep away, uplift, etcetera. It is not an art at all unless it does so.

Now, making connections among the four statements I have quoted from Olson, Corrigan, Koestler, and Brecht, you can see that the responsibility the actor has chosen to shoulder is at once simple and great and that the most important thing is not so much truth in itself as being truthful to whatever truth is being shown in the play. For this to be achieved, great clarity is needed.

Inflecting clearly is one of the ways of achieving clarity. You have seen from the examples earlier in this chapter how the structure of the lines influences the characterization through the voice, and you will be hearing more about this important point throughout this book. What follows is an exercise you can use for different inflections. I remind you that these are only exercises, and that the questions following them are on no account intended to dictate any single interpretation.

Exercise and Questions

Suddenly Last Summer, Tennessee Williams

CATHERINE: Down! Oh, I ran down, the easier direction to run was down, down, down, down!—The hot, white, blazing street, screaming out "Help" all the way, til . . .

DOCTOR: What?

CATHERINE: Waiters, police, and others—ran out of the buildings and rushed back up the hill with me. When we got back to where my Cousin Sebastian had disappeared in the flock of featherless little black sparrows, he—he was lying naked as they had been naked against a white wall, and this you won't believe, nobody *has* believed it, nobody *could* believe it, nobody, nobody on earth could possibly believe it, and I don't *blame* them!—They had *devoured* parts of him. (MRS. VENABLE *cries out softly*) Torn or cut parts of him away with their hands or knives or maybe those jagged tin cans they made music with, they had torn bits of him away and stuffed them into those gobbling fierce little empty black mouths of theirs. There wasn't a sound anymore, there was nothing to see but Sebastian, what was left of him—that looked like a big white-paper-wrapped bunch of red roses that had been *torn, thrown, crushed!*—against that blazing white wall . . .

Here, at the last few moments of the troubling play, the character is in a state of highest anxiety; nevertheless, or even perhaps because of the tension caused by this awful memory that her relatives are seeking to lobotomize out of her, her sentence structure is fluent, if a little diffused in focus.

1. Would you inflect downward on the *down*'s? Why? What about *street*? Might it perhaps be best lifted, as *way* might be, so that the interrupted *til* can sound all the more like a self-interruption, creating suspense in the audience and in the doctor? What would be the virtue of continued downward inflections in this speech, if any?

2. What would you do with *others*? Of course, if you are playing the part with a southern accent (as is, to a degree, proper, mirroring as it does not only the playwright's intentions but also his own cadences), there are likely to be many more upward inflections anyway, even though many southerners, Tennessee Williams included, have a habit of inflecting downward when merely reading aloud.

Comprehending the Script and Absorbing the Lines: Speech Patterns, Focus, and Emphasis

> "Simply the thing I am
> Shall make me live."
>
> (Parolles in *All's Well That Ends Well,* IV, iv, 369–70)

Characters in plays speak the way they feel and are what they say. If characters lie, they feel like lying, and if they adopt a social attitude to the vocabulary of a script, they want to or need to or have to. This chapter shows you how actors are expected to respond to the script. Here you will encounter plays of many different kinds, and you will find many opportunities to exercise your developing skills until you can master them.

While I was writing this book I was in correspondence with Sir

Alec Guinness, who gave the following deceptively simple piece of advice about approaching any passage to get at its meaning: "Give emphasis firstly to the verb, secondly to the noun and lastly (if at all) to adverb and adjective, and never emphasize a personal pronoun except for a particularly good reason." As you read through the extracts and the comments that follow in this chapter, you should remember that advice, which I will discuss later in much more detail.

COMPREHENDING THE SCRIPT

TANNER . . . I have something to say which I beg you to hear. (*Ann looks at him without the slightest curiosity, but waits apparently as much to finish getting her glove on as to hear what he has to say*) I am altogether on your side in this matter. I congratulate you, with the sincerest respect, on having the courage to do what you have done.[1]

This speech from Shaw's *Man and Superman* is from the playwright's final version and is neither sacred nor especially worthy of praise. In fact, the speech is very ordinary. However, the character who utters these lines was created in them and in others, and outside, before, or after the play never utters anything else besides these words and the rest of his lines as written in the script. The character cannot utter anything else because he is a fiction.

MESSENGER O, my good lord, the Duke of Cornwall's dead;
Slain by his servant, going to put out
The other eye of Gloucester.

These lines, from *King Lear*, Act IV, Scene ii, are no more holy than Shaw's. The character who utters them is created in them and in a few more that follow, does not say anything else, and cannot. The character is a fiction born of the author and has no life other than in these lines and in the imaginations of the spectators. An actor who changes the lines would create a different character and never appear in Act IV, Scene ii, of *King Lear* on any stage anywhere. That actor would be an author instead.

An actor who, for instance, persists in saying, "My good lord, O, the Duke of Cornwall's dead," or "My dread lord, the Duke of Cornwall's dead, O, my lord, the Duke of Cornwall's dead," stands a chance of being dismissed by the theatre management.

[1]Shaw, *Man and Superman* (London: Penguin, 1946), p. 87.

If, in a production of *Man and Superman*, an actor said, "I have an interesting thing to say that I beg you to hear," that person would be guilty of a theatrical misdemeanor. Why? The actor is the skilled interpreter of the script and, as we shall see when we consider several examples, the playwright is the provider of the actor's lines. Like musical notation, lines are to be followed: they are not used as a starting point for the creation of a character but *are* the character insofar as they contain everything the character can possibly say in the play. There are, of course, myriads of phrases, words, sentences, and paragraphs the character can say in the actor's imagination, but that is where they must stay if the actor is to create the character at all. With the exception of an improvisation, the actor can create only by interpreting what is written. In a play, the actor says what is there.

EXERCISE 1—*TIME AND TIME AGAIN*

This book is not about improvisational theatre but about voice techniques needed to act in a play produced from a script. As in rehearsal, we begin with the script.

Comprehension denotes much more than apprehension and implies a great deal more than a knowledge of the identity and actions of one's character. Obviously, the actor must first discover *how* the character speaks before knowing the *why* of the speech. The character's method and manner can explain the motivation behind the speech. To illustrate this first and major premise, let us build some of the character of Graham in Alan Ayckbourn's play *Time and Time Again*.

This play is a comedy; however, all the techniques we shall be noting can be found in Neil Simon, Bernard Shaw, Tennessee Williams, Congreve, Marlowe, Shakespeare, Molière, Schiller, Strindberg, Ibsen, Pirandello, Lorca—in short, in the scripts of all good playwrights. A "playwright" is not a "playwrite": Just as a shipwright is a builder of ships, so a playwright is a maker and creator of plays, not a mere writer of them. In Anglo-Saxon and Old Scots the words for poets were, respectively, *scop* and *makar; scop* was also used for God the creator; the imaginative creation was plainly regarded by our ancestors as deeper than mere "speech" or "writing." Speaking the playwright's lines, then, with the concomitant movement and facial expression, makes the actor the last and most important creator before the audience's imagination. Throughout this book the terms *audience* and *spectator* are alternated, as neither sound nor spectacle is supreme.

Let's have a look at the beginning of *Time and Time Again*.

ACT I   SCENE 1

A suburban garden. Spring, a sunny, not particularly warm day.

The garden is of the type that is separated, on either side, by fences which conceal other identical suburban gardens. This particular one has a scrap of lawn upon which stands an unattended, ancient lawn-mower. There is also a murky pond, over which presides a battered stone gnome. At one end of the garden we see part of the back of the Victorian terrace house to which it belongs. One of those glass boxed conservatoires, obviously a later attachment to the original outside wall of the house. Through the windows we see garden furniture, tables and chairs, potted plants all in various stages of decay, some hanging from on high, some sprouting from pots circling the floor. A stained glass door leads from this to the rest of the house. Nothing seems in very good repair. At the other end of the garden a small pile of breeze blocks lies just inside the boundary fence, one of those made with concrete posts with wires threaded through them. Beyond this is more grass, being the edge of the local recreation ground.

When the CURTAIN rises, Leonard, a man in his late thirties, is discovered in the conservatory. He is a pale, alert, darting sort of man. He wears a dark suit and a black tie. He breathes on the window and looks out at the garden for a moment. He comes outside and stares at it again. After a moment he removes his jacket and drops it by the pond. Now in his shirt-sleeves and braces he goes to the mower and tries, ineffectually, to push it. He tries a second time, but the blades appear totally jammed. He crouches down to try to mend it.

Graham, a man of forty, stockier, more solidly built, enters the conservatory. He holds a glass of Scotch, and the end of a cigar. He watches Leonard struggling for a moment, before coming out into the garden.

GRAHAM   So, you're out here then. (*Leonard ignores him*) You don't waste much time, do you? (*He flicks the end of his cigar into the pond and goes to the pile of breeze blocks. Kicking them.*) I should clear these while you're at it. Been stuck here since before Christmas. (*He pauses*) You don't believe in wasting time, do you?

LEONARD   (*Looking up*) Eh?

GRAHAM   Straight back and on with it, that's your motto.

LEONARD   (*Absorbed again*) What?

GRAHAM   I mean your mother hasn't been buried ten minutes and you're back
10   here cutting the bloody grass.

LEONARD   I'm not drinking, anyway.

GRAHAM   What do you mean? I'm toasting her on her way, that's all. Seeing
                her off with a toast.

LEONARD   It's a funeral you've been to, you know, not a launching.

15   GRAHAM   What's the harm? She wasn't my mother. I wasn't her son. I was a
                damn fine son-in-law, though I say it myself, but I wasn't her son.

LEONARD   She'd have confirmed that.

GRAHAM   What the hell are you doing?

LEONARD   Writing my memoirs.

20   GRAHAM   You should have greased it last year when you'd finished with it. Thin
                layer of grease over all the working parts.

LEONARD   Thank you. I'll remember that.

GRAHAM   Otherwise when you come to use them next year they've jammed.
                Like that one.

25   LEONARD   Useful tip that.

GRAHAM   Yes.

LEONARD   Except I wasn't here last year.

GRAHAM   Nor you were. Just seems like it.

LEONARD   Yes.

30   GRAHAM   (*Suddenly jovial*) Tell you what, I'll nip upstairs and throw you the nail
                scissors out of the bathroom window. Cut the grass with those. Be
                quicker in the long run. With the nail scissors. Like they did in the
                army. Did you have that? Fatigues. We had this sergeant major. One
                of his favorite little games that—cutting the grass with nail scissors.
35   My God! We had some laughs in those days. Did you ever do that?

LEONARD   Not in the navy.

GRAHAM   Ah.

LEONARD   We used to paint it blue, instead.

GRAHAM   Blue?

40   LEONARD   The grass. It was a secret Admiralty device to run the enemy aground.*

GRAHAM   (*Puzzled*) I never heard of them doing that.

LEONARD   It was just an experiment.

GRAHAM   (*Shaking his head*) ! never heard of that.

LEONARD   They had to abandon it eventually. It confused the R.A.F. When they
45   flew over it, they weren't sure which way up they were. Half bomber
               command were flying upside down at one time.

GRAHAM   I don't believe that for a minute. You're making the whole thing up.
               That's a pack of lies.

LEONARD   That's just what the Air Ministry said.

50   GRAHAM   I came out to have a word with you. Now then, I've invited young
               Peter back to tea.

LEONARD   How nice.

GRAHAM   I'll remind you he took care of a lot of the arrangements for your
               mother's funeral. Arrangements one might have hoped, others could
55   have dealt with themselves. So, as a small way of sayi~g thanks I've
               invited Peter and his girl to tea.

LEONARD   Good to see you keeping up relations with your employees. (*A dog
               barks in the distance*)

GRAHAM   Oh, yes, I've got plans for young Peter, don't you worry. A very bright
60   young man, that. He'll get on in this world. He's got a style about
               him. And a very presentable young fiancée, too. You see her? Very
               nice. Don't blame him, keeping her hidden away all this time . . . (*He
               leers*)

LEONARD   You fancy her, then?

65   GRAHAM   The point I'm making is this. If you intend to grace us with your

presence at teatime, may I remind you they have not come to hear the story of your life . . .

LEONARD   You amaze me.

GRAHAM   Maybe I do. But I don't want a repetition of last Friday. When George
70   Walker was here to dinner with his wife. All that embarrassing
          scene . . .

LEONARD   What was that?

GRAHAM   All that argument about—sexual incompatibility and so on . . .

LEONARD   Oh. I thought that livened things up a bit.

75   GRAHAM   Oh yes, fascinating. By the time we got to the flan you'd practically
          broken up their marriage. Her in floods of tears and him with his blood
          pressure at boiling point . . . I'll have you know he's one of my most
          important clients.

LEONARD   I'm sorry. I thought that all went rather well.

80   GRAHAM   Well, it damn well didn't. It's cost me a fortune in drinks ever since.
          Just don't trail your failure through my house like—a pair of muddy
          boots.

LEONARD   That's awfully poetic. Please wipe your soul.

GRAHAM   And that's another thing. We don't want another of your damn poetry
85   recitals either. You know your trouble?

LEONARD   (*Who has been looking out over the recreation field*) Ah, they're taking
          up the goal-posts.

GRAHAM   Where?

LEONARD   Over there. Removing the goal-posts . . .

90   GRAHAM   Oh yes. You know what your trouble is. (*He tinkers with the lawn-
          mower*)

LEONARD   Probably has tremendous local significance. Some primitive, subur-
          ban, spring fertility dance, no doubt. First, four little men, symbolically
          dressed in blue overalls—symbolic of what, I don't know . . . Never
95   mind. Men in symbolic blue overalls spill on to the field from their

grey truck to perform the Annual Uprooting the Goal-Posts Ritual. The significance of the goal-posts is perfectly clear, of course. Two male uprights thrusting from the borough council's green soil to support, at each end, the dormant horizontal female crossbar. Soon to be awakened from her winter slumbers by the rough hands of the Parks Department employees . . .

100

GRAHAM You need a spanner on this. Get the blades off . . .

LEONARD And down she comes . . .

GRAHAM Rusted in, this has.

105 LEONARD Go careful with her, men! In her, rest all the parish's hopes of fertility . . . "Spring, the sweet Spring, is the year's pleasant king: Then blooms each thing, then maids dance in a ring . . ." (*Joan, a woman in her early twenties, enters the conservatory with a tray of tea things and starts unloading them on the table*)

110 GRAHAM What are you on about now?

LEONARD I sing in praise of all women and the fruit that they will bear . . . (*Seeing Joan through the window*) Good gracious. Talk of the devil . . .

GRAHAM Here, now listen. Don't you start on about all that stuff again. Just as
115 we're going to have tea. I warned you.

LEONARD (*Back to the recreation field*) Whoops! He nearly dropped her on his head. That would have added a new dimension to the ceremony. "Acolyte coshed by earth mother . . ."

GRAHAM Hey. If you're making some sort of snide references to me and Anna
120 with all this talk of fertility and so on . . .

LEONARD What?

GRAHAM The doctor told her it would be injurious to her health. That's the only reason we haven't had any children. Not that it's any of your business. (*The dog barks again, nearer*) I'm as—as the next man. You can't
125 talk. You've had three and look where that got you . . .

LEONARD Here.

GRAHAM Quite. Remember that. (*Anna, in her late thirties, enters the conservatory with teapot and milk jug*)

LEONARD   Come on, lads! (*The dog barks again, very close*) Get stuck in, there!

130   GRAHAM   I don't think that's fitting behavior in your funeral suit.

LEONARD   Why not? It's my suit for all seasons. Wedding, divorce, Coronation, Trooping the Color—Mother said I was christened in it. (*Joan exits with her tray*)

ANNA   (*Calling*) Graham! Leonard! (*She closes the door, sits and pours tea*)

135   GRAHAM   Ah! Sounds like tea. Are you coming in and behaving properly?

LEONARD   I don't think I could honestly trust myself. I'd better have it out here . . .

GRAHAM   It's freezing cold . . .

LEONARD   With Bernard.

140   GRAHAM   Bernard? Who the hell's Bernard?

LEONARD   (*Indicating the gnome*) Bernard.

GRAHAM   Oh, my God!

LEONARD   The last of the great coarse-fishing gnomes.

GRAHAM   Come on, Leonard. For heaven's sake. You can't sit out here. They'll
145   think something's the matter with you.

LEONARD   Tell them I'm meditating. You can't have it both ways. Either I come in there and embarrass you or I stay out here and embarrass you.

GRAHAM   I just wish to hell you'd go . . .

LEONARD   Then I could ring you up and embarrass you.

150   GRAHAM   Look. I'll remind you that as from last Wednesday, this house no longer belongs to your mother, you know. It belongs to me. Me. You remember that.

LEONARD   Oh. I thought it belonged to your wife, somehow.

GRAHAM   All right. But if I decide to sling you out, she's not going to argue with
155   me, I can tell you that . . . (*He moves away to the conservatory*)

(*Conservatory wall slides away*)

Establishing a Speech Pattern

The Scotch and the cigar give Graham a feeling of some relaxation and power. His opening line begins to establish his speech pattern, the way he will talk and think throughout the play. He does not say:

> So you're out here, then.

That is too fluent for what we later come to know of Graham. The playwright's punctuation has dictated most of the inflection by placing the comma after "So," producing the following rhythm:

> / ◡ / / ◡
> So, you're out here then.[2]

After Leonard ignores him, Graham does not say:

> You don't waste much time.

Instead, Graham turns his statement into something of a taunt by making it a question, at once acknowledging that Leonard—naturally enough since this takes place only a few hours after his mother's funeral—has not replied and phrasing the remark in such a way as to encourage a reply this time:

> You don't waste much time, do you?

So far, then, it is clear for the actor playing the part that Graham is in command of whatever situation is about to develop. Graham's three sentences that follow are of approximately the same length as the ones we have looked at, each having either three or four stresses.[3] Graham's entire opening remarks, then, plainly establish his speech pattern. The shortish sentences are indicative of a man used to authority, obedience, and, as we shall see, rudeness.

> / ◡ / / ◡ ◡ / / (/) ◡ / / ◡
> So, you're out here then. You don't waste much time, do you?
> ◡ ◡ / / ◡ ◡ /◡
> I should clear these while you're at it.
> ◡ / ◡(/)◡ ◡ / / ◡
> Been stuck here since before Christmas.

[2]See notes in Chapter 3 for a full explanation of the meter and inflection markings used.
[3]There are, of course, other ways of stressing these lines. Whichever way one does it, however, the sentences remain of nearly equal length.

After Leonard's "Eh?" Graham is made to speak in the same brusque way. Again as in "Been stuck here since before Christmas," Graham omits the normal verb at the beginning of the sentence in "Straight back and on with it, that's your motto." The actor should realize by now that this is the speech of a British army officer, probably at the rank of major.

How Can Absence of Punctuation Affect Vocal Characterization?

Just as no actor would wish to bring monotony even to a monotonous character except for a brief effect, few playwrights will allow the speech patterns of a character to be unvaried. The next line given Graham is an assertive sentence *without punctuation*. The lack of a comma after "I mean" gives the line much impetus and indicates that the character is intent on maintaining what he considers to be the upper hand in the interchange:

> I mean your mother hasn't been buried ten minutes and you're back here cutting the bloody grass.

It is interesting for the actor to note that the line is far from slow and runs as if Graham *needs* to justify his previous statements. "Ten minutes" recurs throughout the play as one of Graham's favorite phrases and is a verbal tic like the "eh?" Ibsen gave to George Tesman in *Hedda Gabler*. This verbal tic has a rich reason and even a motivation behind it, however: Graham is a fastidious man and although blustery, he has the habit of timing things and, moreover, timing them wrongly. Graham would make what sounds like an accurate pronouncement about something rather than remain silent.

Repetition is a Clue to Character

Of course, Leonard notices that Graham is drinking Scotch, and Graham replies defensively, "What do you mean? I'm toasting her on her way, that's all. Seeing her off with a toast." The actor is to use the repetition of *toast* naturally to advantage in this exposition of the play, conveying as much of his character as can be felt in what he says. There is always a reason behind such repetition, which is as common to naturalistic drama as to life. The point is neither that the character was inaudible on *toast* and feels the need to repeat it in order to make it heard, nor that he can't hear himself, since we find later in the play that Graham does listen to himself and occasionally realizes the idiocy or inappropriateness of what he has said. I think rather the point is that Graham is simply weak and making bold attempts to appear strong, which, at any rate, is the essence of the character developing in the play.

Graham's reply to Leonard's "It's a funeral you've been to, you know, not a launching" (a remark whose patterns are, with the medial insertion "you know," obviously quite different from Graham's) is, as far as we know at this point, standard to the character. There are three very short sentences followed by a sentence with three short clauses.

Repetition by no means invariably indicates a weakness; one glance at line 20 will show us that. Graham is looking at the lawnmower that Leonard is crouched over:

> You should have greased that last year when you'd finished it. Thin layer of grease over all the working parts.

Here, *grease* gets it, and the repetition is surely born of custom. Graham knows what he's talking about, and the only weakness is that he feels it necessary to show that he knows.

Rhythmic Similarities

At line 30 it is plain that Leonard mocks Graham. Ayckbourn gives a stage direction—"suddenly jovial"—to mark Graham's decision to take a new approach in his play for power over Leonard. The lines Graham says now are rhythmically similar to those he has uttered up to this point, as are the grammatical constructions that carry them: verbs omitted, snappy phrases, even one-word sentences. Graham's speech concludes with his merry question "Did you ever do that?," which contains perhaps the merest trace of well-concealed sarcasm, topped by Leonard's laugh-line "Not in the navy," which is best followed quickly by Graham's "Ah." Graham is foiled again.

How Sound Produces Facial Expression

Graham's "Blue?" is an excellent line to say; its plosive *bl* (see Chapter 3) gives great opportunity to the muscles of the lips, providing just about all the facial reaction necessary. We shall find frequently that the only facial expression work needed is produced by the words one's character has to say.

A Problem of Personal Pronouns

I can see now that the repeated *I*'s of "I never heard of them doing that" and "I never heard of that" need the attention that I did not give them myself when I played Graham in Montreal in 1980. While it is satisfactory to use the same inflection on both "I never heard's," which makes Graham appear as an innocent buffer of Leonard's barbs, what Ayckbourn seems to have intended is to convey more of Graham's self-possession and self-obsession. Graham's next line of dialogue, where he attempts to save himself from the merciless and ironic casualness of Leonard, reverts to the safety of his good old short sentences. This time, however, the power of these sentences is tremendously diminished. The moment is instructive for the audience in that a method of discourse that worked before has been amended because of what has preceded it the second time around in the lines of another character. Already in the play's first minute and a half, there is a minor resolution of what will be a major conflict.

With "I came out to have a word with you. Now then, I've invited young Peter back to tea," Graham is playing no more games of stylistic supremacy; he takes a more direct attack on Leonard, openly assuming authority warmed by the slight friendliness of "Now then." This different approach to Leonard is continued in the coldly admonishing "I'll remind you" and the distantly formal "Arrangements one might have hoped, others could have dealt with themselves."

We can see that in Graham there is a nice mixture of formality and near-childish petulance. The logical introduction of "So, as a small way of saying thanks" has in it something of "See? I'm right and you're wrong."

The lines beginning at 59 dispel any doubts the actor might have about the British army speech patterns of some of Graham's speech. If the view is questioned that Graham is weak and uses many words to attempt to appear strong, the actor need only attend to Graham's "The point I'm making is this," which entirely avoids Leonard's "You fancy her, then?"

Different Speech Patterns

For the remainder of this expository interchange, Graham and Leonard proceed with their own speech patterns. Graham has "If you intend," "may I remind you," "I don't want," "I'll have you know," and "Quite. Remember that," and he climaxes the scene with the most brazen admission of self-importance he has uttered so far:

Look. I'll remind you that as from last Wednesday, this house no longer belongs to your mother, you know. It belongs to me. Me. You remember that.

This is the quintessential Graham Baker that the actor and audience know up to this point. The short (sometimes monosyllabic) sentence, the first-person pronoun, the command, and the assumption of attention and the utter need to have it are the shape of the man the actor must embody and articulate.

HOW CAN YOU APPLY WHAT YOU HAVE JUST READ TO OTHER SCENES AND CHARACTERS?

As this chapter proceeds, in your own mind you will be adding questions and answers; but take the following ones with you to everything we will cover, and you will eventually have a rich series of vocal approaches to any role in any scene. The following is another checklist, based on what you have read so far, and it will get longer later.

An Actor's Checklist for Vocal Character Work

1. Speech Pattern
Establish a speech pattern from early in the scene.

2. Punctuation
How does the punctuation affect the meaning and the mood and therefore the character?

3. Repetition
Which repeated phrases or ideas or words make up this character?

4. Rhythmic Similarities
Which rhythmic similarities are there between your character's speech and that of the others? Does this similarity mean mockery? Influence? Flattery? What?

5. Sounds for the Face
Are there sounds in your character's lines that produce certain facial expressions as a significant guide to characterization?

6. Main Words

What are the main words, using Alec Guinness's order of importance in emphasis: verb first, noun second, adverb and adjective third?

7. Pronouns

Is there—again using Alec Guinness's advice—particularly good reason to emphasize any of the personal pronouns? (Remember they are *very rarely* emphasized. There are other elements of the sentences that convey the idea without such a crude signal.)

8. Differences

Sum up the differences in speech pattern between your part and the others without worrying too much about the others.

FOUR CHARACTERS FROM *DESIRE UNDER THE ELMS* AND THEIR SPEECH PATTERNS

A Few Preliminary Words on Mimicry

All actors are imitators of experience; most of us have been, in our youth and since, mimics and parodists. Yet many successful and beloved performers have types of voices and even modes of speech that cannot change very much. For instance, we have seldom heard Gielgud do an accent or dialect; on the other hand, Olivier has often altered the melody of his voice, its pitch, and its quality. We will all acknowledge that there is a special pleasure to be gained from watching an actor sink into a part to the extent that the "self" is now the character, although we still leave the theatre saying "Maggie Smith was wonderful in *As You Like It*," rather than "*As You Like It* was wonderful and Maggie Smith was in it, wonderful too."

However, the lot of the "character actor" is not to be remembered as much as the role, although of course most effective actors will always strive for some sort of identification. "It seems to me," said Herbert Beerbohm Tree in an address to the Royal Institution,[4] "in

---

[4]In London on May 26, 1893. This was the first time anyone from the theatrical profession was invited to address the Institution: Tree had been honored with a knighthood some years before. That he was able to act in Ibsen is probably a tribute to his diminishing his personality in the role, for later in the same address he remarks: "I must confess that, judged by Ibsen's plays, Scandinavia, in its sordid Suburbanism, seems to me an undesirable abiding-place."

spite of all that certain writers are never tired of dinning into our ears, that the higher aim of the artist is to so project his imagination into the character he is playing that his own individuality becomes merged in his assumption. This indeed seems to me the very essence of the art of acting.''

Typecasting has always been part of the theatre. Thomas Heywood's *Apology for Actors* (1612) says: "Actors should be picked out personable according to the parts they present . . ." and in the theatre, what is true of the body can be equally true of the voice. Heywood goes on:

> They should rather be scholars, that though they cannot speak well, know how to speak; or else to have that volubility that they can speak well, though they understand not what, and so both imperfections may by instructions be helped and amended: but where a good tongue and a good conceit both fail, there can never be a good actor.

Much can be said about these statements, and help can be got from them on the matter of dialect and accent called for in a part. Heywood was talking of a knowledge of sentence formation, metaphor, and argumentation when he used the word "scholar." In the sixteenth and seventeenth centuries, the boys of King's School, Canterbury and St. Paul's school in London—and many other pupils in schools not necessarily primed for particular preparation for the stage as a career—came to know most of what there is to know about "tropes and figures," that is, structures of speech and images used in poetry and discourse. This knowledge may have made it easier for the boys to be mimics. While, to the Elizabethans, verisimilitude in the rendering of provincial accents and dialects was not required, and any speech deviant from that of metropolitan London was generally reserved for ridicule or color of a satirical sort, the theatre today calls for more accuracy. Thomas Dekker's Dutchman parody in *The Shoemaker's Holiday*, for instance, is created out of a Londoner's ignorance and wonder and is not drawn from any life other than that of Dekker's imaginative prejudice; the Dutchman would be amusing today only if played with a Dutch accent as recognizably accurate as possible. The role of the Dutchman is minor, with a particular qualification required for the actor who plays it: the ability to mimic a Dutch accent.

The following is an extract from *The Shoemaker's Holiday*, Act

II, Scene iii, in which Sir Hugh Lacy, Earl of Lincoln, is imitating a Dutchman to a group of London shoemakers and apprentices—all members of "the gentle craft."

FIRK   . . . are you of the gentle craft?

LACY   Yaw, yaw, ick bin den skomawker.

FIRK: . . . Have you all your tools, and good Saint Hugh's bones to smooth up your work?

LACY   Yaw, yaw, be niet vorveard. Ick hab all de dingen voour mack skooes groot and cleane. [*Cleane* comes from *klein,* meaning *small.*]

EYRE   Ick weet niet wat yow seg; ick verstaw you niet.

That is a terrible imitation. Fortunately, in this scene, the imitation is meant to be an Englishman's idea of what a Dutchman sounds like. English audiences have apparently found the scene hilarious—really just a cheap piece of what one can even call vaudeville, but fun of a kind.

Work out what Lacy is saying. Then answer the following questions and compare your answers to those of your partner or teacher or group.

1. How did you work it out? What words gave you the clues?
2. Which words would you have to emphasize in performance to get the meaning across?
3. Which sounds particularly make you sound as if your language is not English?
4. Make a list of unusual jaw and lip movements in the pronunciation of these lines.

We can see, then, that the assimilation and presentation of the muscular labial contractions and dental workings necessary to produce the "standard Dutch accent" are relatively simple affairs. Because we live in a world of rapid communication, the more accurate the imitation the more pleasure it will give even though in this scene from *The Shoemaker's Holiday,* the joy intended is small, perhaps even mean. Let us turn our attention to something "better."

DESIRE UNDER THE ELMS

"They lay aside the learned dialect and reveal the powers of common speech." (H. Reid, 1857)

In *Desire under the Elms*, Eugene O'Neill has set a passionate story of greed and possessiveness in what for his audience was an ironic location: the quiet farmland of New Hampshire. O'Neill's people speak so plainly that, like the women in Synge's *Riders to the Sea*, their uttered thoughts approach poetry. This question of elevated language is not what concerns us here, but the translation of the playwright's rhythms into sound. Simeon and Peter, at the end of the first unit of Act I, are given strange euphonious utterances, the most dialectal of which is the New England "Ayeh."

Dialect is Speech Pattern

The brothers are distinguished largely by their similarity. If, ignoring the clearly implicit instructions of the playwright, their similarity is emphasized, the brothers would become little more than caricatures, which indeed happened in the fifties film (with Burl Ives and Sophia Loren), where Simeon and Peter were quite interchangeable in speech as well as in character. Some of the interchangeability is part of O'Neill's point, but another, equally rich point is the relationship between these two men that is affecting in its gnarled simplicity. The following is a section from the short Part I, Scene 1.

SIMEON and PETER come in from their work in the fields. They are tall men, much older than their half-brother (SIMEON is thirty-nine and PETER thirty-seven), built on a squarer, simpler model, fleshier in body, more bovine and homelier in face, shrewder and more practical. Their shoulders stoop a bit from years of farm work. They clump heavily along in their clumsy thick-soled boots caked with earth. Their clothes, their faces, hands, bare arms and throats are earth-stained. They smell of the earth. They stand together for a moment in front of the house and, as if with the one impulse, stare dumbly up at the sky, leaning on their hoes. Their faces have a compressed, unresigned expression. As they look upward, this softens.

SIMEON	(*Grudgingly*) Purty.
PETER	Ay-eh.
SIMEON	(*Suddenly*) Eighteen years ago.
PETER	What?

5	SIMEON	Jenn. My woman. She died.
	PETER	I'd fergot.
	SIMEON	I rec'lect—now an' agin. Makes it lonesome. She'd hair long's a hoss' tail—an yaller like gold!
10	PETER	Waal—she's gone. (*This with indifferent finality—then after a pause*) They's gold in the West, Sim.
	SIMEON	(*Still under the influence of sunset—vaguely*) In the sky!
	PETER	Waal—in a manner o' speakin'—thar's the promise. (*Growing excited*) Gold in the sky—in the West—Golden Gate—Californi-a!—Golden West!—fields o' gold!
15	SIMEON	(*Excited in his turn*) Fortunes layin' just atop o' the ground waiting' t' be picked! Solomon's mines, they says! (*For a moment they continue looking up at the sky—then their eyes drop*)
20	PETER	(*With sardonic bitterness*) Here—it's stones atop o' the ground—stones atop o' stones—makin' stone walls—year atop o' year—him 'n' yew 'n' me 'n' then Eben—makin' stone walls fur him to fence us in!
25	SIMEON	We've wuked. Give our strength. Give our years. Plowed 'em under in the ground,—(*he stamps rebelliouslyl*)—rottin'—makin' soil for his crops! (*A pause*) Waal—the farm pays good for hereabouts.
	PETER	If we plowed in Californi-a, they'd be lumps o' gold in the furrow!
	SIMEON	Californi-a's t'other side o' earth, a'most. We got t' calc'late—
30	PETER	(*After a pause*) 'Twould be hard fur me, too, to give up what we've 'arned here by our sweat. (*A pause. EBEN sticks his head out of the dining-room window, listening*)
	SIMEON	Ay-eh. (*A pause*) Mebbe—he'll die soon.
	PETER	(*Doubtfully*) Mebbe.
35	SIMEON	Mebbe—fur all we knows—he's dead now.

PETER	Ye'd need proof.
SIMEON	He's been gone two months—with no word.
PETER	Left us in the fields an evenin' like this. Hitched up an' druv off into the West. That's plum onnateral. He hain't never been off this farm 'ceptin' t' the village in thirty year or more, not since he married Eben's maw. (*A pause. Shrewdly*) I calc'late we might git him declared crazy by the court.
SIMEON	He skinned 'em too slick. He got the best o' all on 'em. They'd never b'lieve him crazy. (*A pause*) We got t' wait till he's under ground.
EBEN	(*With a sardonic chuckle*) Honor thy father! (*They turn, startled, and stare at him. He grins, then scowls*) I pray he's died. (*They stare at him. He continues matter-of-factly*) Supper's ready.
SIMEON AND PETER	(*Together*) Ay-eh.
EBEN	(*Gazing up at the sky*) Sun's downin' purty.
SIMEON AND PETER	(*Together*) Ay-eh. They's gold in the West.
EBEN	Ay-eh. (*Pointing*) Yonder atop o' the hill pasture, ye mean?
SIMEON AND PETER	(*Together*) In Californi-a!
EBEN	Hunh? (*Stares at them indifferently for a second, then drawls*) Waal—supper's gittin' cold. (*He turns back into kitchen*)
SIMEON	(*Startled—smacks his lips*) I air hungry!
PETER	(*Sniffing*) I smells bacon!
SIMEON	(*With hungry appreciation*) Bacon's good!
PETER	(*In same tone*) Bacon's bacon! (*They turn, shouldering each other, their bodies bumping and rubbing together as they hurry clumsily to their food, like two friendly oxen toward their evening meal. They disappear around the right corner of house and can be heard entering the door*)

CURTAIN

Two Speech Patterns

Clearly, Simeon speaks in slightly more complex sentences than does Peter; he is also given to the pause in place of conventional grammatical transitions and connectives. Look at the brothers' speech patterns side by side and don't consider, for the moment, their "accent":

SIMEON	PETER
Eighteen years ago.	What?
Jenn. My woman. She died. I rec'lect—now an' agin. Makes it lonesome. She'd hair long's a hoss' tail—an' yaller like gold!	I'd fergot.
	Waal—she's gone. They's gold in the West, Sim.

Thinking about these lines without regard for the situation the men find themselves in and even without O'Neill's parenthetical stage directions can only make us clarify that situation. Peter is brief, even terse; Simeon is more of a rambler: Remember that he speaks as he does because he is what he says. Simeon has marginally more brains than his brother and is at the same time marginally more "romantic." All the audience knows of the brothers so far is that Peter is the more practical of the two and this distinction should be made clear. Peter's "They's gold in the West, Sim!" tells *where* the gold is, and Simeon's "yaller like gold," akin to his remark about his wife's hair, is a simile. Before we go on to the rest of their interchange, note that although Simeon speaks with pauses, the remarks around them are grammatically connected by "My . . . She . . . now . . . an'."

SIMEON	PETER
In the sky! **(Simeon raises gold beyond its mere location, augmenting Peter's** "in the West")	
	Waal—in a manner o' speakin'—thar's the promise. Gold in the sky—in the West— Golden Gate—Californi-a Golden West—fields o' gold!

Fortunes layin' just atop o' the ground waitin' t' be picked! Solomon's mines, they says! **(This is almost a complete sentence, almost two. While he has picked up Peter's excitement, he retains his own pattern of speech)**

Here—it's stones atop o' the ground—stones atop o' stones— makin' stone walls—year atop o' year—him 'n' yew 'n' me 'n' then Eben—makin' stone walls fur him to fence us in! **(Peter's speech is generally devoid of the connectives found in Simeon's)**

(And now an interesting thing happens: From the excitement of their common desire, Simeon adopts Peter's patterns) We've wuked. Give our strength. Give our years. Plowed 'em under the ground,—rottin'—makin' soil for his crops! (*A pause*)

Give and Take

What explains this manner of Simeon's speech? We need not trouble ourselves with the question of inspiration or perspiration or drink on O'Neill's part. What he has written is what the actor has, and the actor can see a great deal of "give and take" between these two brothers to the extent that while they do not speak the same way from the start, their common lusts, envies, and resentments cause them to influence each other's speech. We shall see later in the powerful love scene between Eben and Abbie how effective this give and take is in the representation of a "romantic relationship."

How a Harmonic Relationship is Shown

Let us continue with this first scene and observe what happens.

SIMEON
Waal—the farm pays good for hereabouts.
(Like many romantics, Simeon is hesitant about practicalities.

PETER

This is an important small reversal for the character, rounding him out already, so early in the play)

If we plowed in Californi-a, they'd be lumps of gold in the furrow!
(A straightforward, innocent continuation of his soon-to-be-avowed intent, this is an indication of the way in which Peter, the slightly simpler, persuades his brother)

Californi-a's t'other side o' earth a'most. We got t' calc'late—
(Note how near an echo *calc'late* is of *rec'lect*. This is a gift for the actor, establishing a recognizable trait for the audience)

'Twould be hard fur me, too, to give up what we've 'arned here by our sweat.
(Again forthright, direct. He can speak only what is on his mind)

Ay-eh.
(The last time this was uttered—less than 40 seconds ago—it was by Peter. Although every character in the play says it, since it is—and is still—a common regional expression from mid-New Hampshire to the Maine coast, here it serves well the similarity and indeed the harmony of the two brothers.)
Mebbe—he'll die soon.

Mebbe.
(Characteristically short for Peter)

Mebbe—fur all we knows—he's dead now.
(Three *mebbe*'s, two of them Simeon's)

Ye'd need proof.
(The typical terse Peter phrase)

He's been gone two months—
with no word.
(**Rambling Simeon again, with
the connective *with* after his
pause**)

Left us in the fields an evenin'
like this. Hitched up an' druv
off into the West. That's plum
onnateral. He hain't never been
off this farm 'ceptin' t' village
in thirty year or more, not since
he married Eben's maw.
(**Note how Peter's speech
begins with two sentences
without subjects. Had Simeon
said this, he might have put it
this way: He's left us in the
fields—an' hitched up and
druv . . .**)

Similarities and a Problem

I calc'late we might git him
declared crazy by the court.
(**This is a quietly brilliant
moment. Peter also says
calc'late. But the audience had
to think the brothers were
different at first before
accepting their similarities.
This last phrase—"declared
crazy by the court"—is
abnormally correct for Peter
grammatically. How is the
actor to handle it? The phrase
is not Peter's original language,
of course . . . he had learned it
in the village and only thus has
its good grammar become part
of his own speech, reserved for
occasions of heightened
emotion like this**)

This kind of "foreign" phrasing is found frequently in well-written dialogue and is not always easy to act. What if the actor said: "I calc'late we might git him *declared crazy* by the court"? That would not do because it would not show social influence in addition to the already present resentful guile. If the actor indulged in unindicated pauses such as: "I calc'late we might . . . git him *declared crazy* . . . by the court," there would be far too many rapid shifts of thought and intention for any audience to take in. Both ways of speaking it, however, make the last phrase a natural part of the character's vocabulary. But this is not the point. Peter has heard that such things as certification of the mentally unfit exist but is not totally familiar with them from practice.

"Git him declared crazy by the court" is perfect for conveying the half-educated man particularly because of the contrast between the last fluent phrase and the regional, low "git."

Togetherness of Purpose

SIMEON
He skinned 'em too slick. He got the best o' all on 'em. They'd never b'lieve him crazy. (*A pause*) We got t' wait—till he's under ground.
(Note that these brothers speak in concrete terms. Simeon does not say "underground," which would conjure up the merest concrete image; he gives two words, strongly emphasizing not only what death is in the country but also the fact that he lives there, *on* the "ground")

EBEN

SIMEON AND PETER

Ay-eh.

Ay-eh. They's gold in the West.
(The brothers are in concert now, complete harmony against the usurping brother

EBEN
Supper's ready.

Sun's downin' purty.

**Eben; like children, they're still
taking half their troubles to
him at the same time as
flaunting their intent in front of
him)**

Ay-eh. Yonder atop o' the hill
pasture, ye mean?

In Californi-a!
**(The remainder of this very
musical scene is self-
explanatory, the two brothers
alternating between solo
dialogue and unison)**

Scene Study

Quite early in the play the brothers go off to California. You should get a copy of *Desire under the Elms* and work on these two characters. The following is a list of things to look for, to guide you through your rehearsing. Perhaps if you are taking the kind of course that allows for student-directed scenes for presentation, you might get a director. (The scene that follows is for one male, one female, so don't give up if you don't want a two-male scene.)

Checklist

1. What phrases I speak are similar to those of the other character? Why? What does this mean?
2. What rhythms and stresses do I share with the other character? Why? What does this mean?
3. Where do we utter similar sounds? How can I use this to show a side of our relationship?
4. Does my vocabulary differ from the other character's? My use of it? How? Where? What?
5. In what other ways can I use the rhythms and patterns of my role to create the character?

Eben and Abbie (Part III, Scene 2)

With Simeon and Peter we have seen how the playwright has characters influence each other in their speech patterns. Let us turn to a scene of very heightened emotion between old man Ephraim Cabot's new young wife Abbie and her lover Eben, his son by his first marriage. The scene is one of the strongest in American theatre, and some people would go so far to call it melodramatic, which it certainly can be, and I think the rapid fall of the curtain at the end of it makes it so, unless of course the performances are overstated. However, the scene has so many subtleties that it can and should be a *tour de force*, not of ranting but of human observation.

ABBIE   Eben! Ephraim! (*She tugs at the hand on EBEN's throat*) Let go, Ephraim! Y're chokin' him!

CABOT   (*Removes his hand and flings EBEN sideways full length on the grass, gasping and choking. With a cry, ABBIE kneels beside him, trying to take his head on her lap, but he pushes her away. CABOT stands looking down with fierce triumph*) Ye needn't t've fret, Abbie, I wa'n't aimin't' kill him. He hain't wuth hangin' fur—not by a hell of a sight! (*More and more triumphantly*) Seventy-six an' him not thirty yit—an' look what he be fur thinkin' his Paw was easy! No, by God, I hain't easy! An' him upstairs, I'll raise him t' be like me! (*He turns to leave them*) I'm goin in an' dance!—sing an' celebrate! (*He walks to the porch— then turns with a great grin*) I don't calc'late it's left in him, but if he gits pesky, Abbie, ye just sing out. I'll come a-runnin' an' by the Etarnal, I'll put him across my knee an' birch him! Ha-ha-ha! (*He goes into the house laughing. A moment later his loud "whoop" is heard*)

ABBIE   (*Tenderly*) Eben. Air ye hurt? (*She tries to kiss him but he pushes her violently away and struggles to a sitting position*)

EBEN   (*Gaspingly*) T' hell—with ye!

ABBIE   (*Not believing her ears*) It's me, Eben—Abbie don't ye know me?

EBEN   (*Glowering at her with hatred*) Ay-eh—I know ye—now! (*He suddenly breaks down, sobbing weakly*)

ABBIE   (*Fearfully*) Eben—what's happened t' ye—why did ye look at me 's if ye hated me?

EBEN   (*Violently, between sobs and gasps*) I do hate ye! Ye're a whore—a damn trickin' whore!

ABBIE   (*Shrinking back, horrified*) Eben! Ye don't know what ye're sayin'!

EBEN   (*Scrambling to his feet and following her—accusingly*) Ye're nothin' but a stinkin' passel o' lies! Ye've been lyin' t' me every word ye spoke, day an' night, since we fust—done it. Ye've kept sayin' ye loved me . . .

30 ABBIE   (*Frantically*) I do love ye! (*She takes his hand but he flings hers away*)

EBEN   (*Unheeding*) Ye've made a fool o' me—a sick, dumb fool—a-purpose! Ye've been on'y playin' yer sneakin', stealin' game all along—gittin' me t' lie with ye so's ye'd hev a son he'd think was his 'n, an' makin' him promise he'd give ye the farm and let me eat dust, if ye did git him a

35   son! (*Staring at her with anguished, bewildered eyes*) They must be a devil livin' in ye! T'ain't human t' be as bad as that be!

ABBIE   (*Stunned—dully*) He told yew . . . ?

EBEN   Hain't it true? It hain't no good in yew lyin'.

ABBIE   (*Pleadingly*) Eben, listen—ye must listen—it was long ago—afore we
40   done nothin'—yew was scornin' me—goin' t' see Min—when I was lovin' ye—an' I said it t' him t' git vengeance on ye!

EBEN   (*Unheedingly. With tortured passion*) I wish ye was dead! I wish I was dead along with ye afore this come! (*Ragingly*) But I'll git my vengeance too! I'll pray Maw t' come back t' help me—t' put her cuss on yew an'
45   him!

ABBIE   (*Brokenly*) Don't ye, Eben! Don't ye! (*She throws herself on her knees before him, weeping*) I didn't mean t' do bad t' ye! Fergive me, won't ye?

EBEN   (*Not seeming to hear her—fiercely*) I'll git squar' with the old skunk—
50   an' yew! I'll tell him the truth 'bout the son he's so proud o'! Then I'll leave ye here t' pizen each other—with Maw comin' out o' her grave at nights—an' I'll go t' the gold fields o' Californi-a whar Sim an' Peter be!

ABBIE   (*Terrified*) Ye won't—leave me! Ye can't!

EBEN   (*With fierce determination*) I'm a-goin', I tell ye! I'll git rich thar an' come
55   back an' fight him fur the farm he stole—an' I'll kick ye both out in the road—t' beg an' sleep in the woods—an' yer son along with ye—t' starve an' die! (*He is hysterical at the end*)

ABBIE   (*With a shudder—humbly*) He's yewr son, too, Eben.

EBEN   (*Torturedly*) I wish he never was born! I wish he'd die this minit! I wish
60   I'd never sot eyes on him! It's him—yew havin' him—a-purpose t' steal— that's changed everythin'!

ABBIE   (*Gently*) Did ye believe I loved ye—afore he come?

EBEN   Ay-eh—like a dumb ox!

ABBIE   An, ye don't believe no more?

65 EBEN   B'lieve a lyin' thief! Ha!

ABBIE   (*Shudders—then humbly*) An' did ye r'ally love me afore?

EBEN   (*Brokenly*) Ay-eh—an' ye was trickin' me!

ABBIE   An' ye don't love me now!

EBEN   (*Violently*) I hate ye, I tell ye!

70 ABBIE   An' ye're truly goin' West—goin' t' leave me—all account o' him being born?

EBEN   I'm a-goin' in the mornin'—or may God strike me t' hell!

ABBIE   (*After a pause—with a dreadful cold intensity—slowly*) If that's what his comin's done t' me—killin' yewr love—takin' yew away—my on'y joy—
75   the on'y joy I ever knowed—like heaven t' me—purlier'n heaven—then I hate him, too, even if I be his Maw!

EBEN   (*Bitterly*) Lies! Ye love him! He'll steal the farm fur ye! (*Brokenly*) But t'ain't the farm so much—not no more—it's yew foolin' me—gittin' me t' love ye—lyin' yew loved me—jest t' git a son t' steal!

80 ABBIE   (*Distractedly*) He won't steal! I'd kill him fust! I do love ye! I'll prove t' ye . . . !

EBEN   (*Harshly*) T'ain't no use lyin' no more. I'm deaf t' ye! (*He turns away*) I hain't seein' ye agen. Good-by!

ABBIE   (*Pale with anguish*) Hain't ye even goin' t' kiss me—not once—arter all
85   we loved?

EBEN   (*In a hard voice*) I hain't wantin' t' kiss ye never agen! I'm wantin t' forgit I ever sot eyes on ye!

ABBIE   Eben!—ye mustn't—wait a spell—I want t' tell ye . . .

EBEN   I'm a-goin' in t' git drunk. I'm a-goin' t' dance.

90 ABBIE   (*Clinging to his arm—with passionate earnestness*) If I could make it—

's if he'd never come up between us—if I could prove t' ye I wa'n't schemin' t' steal from ye—so's everythin' could be jest the same with us, lovin' each other jest the same, kissin' an happy the same's we've been happy afore he come—if I could do it—ye'd love me agen, wouldn't
95   ye? Ye'd kiss me agen? Ye wouldn't never leave me, would ye?

EBEN   (*Moved*) I calc'late not. (*Then shaking her hand off his arm—with a bitter smile*) But ye hain't God, be ye?

ABBIE   (*Exultantly*) Remember ye've promised! (*Then with strange intensity*) Mebbe I kin take back one thin' God does!

100   EBEN   (*Peering at her*) Ye're gittin' cracked, hain't ye? (*Then going towards door*) I'm a-goin' t' dance.

ABBIE   (*Calls after him intensely*) I'll prove t' ye! I'll prove I love ye better'n . . . (*He goes in the door, not seeming to hear. She remains standing where she is, looking after him—then she finishes desperately*) Better'n everythin'
105   else in the world!

    I tremble whenever I read this scene, the passions fly back and forth so quickly and intensely. Before you proceed with your own scene study, let me take you through a few of the scene's rich and subtle points.

ABBIE

1. It's me, Eben—Abbie—don't ye know me?

3. Eben—what's happened t' ye—why did ye look at me 's if ye hated me?
(**Both characters are speaking in broken phrases because of the breathlessness, hatred, and pain**)

EBEN

2. Ay-eh—I know ye—now!
(**This repetition of *know* is as natural as can be, tragic in the circumstances and affecting. I don't think emphasis is expected to be placed on *know*, however, as the shift in mood is covered suddenly and theatrically by *now***)

4. I do hate ye! Ye're a whore—
a damn trickin' whore!
(**Eben is establishing a habit of
repetition simple to act if not
underlined. The repetition is
underlining enough**)

Let us reexamine the dialogue for its rhythm.

1. ∪/:/∪::/∪::/∪/∪∪?

2. /∪::/∪::/!

3. /∪::/∪/∪::/∪∪/∪∪∪∪/∪∪?

4. ∪//∪::∪∪/::∪//∪/!

The first most obvious difference between the rhythms of these speeches is that Abbie's lines have insistent, questioning feminine endings and Eben's have assertive masculine endings, which also continues in the subsequent couple of speeches:

ABBIE

/ ∪　∪ /　∪　∪ ∪
Eben! Ye don't know what ye're

/ ∪
sayin'!

EBEN

∪　/ ∪　∪ ∪ / ∪
Ye're nothin' but a stinkin'

/ ∪ ∪ /　∪　　∪ /
passel o' lies! Ye've been lyin'

∪　/ ∪ ∪ /　∪ /　　/
t' me every word ye spoke, day

∪　/　∪　　∪ /　/
and night, since we fust—done

∪　∪　　/ / ∪　∪ /
it. Ye've kept sayin' ye loved

∪
me . . .

But what is happening to Eben and to the mouth of the actor who plays him? Eben's assertive rhythms give up when, now ashamed and regretful, he recollects the first sexual encounter with Abbie. "Made love" would have a masculine ending: "done it" is feminine, as is his pathetic half-plea for reassurance that is in fact a condemnation, "Y've kept sayin' ye loved me."

/ /　∪
I do love ye!

. . . listen to what happens:

∪　　/　∪ ∪ / ∪ ∪ ∪ /
Ye've made a fool o' me—a sick

/　/　∪ / ∪
dumb fool—a-purpose!

Tight with rage, Eben speaks with Abbie's rhythms for the first time in the scene. The rest of that speech vacillates between the two kinds of line-ending, while Eben gathers his strength, as it were, for his continued rage. Thereafter, Eben's lines, heartfelt as they are, bristle and damn with strong endings:

> I'll get my vengeance too / cuss on yew an' him / the old skunk /
> whar Sim an' Peter be / farm he stole / out in the road / sleep in
> the woods / starve an' die / I wish he was never born.

When, in response to Abbie's "He's yewr son, too, Eben," Eben is speaking about the baby, he once again lapses into the tenderness (for him) of feminine endings:

> I wish he'd die this minit! I wish I'd never sot eyes on him!
> It's him—yew havin' him—a-purpose t' steal—that's changed
> everythin'!

In a beautiful reversal of powers, O'Neill lets Abbie now, get the upper hand in the interchange and gives her masculine stresses on which to end her lines, while Eben fumbles tearfully along with almost puny ones:

ABBIE Did ye believe I love ye—afore he come?

EBEN Ay-eh—like a dumb ox!

ABBIE An' ye don't believe no more?

EBEN B'lieve a lyin' thief! Ha!

5 ABBIE An' did ye r'ally love me afore?

EBEN Ah-ey—an' ye was trickin' me!

ABBIE An' ye don't love me now!

EBEN   I hate ye, I tell ye!

ABBIE   An' ye're truly goin' West—goin' t' leave me—all account o' him being born?

EBEN   I'm a-goin' in the mornin'—or may God strike me t' hell!

We can now see easily that in his sudden determination to leave Abbie, the child she bore him, and the farm, Eben ends this passage of stichomythia with a strong stress.

Actors and actresses must sensitize themselves to this kind of musical interplay between characters in order to perform satisfactorily in carefully constructed dialogue of this kind. It is clear, for instance, that each character has an individual music and rhythm and that the two "types" are at passionate war. O'Neill need not really have written a complete stage direction such as "after a pause—with a dreadful cold intensity—slowly" (although the "slowly" is perhaps helpful) because Abbie's speech, which follows these particular directions, *is* precisely what he describes it as being:

> If that's what his comin's done t' me—killin' yewr love—takin' yew away—my on'y joy—the on'y joy I ever knowed—like heaven t' me—purtier 'n heaven—then I hate him, too, even if I be his Maw!

Abbie regains her quieter, feminine-ended speech in a few seconds, when, "distractedly," she says:

> ‿ / (‿) ‿ / ‿ (‿)
> He won't steal! I'd kill him fust!
> ‿ / / ‿ ‿ / ‿
> I do love ye! I'll prove t' ye . . . !

When Abbie is "all-woman," albeit a fiendish one at this point, she reverts to what O'Neill could well have called feminine wiles, and all her lines have weak endings:

> (*Clinging to his arm—with passionate earnestness*) If I could make it—'s if he'd never come up between us—if I could prove t' ye I wa'n't schemin' t' steal from ye—so's everythin' could be jest the same with us, lovin' each other jest the same, kissin' an' happy the same's we've been happy afore he come—if I could do it—ye'd love me agen, wouldn't ye? Ye'd kiss me agen? Ye wouldn't never leave me, would ye?

This great speech is not a model of rhetoric, nor is it meant to be, but it does have the desired effect on Eben. Why? The speech represents the image of womanhood to him—his image of what a woman means to a man; poor Eben.

> I calc'late not. (*Then shaking her hand off his arm—with a bitter smile*) But ye hain't God, be ye?

In its emphasis on low wide ee's, this thin, sparse, teeth-bared line is—if anything in the play is—man addressing woman in a challenging female voice.

Of course, Abbie becomes a murderess overnight. This development in her character is boldly delineated by the playwright and the actress in the magnificent tension between weak and strong endings in the final lines of the scene:

> I'll prove t' ye! I'll prove I love ye better'n (. . . *then she finishes desperately*) better'n everythin' else in the world.

First, on page 116, look again at the checklist for scene study from the scenes between the two brothers, Simeon and Peter. You will see that all those questions apply equally well to the scene between Eben and Abbie you've just looked at.

EXERCISE

Choose a scene with two characters and approach with what you have learned so far from working through this chapter of the book. Always use the Checklist. Soon you will find that your character springs from the lines and provides you with emotions and shades of feeling that you might have a difficult time conjuring up in any other ways.

Vocal Balance and Variety Can Come From Sentence Structure.

Variety of Pitch: This book is intended to stimulate aspiring young professional actors and actresses; and the theatre profession, since its inception and all through its history in various civilizations, offers many more parts for men than for women. This condition has been—and still is—a fact of the life of the theatre. Student actors in theatre schools, universities, colleges, and even high schools must be aware of another fact: There are many more aspiring actresses than aspiring actors. Whenever I attend a casting call for movies or an audition for

a stage play, most of my companions in the waiting room are actresses, unless the show has been announced as totally male. Thus,
the preponderance of male speeches in this book is merely an honest
reflection of the reality of professional theatre—indeed, of the "en-
tertainment industry" in general. However, the scenes are interesting
enough for women to read the male parts.

The Female Voice and Symmetry

Of course, there really is a reason for the disproportion of male and
female parts, and it is due not only to the patriarchal societies that
have produced our greatest theatre by having men play the parts, or
to the leadership men have shown—at the expense of the creativity
of women—in the arts through the centuries; the reason could also
be the natural result of a *desire on the part of any audience to have
vocal variety.*

The Belgian playwright Ghelderode wrote a play in the late fifties
titled *Seven Women at the Tomb.* One of the things that makes the
play very difficult to perform successfully, and one of the things that
makes it almost boring at times is the high pitch of the vocal experience: the total reliance on female voices, the emphasis on the treble
clef—like a pianist not playing much below middle C. There is no
denying that it is uncomfortable for an audience to sit in the same
seats for two hours and hear nothing below a certain note. Imagine a
discotheque without the electric bass to provide its base. Imagine a
Joan Armatrading, Juice Newton, Pink Floyd minus the ground bass:
The experience is insufficiently rounded. The subject would take a
longer essay than these brief notes to discuss; suffice it to say that
directors of plays, films, shows, directors of anything to which people
are invited as paying guests will seldom willingly mount a production
without the variety I've been speaking about.

Earlier in this book (in the section on Projection) I mentioned
Agnes of God, a play concerning—and played by—three women. The
casting was brilliant. Against the mezzo-soprano of Geraldine Page
and the soprano of Amanda Plummer, we got the husky alto of Elizabeth Ashley, and the show was played in front of a giant wooden
sounding-board that had the effect of deepening the voices of the first
two actresses. The experience as altogether superb. The audience was—
as it usually is at a Broadway show—a cross-section of the humanity
able to afford the price of a theatre ticket, and they were satisfied with
the aural experience of the evening because there was such a well-
chosen variety of timbres and pitches on the stage. The wooden stage
and the deep tones of Elizabeth Ashley were a necessary counterbass,

as it were, to Page and Plummer. Further, the sounding board of the set created a pleasurable boom that offset any shrillness that might have been present in the vocal characterizations of those actresses. It is interesting to note that when Elizabeth Ashley went on vacation from the show for a few weeks, her substitute was Diahann Carroll, whose voice is not high pitched.

What I have been saying is not intended to discourage the talented actress from seeking a career in acting, but it is obvious that I'm calling for some kind of caution about the pitch of the voice. Let us look at *Who's Afraid of Virginia Woolf?*, and use this brilliant and indeed epoch-making play by the young Edward Albee as a basis for a discussion of the problem as you might usefully consider it. When variety of the actual pitch of the actors' voices is not possible, it is particularly necessary to attend carefully to the variety of the sentence structure. Quite often, changes in shape and tempo can be exciting substitutes for tonal variety, as we shall soon see.

In the first New York production of *Who's Afraid of Virginia Woolf?*, Martha was played by Uta Hagen and Honey by Melinda Dillon. This fine cast, completed by Arthur Hill as George and George Grizzard as Nick, can be heard on Caedmon records and makes a most interesting comparison with the record of the movie, which is also available from record-lending libraries and is even still in stores, with Elizabeth Taylor, Sandy Dennis, Richard Burton, and George Segal. Alan Schneider directed the stage production, and Mike Nichols the film. In each version it was important for the director to have a vocal balance, and in the play we had Uta Hagen slightly deeper than Arthur Hill, in the film Richard Burton deeper than Elizabeth Taylor. Sandy Dennis and Melinda Dillon both have "thin" voices but with depths and eccentricities that round them out. In fact, there are very few working actresses who are not capable of diving below the treble clef to provide the simple variety that every audience unwittingly craves. Why do people crave this fullness?

The Audience's Desire for Symmetry

Apart from an instinctive desire for *symmetry* that exists in everyone, there is a desire for richness, and I don't mean mere money and property, although the acquisition of those things is in itself a symptom of the same need. Let me explain what is meant by this desire for symmetry and order and how it is connected to the desire for a fulfillment that includes an aural need for the bass and treble pitches to exist in the same aural experience. I'm sure some of you have felt, when walking along a sidewalk, that you want to pace yourselves in such a way as to hit either all the cracks (if they are regular) or none of them. Of course, the childhood game of hopscotch satisfies this basic, primitive, and instinctual urge. Those of you who dress formally know how out of sync you feel when an element in your dress is askew: a necktie, a bow, a ribbon, an undone shoelace, a snot in the nostril, hair out of place. You know what I'm talking about when I say "out of place." You know that it's to do not only with the mean desire to conform; that's not at all close to the main reason we want to have order, why we have to be symmetrical. We are reflecting our inner, emotional, and even our sexual selves when we want to be "neat" or "tidy" or "in order," and of course, in turn, these inner selves are reflections of an order we perceive (or that we hope is there, at any rate, or that we wish were there, or that perhaps we are convinced by religion is there) in the universe around and beyond us.

When you sit on a chair, you are committing an act that you hope will make you "comfortable." What is comfort?; symmetry. In 1648, Robert Herrick wrote a sweet poem about the attractiveness of form and the deliciousness of deviation from it. However, with nothing to deviate from, such pleasure is utterly impossible. As Van Gogh said, "The world is a study of God that has turned out badly"; he continued, saying that the artist's job is to impose form or order on the chaos. That is indeed one way of looking at it. Twenty centuries ago, Plato said that all art is an aspiration toward the order already there. Either way, and whichever position the artist takes from which to work at a craft, order and form are the tools for the message to be understood at all. The "given" in Herrick's poem is that there is an ordered dress from which the woman has deviated. Without the initial order, variations from it cannot be understood or appreciated.

> A sweet disorder in the dress
> Kindles in clothes a wantonness.
> A lawn about the shoulders thrown
> Into a fine distraction;
> An erring lace, which here and there
> Enthralls the crimson stomacher;
> A cuff neglectful, and thereby
> Ribbons to flow, confusedly;
> A winning wave, deserving note,
> In the tempestuous petticoat;
> A careless shoestring, in whose tie
> I see a wild civility;
> Do more bewitch me than when art
> Is too precise in every part.

Herrick needs order before he can appreciate disorder or even desire it; so do we. How can we possibly know what morning is before having gone through night?

Finding a Physical Center

As you read this, you are probably sitting down in a chair. You have sought the position that puts you in the best relation to yourself, puts your surroundings in the most acceptable relation to your mind and body—for the time you have decided to spend reading at any rate. You have "placed yourself" so that, by being a comfortable part of your surroundings, you are more yourself. It is possible that you may be uncomfortable without knowing it because you are fascinated by what you are reading, although that is unlikely because of the amount of attention required for what you're doing. Examine the position you are in. You will find its elements very ordered, even if your legs are pressing against each other to impede blood circulation. My point is that you are *in harmony,* you have a *sense of order* you are reflecting in your posture, in the arrangements of your bodily parts.

Now—is there music playing? Were you conscious of it if there was? As I'm typing this the radio is playing some German songs I happen to like particularly, and my own sense of order is becoming dissipated; that's better; I've switched it off. And what an ordered act *that* was—very satisfying. I needed not only the concentration but also the shifting of the body. My comfort depended on other things than my simple position in front of the typewriter. For my position to be psychically complete and full, I needed the absence of music at that time. Around me familiar things put me at ease, and—although I am by nature a very untidy person who leaves things lying around more often than I really want to—they are in order. The pictures on the wall, for instance, have been placed there by my instinct, and therefore, I would say, also by my desire for order, even though to a casual observer they may appear randomly hung. My cigarette package is near at hand not only for convenience but also because of my years-old ritual of having it close when I type. Then, of course, there is the straightness of the lines produced by the typewriter—an order I cannot produce by hand however much I yearn for it.

Balance, Variety, Richness

Apart from violinists, few people could bear to hear in a week more than one solo violin recital without piano accompaniment, for instance. Why does a concert of unharmonized *a cappella* singing pall so soon? Why do we desire harmony? Because one voice is not enough, one *tone,* one pitch, is not enough, and it does not reflect the comfort and order of which I have been speaking. Why did Monteverdi set such glorious nine-part harmonies to his church choir music in the seventeenth century? So that the congregation could experience a *general fulfillment.* What made opera such a popular form of theatrical art from Purcell and Handel as far as Puccini and Wagner? Its fullness, of course. With the exception of the popular extracts sung by Pavarotti and Placido Domingo, why has opera sunk in mass appeal since the beginning of this century? One theory is that the music of the masses since the fifties has provided sufficient ground bass. Another reason, of course, is that opera is so removed from the level of life as it is lived and that musical comedy like *Oklahoma!* and *Cats,* while even further removed, deals with less harmful and thought-provoking themes; it is easy to note nonetheless that both examples of musical theatre I've mentioned use all the resources of large orchestras, choruses, or amplification to provide the "richness" for which the audience goes to the theatre or the cinema in the first place.

George and Nick in *Who's Afraid of Virginia Woolf?*

I would quite like to labor further the point about the need for balance, variety, and richness in any vocal makeup of a production, but rather than theorize, an analysis of one scene from *Who's Afraid of Virginia Woolf?* will serve the point just as well because it will become plain in the course of the discussion and the accompanying exercises that one of the things that makes Albee's tormenting and searing piece such a magnificent play is the very richness of variety we have been talking about.

Let us look at the famous beginning of Act II, which Albee has bitterly and excitingly labeled "Walpurgisnacht."[5] Honey has been vomiting, and she and Martha are upstairs. Everyone is very drunk, and it is about three in the morning.

---

[5]*Walpurgisnacht,* Night of the Witches, has been held for many centuries on the Brocken, a mountain in northern Germany associated with supernatural affairs. The witches dance there after midnight before May Day. Witches and warlocks cast spells and are considered androgynous, although they have intercourse with the Devil.

GEORGE by himself: NICK re-enters.

NICK (*After a silence*) I . . . guess . . . she's all right. (*No answer*) She's . . . frail. (*GEORGE smiles vaguely*) I'm really very sorry.

GEORGE (*Quietly*) Where's my little yum yum? Where's Martha?

NICK She's making coffee . . . in the kitchen. She . . . gets sick quite
5 easily.

GEORGE (*Preoccupied*) Martha? Oh no, Martha hasn't been sick a day in her life, unless you count the time she spends in the rest home . . .

NICK (*He, too, quietly*) No, no; *my* wife . . . *my* wife gets sick quite
10 easily. Your wife is Martha.

GEORGE (*With some rue*) Oh, yes . . . I know.

NICK (*A statement of fact*) She doesn't really spend any time in a rest home.

GEORGE Your wife?

15 NICK No. Yours.

GEORGE Oh! Mine. (*Pause*) No, no, she doesn't . . . *I* would; I mean if I were . . . her . . . she . . . *I* would. But I'm not . . . and so I don't. (*Pause*) I'd like to, though. It gets pretty bouncy around here sometimes.

20 NICK (*Cooly*) Yes . . . I'm sure.

GEORGE Well, you saw an example of it.

NICK I try not to . . .

GEORGE Get involved. Um? Isn't that right?

NICK Yes . . . that's right.

25 GEORGE I'd imagine not.

NICK I find it . . . embarrassing.

	GEORGE	(*Sarcastic*) Oh, you do, hunh?
	NICK	Yes. Really. Quite.
30	GEORGE	(*Mimicking him*) Yes. Really. Quite. (*Then aloud, but to himself*) IT'S DISGUSTING!
	NICK	Now look! I didn't have anything . . .
35	GEORGE	DISGUSTING! (*Quietly, but with great intensity*) Do you think I like having that . . . whatever-it-is . . . ridiculing me, tearing me down, in front of . . . (*Waves his hand in a gesture of contemptuous dismissal*) YOU? Do you think I *care* for it?
	NICK	(*Cold—unfriendly*) Well, no. . . I don't imagine you care for it at all.
	GEORGE	Oh, you don't imagine it, hunh?
	NICK	(*Antagonistic*) No . . . I don't. I don't imagine you do!
40	GEORGE	(*Withering*) Your sympathy disarms me . . . your . . . your compassion makes me weep! Large, salty, unscientific tears!
	NICK	(*With great disdain*) I just don't see why you feel you have to subject *other* people to it.
	GEORGE	*I?*
45	NICK	If you and your . . . wife . . . want to go at each other, like a couple of . . .
	GEORGE	*I!* Why *I* want to!
	NICK	. . . animals, I don't see why you don't do it when there aren't any . . .
50	GEORGE	(*Laughing through his anger*) Why, you smug, self-righteous little . . .
	NICK	(*A genuine threat*) CAN . . . IT . . . MISTER! (*Silence*) Just . . . watch it!
	GEORGE	. . . scientist.

55	NICK	I've never hit an older man.
	GEORGE	(*Considers it*) Oh. (*Pause*) You just hit younger men . . . and children . . . women . . . birds. (*Sees that NICK is not amused*) Well, you're quite right, of course. It isn't the prettiest spectacle . . . seeing a couple of middle-age types hacking away at each other, all red in the face and winded, missing half the time.
60		
	NICK	Oh, you two don't miss . . . you two are pretty good. Impressive.
	GEORGE	And impressive things impress you, don't they? You're . . . easily impressed . . . sort of a . . . pragmatic idealism.
65	NICK	(*A tight smile*) No, it's that sometimes I can admire things that I don't admire. Now, flagellation isn't my idea of good times, but . . .
	GEORGE	. . . but you can admire a good flagellator . . . a real pro.
	NICK	Unh-hunh . . . yeah.
70	GEORGE	Your wife throws up a lot, eh?
	NICK	I didn't say that . . . I said she gets sick quite easily.
	GEORGE	Oh. I thought by sick you meant . . .
	NICK	Well, it's true . . . she . . . she does throw up a lot. Once she starts . . . there's practically no stopping her . . . I mean, she'll go right on . . . for hours. Not all the time, but . . . regularly.
75		
	GEORGE	You can tell time by her, hunh?
	NICK	Just about.
	GEORGE	Drink?
	NICK	Sure. (*With no emotion, except the faintest distaste, as GEORGE takes his glass to the bar*) I married her because she was pregnant.
80		
	GEORGE	(*Pause*) Oh? (*Pause*) But you said you didn't have any children . . . When I asked you, you said . . .

NICK	She wasn't . . . really. It was a hysterical pregnancy. She blew up, and then she went down.
85 GEORGE	And while she was up, you married her.
NICK	And then she went down. (*They both laugh, and are a little surprised that they do*)
GEORGE	Uh . . . Bourbon *is* right.
90 NICK	Uh . . . yes, Bourbon.
GEORGE	(*At the bar, still*) When I was sixteen and going to prep school, during the Punic Wars, a bunch of us used to go into New York on the first day of vacations, before we fanned out to our homes, and in the evening this bunch of us used to go to this gin mill owned by the gangster-father of one of us—for this was during the Great Experiment, or Prohibition, as it is more frequently called, and it was a bad time for the liquor lobby, but a fine time for the crooks and the cops—and we would go to this gin mill, and we would drink with the grown-ups and listen to the jazz. And one time, in the bunch of us, there was this boy who was fifteen, and he had killed his mother with a shotgun some years before—accidentally, completely accidentally, without even an unconscious motivation, I have no doubt, no doubt at all—and this one evening this boy went with us, and we ordered our drinks, and when it came his turn he said, "I'll have bergin . . . give me some bergin, please . . . bergin and water." Well, we all laughed . . . he was blond and he had the face of a cherub, and we all laughed, and his cheeks went red and the color rose in his neck, and the assistant crook who had taken our order told people at the next table what the boy had said, and then they laughed, and then more people were told and the laughter grew, and more people and more laughter, and no one was laughing more than us, and none of us more than the boy who had shot his mother. And soon, everyone in the gin mill knew what the laughter was about, and everyone started ordering bergin, and laughing when they ordered it. And soon, of course, the laughter became less general, but it did not subside, entirely, for a very long time, for always at this table or that someone would order bergin and a new area of laughter would rise. We drank free that night, and we were bought champagne by the management, by the gangster-father of one of us. And, of course, we

125   suffered the next day, each of us, alone, on his train, away from New York, each of us with a grown-up's hangover . . . but it was the grandest day of my . . . youth. (*Hands NICK a drink on the word*)

NICK   (*Very quietly*) Thank you. What . . . what happened to the boy . . . the boy who had shot his mother?

GEORGE   I won't tell you.

130   NICK   All right.

GEORGE   The following summer, on a country road, with his learner's permit in his pocket and his father on the front seat to his right, he swerved the car, to avoid a porcupine, and drove straight into a large tree.

135   NICK   (*Faintly pleading*) No.

GEORGE   He was not killed, of course. And in the hospital, when he was conscious and out of danger, and when they told him that his father *was* dead, he began to laugh, I have been told, and his laughter grew and he would not stop, not until after they jammed
140   a needle in his arm, not until after that, until his consciousness slipped away from him, that his laughter subsided . . . stopped. And when he was recovered from his injuries enough so that he could be moved without damage should he struggle, he was put in an asylum. That was thirty years ago.

145   NICK   Is he . . . still there?

GEORGE   Oh, yes. And I'm told that for these thirty years he has . . . not . . . uttered . . . one . . . sound. (*A rather long silence: five seconds, please*) MARTHA! (*Pause*) MARTHA!

NICK   I told you . . . she's making coffee.

150   GEORGE   For your hysterical wife, who goes up and down.

NICK   Went. Up and down.

GEORGE   Went. No more?

NICK   No more. Nothing.

	GEORGE	(*After a sympathetic pause*) The saddest thing about men . . .
155		Well, no, one of the saddest things about men is the way they
		age . . . some of them. Do you know what it is with insane
		people? Do you? . . . the quiet ones?

NICK   No.

GEORGE   They don't change . . . they don't grow old.

160   NICK   They must.

GEORGE   Well, eventually, probably, yes. But they don't . . . in the usual sense. They maintain a . . . a firm-skinned serenity . . . the . . . the under-use of everything leaves them . . . quite whole.

NICK   Are you recommending it?

165   GEORGE   No. Some things are sad. (*Imitates a pep-talker*) But ya jest gotta buck up an' face 'em, 'at's all. Buck up! (*Pause*) Martha doesn't have hysterical pregnancies.

NICK   My wife had *one*.

GEORGE   Yes. Martha doesn't have pregnancies at all.

170   NICK   Well, no . . . I don't imagine so . . . now. Do you have any other kids? Do you have any daughters, or anything?

GEORGE   (*As if it's a great joke*) Do we have any *what*?

NICK   Do you have any . . . I mean, do you have only one . . . kid . . . uh . . . your son?

175   GEORGE   (*With a private knowledge*) Oh no . . . just one . . . one boy . . . our son.

NICK   Well . . . (*Shrugs*) . . . that's nice.

GEORGE   Oh ho, ho. Yes, well, he's a . . . comfort, a bean bag.

NICK   A what?

180   GEORGE   A bean bag. Bean bag. You wouldn't understand. (*Over-distinct*) Bean . . . bag.

NICK	I *heard* you . . . I didn't say I was deaf . . . I said I didn't understand.
GEORGE	You didn't say that at all.
185 NICK	I meant I was *implying* I didn't understand. (*Under his breath*) For Christ's sake!
GEORGE	You're getting testy.
NICK	(*Testy*) I'm sorry.
GEORGE 190	All I said was, our son . . . the apple of our three eyes, Martha being a Cyclops . . . our son is a bean bag, and you get testy.
NICK	I'm sorry! It's late, I'm tired, I've been drinking since nine o'clock, my wife is vomiting, there's been a lot of screaming going on around here . . .
GEORGE 195	And so you're testy. Naturally. Don't . . . worry about it. Anybody who comes here ends up getting . . . testy. It's expected . . . don't be upset.
NICK	(*Testy*) I'm not upset!
GEORGE	You're testy.
NICK	Yes.
200 GEORGE	I'd like to set you straight about something . . . while the little ladies are out of the room . . . I'd like to set you straight about what Martha said.
NICK	I don't . . . make judgments, so there's no need, really, unless you . . .
205 GEORGE	Well, I want to. I know you don't like to become involved . . . I know you like to . . . preserve your scientific detachment in the face of—for lack of a better word—Life . . . and all . . . but still, I want to tell you.
NICK	(*A tight, formal smile*) I'm a . . . guest. You go right ahead.
210 GEORGE	(*Mocking appreciation*) Oh . . . well, thanks. Now! That makes me feel all warm and runny inside.

NICK		Well, if you're going to . . .
MARTHA'S VOICE		HEY!
NICK		. . . if you're going to start that kind of stuff again . . .
215	GEORGE	Hark! Forest sounds.
	NICK	Hm?
	GEORGE	Animal noises.
	MARTHA	(*Sticking her head in*) Hey!
	NICK	Oh!
220	GEORGE	Well, here's nursie.

Nick lacks George's sour irony, and when he says of Honey, "She's . . . frail," he means it. Note that George's speech is quite fluent, as opposed to Nick's, which is fraught with ellipses caused by nervousness, drink, insecurity, and the kind of slow sincerity that, at his relatively young age and position at work, forms much of his character as we have come to know it in the course of Act 1 ("Fun and Games"). Nick's pauses reflect these things, whereas George's are much more ruminative. You can see from the first few lines of dialogue that George is in control of such a phrase, particularly in a situation where minivictories count as power.

EXERCISES AND COMMENTS

Borrowed Rhythms

From your experience with "strong and weak endings" in the scene between Aston and Davies from *The Caretaker* in Chapter 3, and from your knowledge of rhythms and stresses made clearer by reading about the differences between the speech and Goneril, Regan, and Cordelia in *King Lear* in Chapter 5, you will be able to see right away how Nick's language is weaker than George's, less assertive, or at least with assertions from a position of inferiority. You can notice, too, how Albee has made Nick sound very much like Nick's own wife, and how like Martha's ringing tone is George's, although George's lines are a shade smoother than hers. (By "smooth" please take care to realize that I don't mean the *kind* of rhythm, but that the rhythm is generally uninterrupted.)

In the following speech why does George take on something of Nick's rhythms and style?

> Oh! Mine. (*Pause*) No, no, she doesn't . . . *I* would; I mean if I were . . . her . . . she . . . *I* would. But I'm not . . . and so I don't. (*Pause*) I'd like to, though. It gets pretty bouncy around here sometimes.

George has started to think about his own life with Martha, whereas before in the scene he had been pumping and more or less goading Nick. George's speech therefore becomes more elliptical.

The Mockery of Repetition

How does Nick sufficiently take control of himself to measure up to the challenge forced on him by George, his superior in profession, talk, wit, and experience? Look at these lines, and see what happens:

GEORGE ... (*Waves his hand in a gesture of contemptuous dismissal*) YOU? Do you think I care for it?

NICK (*Cold—unfriendly*) Well, no . . . I don't imagine you care for it at all.

GEORGE Oh, you don't imagine it, hunh?

NICK (*Antagonistic*) No . . . I don't. I don't imagine you do!

The simple, gut-felt repetition of "imagine" is at work in basic mockery and battle. The actor should note that Albee, who frequently italicizes or capitalizes words he means his characters to emphasize, has not done so here, and the subtle verisimilitude of the exchange would be ill-served by any untoward leaning on the repetition of the word "imagine." The repetition makes its needling point sharply without the actor's signaling to the audience what is going on; this is a classic example of the rule I emphasize throughout, that the actor is not doing any good by tampering, before catching the already given essentials.

Nick's Sentence Structure

Nick becomes even more fluent a few seconds later, when he says "with great disdain":

I just don't see why you feel you have to subject *other* people to it.

Here Nick's sentence structure is beautifully in line with the character as it has been established and is being developed. Nick is grammatically proper, as befits a university professor even of biology and also as befits almost any person of the middle class, when drunk. Any actor wanting help with playing a drunk scene—and there are enough occasions when this is required, particularly in drama since the 1930s— can get many hints from *Who's Afraid of Virginia Woolf?*, where Albee has delineated so carefully and so accurately the spoken indications of alcohol poisoning. Nick might just as well have said:

I just don't see why you subject other people to it.

Are "feel" and "you have to" ornaments, then? Are they the products of an author's padding? Not at all. "Have to" is so childlike and breathes with the aspiration of one being put down. "Feel" is Nick's way of trying to seek for one level, any level really, on which he can communicate with the older and apparently more powerful person. The sentence is whining, in fact, and is too long. Nick could indeed have said the version of his line that I have already offered for your consideration. But that is not this playwright's way. Albee is not writing down what sounds good but writing down what sounds weak, which is what he is making of Nick. The monosyllables make the effects, if you listen closely to the line. "Subject," the only polysyllabic word in the line apart from "people," stands out like the sore thumb it is. Also, Nick's courage to use such a word, with its spat final consonants (*ct*), comes from his inner reaction to George's ironic "Your sympathy disarms me" in the previous speech, which ends with the nasty "Large, salty, unscientific tears!" Nick *needs vocabulary* at this moment and comes up with at least something.

Facial Expression and the Actor's Words

The actor can see that facial response is not always necessary. That's not how these characters are working. If every moment were to be given a facial act, the play would last for eight hours instead of the already long three, and the play would become a very dumb show indeed. This is one reason, in fact, why amateur productions of *Who's Afraid of Virginia Woolf?* are seldom successful. It is one thing to live the parts (and living these will, as the experience of the original casts attest, produce near-madness and despair) and quite another to let the audience live them by responding to the lines in an intelligent way.

Look at what happens when George once more regains the upper hand after being disdained by Nick for the older pair's fighting like "a couple of animals" and after the rhythm of the scene has turned with the acceptance of flaggellation as a means of social intercourse:

GEORGE   Your wife throws up a lot, eh?

You can see in the script how Nick reverts to his broken-up speech after this question—until, that is, he succeeds in coming out with his first great confession of the evening, which is uttered with the clarity of drunken truth:

GEORGE   Drink?

NICK   Sure. (*With no emotion, except the faintest distaste, as GEORGE takes his glass to the bar*) I married her because she was pregnant.

GEORGE   (*Pause*) Oh? (*Pause*) But you said you didn't have any children . . . When I asked you, you said . . .

NICK   She wasn't . . . really.

George's Pauses: How the Actor Can Use Them

To actor and audience, what is the function of those pauses in George's speech? Here is what I think. Obviously, at a basic and almost mean level, George is jealous of Nick because of Honey's pregnancy. So, the first pause is to let that sink in—silently. No "histrionics" are called for; the moment is well described as it is. And the second pause after his "Oh?," gives George time to rally his forces for an attack on Nick while thinking sadly to himself about his own desperately barren situation.

Encouraged, in the power play that surges beneath all conversations in the work, by this hint of George's inferiority, which is later to be consolidated by the stronger hints of his impotence and Martha's frigidity, Nick manages another unbroken line:

It was a hysterical pregnancy. She blew up, and then she went down.

Interpersonal Harmony

Now follows a perfect model of "interpersonal harmony" for any actor to study. For the first time in the scene, in fact for the first time in the play between these two characters at any rate, the two men speak with the same fluency and, because of the repetition involved, indeed almost the same cadences:

GEORGE   And while she was up, you married her.

NICK   And then she went down. (*They both laugh, and are a little surprised that they do*)

GEORGE   Uh . . . Bourbon *is* right.

NICK   Uh . . . yes, Bourbon.

An Actor's Analysis of George's "Gin Mill" Speech

It is a warm moment in the general cold, a moment where the two men come closer to each other because of a shared affliction—childlessness. The men laugh for their own reasons, of course, but they do laugh. The moment is very rich, varied, and harmonious.

For whatever reason, vague memories stirred into accurate recountings being the best since the playwright suggests little else, the moment causes George to embark on his tale of the gin mill when he was young during the Prohibition of the thirties. The speech containing the story is so richly constructed and patterned that not to discuss it at this point would be to commit a crime not only against the genius of Albee but also against the future excellence of actors and actresses who read this book, including their sensitivity to nuance of thought and phrase. Whether by design or chance (and with Albee the latter is unlikely), George's long speech about the gin mill comes out of the blue. In this speech the man bares his soul, gets some of the confusions if not straight then at least aired, and voices his basic, sad concerns.

As with Chekhov and Pinter before him, and as with Arthur Miller and Tennessee Williams too, Albee relies heavily on careful repetitions to give chracter, and in the case of this rich, weak, tired, articulate character he has created in *Who's Afraid of Virginia Woolf?*, he has furnished the actor with a goldmine of rhythmic, consonantal, and voweled variety to present one of the most poignant scenes of the theater.

The actor could take several approaches to this scene, and I am only suggesting mine. Generally, it is played more or less motionlessly, so there's very very little movement to think about. George has poured Nick bourbon, the young man's drink, which, in collaboration with the previous discussion about pregnant wives and worries of that kind, has triggered memories of bourbon and youth . . . and, of course, the loss of innocence. Let us look at the speech in the light of the advice from Sir Alec Guinness cited at the beginning of this chapter, which I shall repeat here:

> The only *very* simple advice I give . . . is to give emphasis firstly to the verb, secondly to the noun and lastly (if at all) to adverb and adjective and *never* to emphasize a personal pronoun except for a particular reason.

George's speech is 400 words long; its first sentence is 100 words long; its second sentence has 75 words; the third 95 words; the remaining four sentences are much shorter. What does this structure mean? The actor must know that George is the kind of man who at this kind of moment has in himself (for he *is* what he *says* and he *is* his *manner of speaking*) feelings, desires, and memories that take on precisely this shape and no other. Have a closer look at it:

SENTENCE	TOPIC	NO. OF WORDS	WORDS OR PHRASES REPEATED
No. 1	Setting the time of the visits to the New York gin mill	100	*bunch of us* *this gin mill*
No. 2	Telling the tale of the bergin and the boy	75	*bunch; accidentally; no doubt; bergin; boy; laughter* and *laughing; he, we, us*
No. 3	Boy reddens and laughter begins	95	
No. 4	The general laughter and mockery	30	*gin mill; bergin; everyone; laughter* and *laughing; boy who shot his mother*

SENTENCE	TOPIC	NO. OF WORDS	WORDS OR PHRASES REPEATED
No. 5	Subsidence of laughter	40	*laughter; order bergin*
No. 6	The champagne	20	*gangster-father* (repetition from Sentence No. 1)
No. 7	The hangover on the trains home	35	*each of us*

Now this is really little more than a cursory glance at the structure of the speech. Because it takes an actor much rehearsal, much could be written about each vocal step taken, let alone posture and other insights. But let us see what is happening just with the repeated concepts and perhaps notice some things about their phonetic makeup and then move on to the "grammar" of the sentences.

First, the structure of the speech as given by its repeated concerns in order: (1) When I was sixteen . . . bunch of us . . . this gin mill . . . bunch of us . . . ; (2) boy accidentally no doubt shot his mother . . . ordered bergin . . . boy laughed at . . . ; (3) everyone in gin mill ordered bergin . . . more laughter . . . most laughter from boy who shot his mother . . . ; (4) less laughter . . . ordering bergin . . . ; (5) gangster-father of one of us . . . each of us alone . . . youth.

Now, look at its structure by concept: youth—comradeship—drinking with grown-ups—mysterious murder—getting words wrong and being laughed at—being mocked and imitated—the most vulnerable the one with the loudest laughter—laughter subsides—mockery continues in parts—adult approval by free drinks—adult suffering of solitary hangovers—youth.

Next, let us structure the speech in order of classical dramatic form:

1. exposition
2. rising action and complication
3. & 4. catastrophe
5. anagnorisis (reversal)
6. dénouement
7. anticlimax and resolution

This form can be seen more easily, perhaps, in the following graph:

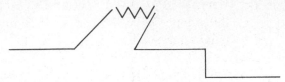

It is vital for the actor to realize that this speech is not structure for the sake of structure (although, as I have often been saying in this book, the theatre can seldom entertain or understand or be understood without it), but to show the audience how George feels, and how he feels in the shape shown above; that is *the shape* of his feeling and of his recollection as well because his recollection is, of course, causing his feeling. The structure and the shape of the speech is of inestimable aid to the actor, as you must know by now, having considered so many scenes from Shakespeare, O'Neill, Williams, Pinter, Ayckbourn, etc. Here what is conveyed to the audience is experienced in the form shown in the graph above.

The components of the first sentence are joined by very informal grammatical connectives that, taken as a whole effect, mean that George is "making it up as he goes along" or speaking in a "stream of consciousness" to a degree, and also that he is possessed by the power of a need in himself to get the story out, however confusing it is to his audience—Nick. Here George is addressing youth from the powerlessness of "age." These connectives are *When, during, before, and, for, as, and, but, and, and, and.* You can see how they dwindle away from formality. By the following connectives the second sentence—the longest one, containing the main unfolding of the "plot"—continues this diminution of formality as the emotion of the recollection becomes more intense: *And, in, there was, and, and, and, . . . , . . . , . . .* Third sentence: *Well, . . . and, and, and, and, and then, and then, and, and, and.* The fourth sentence: *And, and, and.* The fifth sentence: *And, but, for, for, and.* The sixth: *and, by.* The final sentence: *And, away, but.* What more need be said to the alert actor? George's speech begins and ends with the concept of being young. The speech begins and ends formally, beginning with a *when* and ending with a *but* clause. Let's now look at this as a total picture, still considering only the connective words but knowing a lot more about them and the emotional reasons for them:

1. When (during, before) and (for, as) and, but, and, and
2. And (in) there was, and, and, and, and, . . . , . . . , . . .
3. Well, . . . , and, and, and, and, and then, and then, and, and, and

4. And, and, and
5. And, but (for), for, and
6. And, (by)
7. And (away), but

Although the actor cannot help being aware of this pattern if the lines have been responded to with any reasonable attention in rehearsal, it would spoil things to make the audience aware in quite the same way. And this is another of the great parts of our craft: to convey structure without drawing attention to it. When attention is drawn to it (as many British actors used to do in the bad years of Shakespearean acting in the twenties through the fifties), the spectators lose the sense of illusion they came to enjoy. It is hard to decide which is the more useless kind of acting—the "artificial" (emphasizing structure at the expense of the emotional sense) or the "sincere" and talentless.[6] Neither kind of acting is pleasant. So, what does the actor do with all these repetitions of *and* that speckle this speech? Being aware of the repetitions, the actor simply *says them;* if the structure of the speech is grasped, they should come naturally.

Some Hard Work—Please Don't Skip This Bit: Sentence Structure Analysis

"Coming naturally," however, is one thing, and "appearing natural" another. Alec Guinness's advice to actors is of great help with this point. Let me notate the speech according to his basic rules about what to emphasize. I consider this one of the principal exercises of this book, and I hope that you won't also find it wearisome. It's work, after all, and that's what we're here in the theatre to do. The playgoers are the people who pay to have the fun. Our fun comes from having provided them with theirs.

What is the main idea of the first sentence? Because there are so many "and" clauses in the speech, there are more main clauses in these sentences than in usual ones. The first has one really, which is repeated twice, and a second subsidiary main clause.

First Main Idea: a bunch of us used to go into New York

First Repetition: and in the evening this bunch of us used to go to the gin mill

[6]See Geraldine Page's remarks on this, p. 2.

Second Repetition:	and we would go to this gin mill
Second Main Idea:	and we would drink with the grown-ups and listen to the jazz

What are its subordinate clauses? There are four.

First Subordinate Clause:	When I was sixteen and going to prep school
Second Subordinate Clause:	during the Punic wars
Third Subordinate Clause:	before we fanned out to our homes
Fourth Subordinate Clause:	from "for this was during the Great Experiment" to "but a fine time for the crooks and the cops"

The main facts presented in the sentence are, indisputably, "A bunch of us used to go to a gin mill in New York and drink with the grown-ups." The grammar of English being what it is, the author having written his play in English, and the actor and audience transmitting and receiving information in it, we as actors must be able to get the points across in order. So, the "points" of the first sentence are:

> When I was young a bunch of us used to go into New York on the first day of vacations, go to a gin mill and drink with the grown-ups.

All other information—and believe me it is all essential information, adding to character, advancing the story line of the play, providing thoughts for the other character and the audience to ponder—is *subordinate* to these *main points*.

Before we start to decide to which of the subordinate clauses to give emphasis, we have to go through the other six sentences with equal care, marking out the main clauses from the subordinate ones as best we can in a speech like this. As we go along we can summarize and eventually build a "subtext," if you like, of all the main clauses in the speech.

What is the real main clause of the second sentence? And what are the subordinate clauses? The first main clause is repeated, so we can contract it thus:

First Main Idea:	this boy who was fifteen went with us
Second Main Idea:	and he said I'll have bergin and water
First Subordinate Idea:	And one time
Second Subordinate Idea:	in the bunch of us
Third Subordinate Idea:	and he had killed his mother with a shotgun some years before
Fourth Subordinate Idea:	accidentally, completely accidentally
Fifth Subordinate Idea:	I have no doubt, no doubt at all

The "points" of the second sentence, then, are:

> This boy who was fifteen went with us one evening and ordered bergin and water.

So far in the speech, the points are:

> When I was young a bunch of us used to go into New York on the first day of vacation and drink with the grown-ups in a gin mill. One evening this boy who was fifteen went with us and ordered bergin and water.

What of the third sentence? There are eleven main clauses and one subordinating conjunction.

First Main Clause:	we all laughed
Second Main Clause: Combines with Ten Subsequent Main Clauses	he was blond and he had the face of a cherub, and we all laughed, and his cheeks went red and the color rose in his

neck, and the assistant crook
who had taken our order told
people at the next table what
the boy had said, and then they
laughed, and then more people
were told and the laughter
grew, and more people and
more laughter, and no one was
laughing more than us, and
none of us more than the boy
who had shot his mother.

Subordinating Conjunction: Well

Might this indicate that everything is to receive more or less equal emphasis? Probably, as we shall see when we have finished the next four sentences.

SENTENCE NO. 5:
Second Main Clause: it did not subside, entirely, for
a very long time

First Main Clause: the laughter became less
general

Subordinate Clause: always at this table or that
someone would order bergin
and a new area of laughter
would rise

Sentence No. 6 is all one combination of two main clauses:

1:                        We drank free that night

2:                        we were bought champagne by
the management, by the
gangster-father of one of us

The final sentence of the speech has two main clauses and five subordinate phrases:

First Main Clause: we suffered the next day

Second Main Clause:	but it was the grandest day of my . . . youth
First Subordinate Phrase:	each of us
Second Subordinate Phrase:	alone
Third Subordinate Phrase:	on his train
Fourth Subordinate Phrase:	away from New York
Fifth Subordinate Phrase:	each of us with a grown-up's hangover

Let me now put the main "points," as in the main clauses, together and form a ridiculous *Readers' Digest* précis of the sense of the speech as far as its *plot* is concerned:

> When I was young a bunch of us used to go into New York and drink with the grown-ups in a gin mill. One evening this boy who was fifteen went with us and ordered bergin and water. We all laughed . . . he was blond and he had the face of a cherub, and we all laughed, and his cheeks went red and the color rose in his neck, and the assistant crook who had taken our order told people at the next table what the boy had said, and then they laughed, and then more people were told and the laughter grew, and more people and more laughter, and no one was laughing more than us, and none of us more than the boy who had shot his mother. The laughter became less general, but it did not subside for a very long time. We drank free that night, and we were bought champagne by the management. We suffered the next day . . . but it was the grandest day of my . . . youth.

Those are the points, without the supporting subordinate clauses and phrases. As the real speech is constructed so, of course, is George. We now know with certainty that the sentence with the most main clauses (sentence No. 3, the one with the "catastrophe") contains everything. The sentences with many subordinate clauses are likely to concern those thoughts that do not rush in upon him with such force. How natural all this is. The mockery, the terror of adolescence when mistakes are made, and the one who commits the mistake is forced by the pressures of both adult and peer society to laugh them off to avoid the cosmic embarrassment of appearing embarrassed: This is what George remembers with most force.

Now this is not at all to say that the subordinate clauses and phrases are to be thrown away. The playwright doesn't throw them away; just look again at the ideas he repeats:

Bunch of us	This is adolescent comradeship and togetherness remembered.
This gin mill	Not "the gin mill," but "this gin mill," in the idiom of George's youth. Few history professors at a New England college or anywhere else for that matter would normally use "this" in this way. Of course, it is also an appeal to Nick's quality as an audience.
Bunch of us	It is at once a distant and a close way of describing a group of boys on the loose in the big city.
Accidentally	Is George protesting too much? Was *he* the young boy who had killed his mother with a shotgun? Is the boy a figment of George's (and Martha's) imagination? Did the "boy" "kill" Martha by not existing? Neither the actor playing George nor the audience in the theatre need know the answers to these questions, it seems to me. George is confused and drunk and speaks with that kind of mysterious clarity we associate with such a condition, especially after those years with that Martha and her "bobbling melons."
I have no doubt at all:	Same as above.

Bergin	George repeats the word often because he is reliving the time of terror in the speakeasy. Was he one of the ones saying the word over and over again, or was he the one who coined it? Either way, and again I feel that the actor can only arrive at a decision—if he must at all—after playing the part for some time and he finds this out—if at all—by instinct or decides to make a decision about it to get it out of his mind and not go mad himself.
Boy	George does not give him a name. The word *boy* shares the *b* with *bunch* and *bergin*. Why? Speak the speech and you will know; you will become something of George, who in drunkenness sees sounds and structures as a kind of sobriety, and to whose patterns he holds on to for dear life; for George, talk is one way of surviving, drunk or sober; talk gives him identity and revives his memory. Memory—and the sounds it creates when articulated—*is*, after all, for George and for us all, something to hold on to. *Boy* carries with it, too, a much more youthful sense than would a name.
Laughter, laughing	It is obvious that the effect this laughter had on George was profound, and that it still is. He keeps talking about it well after

the speech is over, and both he and Martha and he and Nick laugh. In fact, laughter is a potent image in the play—something to hang on to when other things fail or have always been absent. Laughter is used savagely against other people, against people one "loves," and it is used to cover up the vacuum of many a moment: It is one of the main things the audience comes away from this play remembering.

The boy who shot his mother

Well, for one thing George likes to shock, and he particularly likes to shock the young, and particularly the young Nick. And this repetition is shocking, mainly because it is so seemingly understated, coming at the end of those eleven clauses joined by *and*'s. We should note, therefore, that the last phrases of that great third sentence do *not* read "and no one was laughing more than us—and none of us more than ... *the boy who shot his mother!*" The shock happens precisely because it is slipped in quietly—as the makers of the best horror films and the actors in them well know.[7]

[7]In *The Innocents,* a 1960s movie of Henry James's *Turn of the Screw,* there is a famously terrifying minute when the ghost of Peter Quint appears at the window; there are gauze curtains covering the windows, the camera is motionless, and we think we see a face at the window, then we stop thinking about it because nothing is made of it as Deborah Kerr and two children talk between us and the window. Then we do see the face; it was there all the time. The horror happens to *us,* not to the people on the screen, which is what makes it doubly frightening.

Laughter and bergin

The bergin was the cause of the laughter, and Bourbon and laughter the trigger of this memory ("And then she went down. *They both laugh, and are a little surprised that they do.* Uh . . . Bourbon *is* right. Uh . . . yes, Bourbon"). Repetition of *bergin* recalls the mockery, and the variants of *laughter* reinforce it.

Gangster-father of one of us

If you read through the play, see it, or act in it even as rehearsal scenes, you cannot help noticing that this repetition of odd constructions is very much a habit of George's. To say that he repeats such things because he *likes* to is partly true. He also can't help it. He is also a literate man, a history professor who goads his wife and others repeatedly with grammatical oddities in addition to correcting their speech when he feels it will give him the upper hand in a conversation. Here, "gangster-father of one of us" is complex in tone, as if George is remembering that he used the phrase and found it satisfactory.

Each of us, alone

That each of us *is* alone is one of the themes of the play, and we can see in this phrase how the speech comes full circle in its concerns. The speech begins with "When I was sixteen" and ends with "the grandest day of

my . . . youth." The speech
begins so solitarily, with *I*, but
proceeds to a tension between *I*,
us, and *them*, ending utterly
alone with a youth lost and a
lost youth.

These, then, are the *ideas* and *words* that convey George's feelings. The summary before these ideas and words is the *plot* of his feelings. Is it just a case of "put them together and bingo!! you've got George acted?" Of course not, but the actor who attends to the script with this technique is well on the way to creating George because he has clarified some of George's structure.

Now I shall, as an exercise, list actual verbs that carry these nouns, adverbs, and adjectives on their way. Remember that Alec Guinness does not mean that actors emphasize *all* verbs regardless of their position in the sentence; that would be as tedious as to emphasize personal pronouns, as amateurs almost always do. Rather than list the verbs in a meaningless column of short words, I shall put them in their verb phrases and see where we get to. (*My italics are not yet meant to denote emphasis.* I am simply pointing out verbal phrases, not pointing them. Nor am I listing subordinate *was*'s, *is*'s, etc.)

I *was* sixteen
used to go into New York
before we *fanned out* to our homes
used to go to this gin mill
we *would go* to this gin mill
we *would drink* with the grown-ups
and *listen to* the jazz

That's the first sentence. Let's stop there, and look at the verbs by themselves without their phrases.

was
used to go into
fanned out
used to go
would go to
would drink
(would) listen

Now, obviously *was, used to go into, used to go to, would go to* are such simple and unpointed verbs that the nouns they are concerned with are at least as important: *New York, gin mill,* and *gin mill. But when a verb denotes a distinct and individual act* beyond mere tense and mere motion, when it tells us more than whether or not the action is in the past, present, or future, it is in need of emphasis, as can be seen from this list from the first sentence of the speech. Those verbs in need of emphasis in this sentence, therefore, are *fanned out* and *would drink* and *listen*. In fact, when you put the verbs together, you have the action of the sentence; you have its story: we fanned out, but before we did we drank and listened. Acting is storytelling, however emotional the speech. Without the story the audience doesn't know where it is.

EXERCISE

1. Find the main verbs of the next six sentences of the speech, and discover how clearly you get the plot of the speech and therefore its motive force.

2. Find the main nouns that these verbs propel, and try delivering the speech with slightly less emphasis on them than on the verbs but still much more than you would put on the adverbs and adjectives.

Further Exercises on *Who's Afraid of Virginia Woolf?*

1. Account for the italicized words and phrases and for those Albee has capitalized. What do they do to your characterization?

2. In what ways are the speech patterns of George and Martha similar, and in what ways do they differ? What does this tell the performers playing these two parts?

3. Do Nick and Honey share each other's speech patterns as much as George and Martha do? Why not? What does this tell the actor and actress about their roles?

4. Are the ellipses in the play to indicate only the pauses of drunken people? What do they tell the actor? Be as specific as you can when working this out, and remember that they exist in Albee's other plays, *The Death of Bessie Smith, The Sandbox, The American Dream, Tiny Alice, A Delicate Balance,* as well as in *Who's Afraid of Virginia Woolf?* Compare the ellipses with the pauses in O'Neill's *Desire under the Elms,* discussed in this chapter.

5. How does the language of the characters change toward the end of the play? Why, for instance, is George found in "The Exorcism" using idioms such as "you gotta," and "we all peel labels, sweetie"? Why is his speech such a struggle between the intelligent "well spoken" and the fashionably youthful ("But bones are pretty resilient, especially in the young" and, for instance, "Awww, that was nice. I think we've been having a . . . a real good evening.")?

6. What makes Honey occasionally use strange words ("All right. I'd like a nipper of brandy, please.")?

7. What does it tell the actress about Martha that her language sinks to constructions such as "You moving on the principle the worm turns?"

EXERCISES ON SPEECH PATTERNS: FOCUS AND EMPHASIS

In the following extracts from a wide variety of plays, look for the speech patterns of the characters. Discover individualizing characteristics of speech they have, ways of saying things, word order, vocabulary habits, habits of sentence-length, etc. There are a few specific questions after each extract—not literary analysis but actors' work. You must do these out loud.

Hedda Gabler, Ibsen

HEDDA GABLER   *(Rises, weary, with an air of refusal)* No, no. You mustn't ask me that. I don't want to look at death and disease. I don't want anything to do with ugliness.

GEORGE TESMAN   Well, all right—*(Rushing around)* My hat? My coat? Oh . . . out here in the hall. I just hope I won't be too late, Hedda. Hm?

(Trans. Otto Reinert)

Questions
1. Hedda and George speak quite differently. How can George's first two questions about his hat and coat be handled? Why are they questions and not statements or exclamations?
2. Why are Hedda's sentences and phrases so much smoother (at least by this point in the play) than those of her husband?

The American Dream, Edward Albee

GRANDMA   There you go. Letting your true feelings come out. Old people aren't dry enough, I suppose. My sacks are empty, the fluid in my eyeballs is all caked on the inside edges, my spine is made of sugar candy, I breathe ice, but you don't hear me complain. Nobody hears old people complain because people think that's all old people do. And *that's* because old people are gnarled and sagged and twisted into the shape of a complaint. (*Signs off*) That's all.

Questions

1. Look at the *length* of the sentences here. Why do they begin short and get longer?

2. Why is the fourth sentence so full of short clauses culminating in that final statement?

The Playboy of the Western World, J. M. Synge

CHRISTY   (*Grimly*) It's well you know what call I have. It's well you know it's a lonesome thing to be passing small towns with the lights shining sideways when the night is down, or going in strange places with a dog noising before you and a dog noising behind, or drawn to the cities where you'd hear a voice kissing and talking deep love in every shadow of the ditch, and you passing on with an empty, hungry stomach falling from your heart.

Questions

1. This is not a difficult passage, but repays study by the actor. How would you go about avoiding an obvious rhyme on "towns" and "down?" Is the rhyme meant anyway?

2. Which nouns would you emphasize? Why? Which verbs?

3. What is the rhetorical structure of this speech? Discover its true beginning, middle, and end.

The Cherry Orchard, Chekhov

PISHTCHIK   Wait—I'm hot . . . Most extraordinary event. Some Englishmen came and found on my land some kind of white clay . . . (*To* LYUBOV ANDREEVNA) And four hundred for you . . . Beautiful lady . . . Wonderful lady . . . (*Handing over the money*) The rest later. (*Taking a drink of water*) Just now a young man was saying on the train that some great philosopher recommends jumping off roofs . . . "Jump!" he says, and "therein lies the whole problem." (*With astonishment*) You don't say! Water!

(Trans. Stark Young, the estate of Stark Young)

PISHCHIK   Wait a minute . . . I'm so hot . . . A most extraordinary thing happened. Some Englishmen came along and discovered some kind
of white clay on my land . . . (*To* LYUBOV) Here's four hundred for
you also, my dear . . . enchantress . . . (*gives her the money*) You'll
get the rest later. (*Takes a drink of water*) A young man on the train
was just telling me that some great philosopher advises people to
jump off roofs. "You just jump off," he says, "and that settles the
whole problem." (*Amazed at what he has just said*) Imagine that!
More water, please.

(Trans. Robert Corrigan)

Question

You can see how very different these two translations are (and
there are many more translations of Chekhov, and especially of this
play, than these by Stark Young and Robert Corrigan). But such dis-
tinctions can only help the actor, of course. What do the differences
tell you about the problems of this part?

The Crucible, Arthur Miller

Compare the following two versions of this speech.

ABIGAIL   1 Why, you taught me goodness, therefore you are good.
2 It were a fire you walked me through, and all my
3 ignorance was burned away. It were a fire, John,
4 we lay in fire. And from that night no woman dare
5 call me wicked any more but I knew my answer.
6 I used to weep for my sins when the wind lifted up
7 my skirts; and blushed for shame because some old
8 Rebecca called me loose. And then you burned my
9 ignorance away. As bare as some December tree
10 I saw them all . . . walking like saints to church,
11 running to feed the sick, and hypocrites in their
12 hearts! And God gave me strength to call them liars,
13 and God made men to listen to me, and by God I will
14 scrub the world clean for the love of Him! Oh,
15 John, I will make you such a wife when the world is
16 white again! (*She kisses his hand*) You will be
17 amazed to see me every day, a light of heaven in your
18 house, a . . . (*He rises, backs away, amazed*) Why are
19 you cold?

That is Miller's original, from the Appendix to the 1959 Bantam
edition. Now let us look at a deliberately changed version in which

the punctuation provides some subtle differences and some great ones. If you study these differences carefully and think about the questions I give at the end, you will realize the importance of punctuation in the script.

ABIGAIL   1 Why you taught me goodness; therefore, you are good.
          2 It were a fire you walked me through and all my
          3 ignorance was burned away. It were a fire; John,
          4 we lay in fire. And, from that night, no woman
          5 dare call me wicked any more but I knew my answer.
          6 I used to weep for my sins, when the wind lifted up
          7 my skirts, and blushed for shame, because some old
          8 Rebecca called me loose, and then you burned my
          9 ignorance away. As bare as some December tree, I
         10 saw them all walking like saints to church, running
         11 to feed the sick—and hypocrites in their hearts!
         12 And God gave me strength to call them liars; and
         13 God made men to listen to me; and, by God, I will
         14 scrub the world clean for the love of Him! Oh John,
         15 I will make you such a wife, when the world is white
         16 again! (*She kisses his hand*) You will be amazed
         17 to see me every day, a light of heaven, in your
         18 house, a . . . (*He rises, breaks away, amazed*) Why
         19 are you cold?

Questions

The best way to begin to absorb the important blunders that would be made if the speech were punctuated as in version 2, or if an actress were to interpret the speech according to my wrong-headedly amended punctuation, is to consider the following questions. They are listed according to the line numbers.

1. The semicolon between the two phrases emphasizes the logical process more than the *fact of goodness*—and it is with this that Abigail is obsessed. What differences does the absence of the comma after *Why* make? And the new comma after *therefore*?

3. Is some of the connection between *fire* and *burned* lost by omitting the comma after *through*?

3/4. This is easier to answer. How is importance wrongly taken away from *lay* by the addition of the semicolon and by the clear placement of "John" as an introduction to the second phrase?

4. What difference, what added and unnecessary (although not necessarily utterly wrong) meaning and/or feeling occurs from placing *from that night* apart in a subordinate clause of its own?

6/7/8/9. The first question for these lines is the same as the above. What happens when *when the wind lifted up my skirts* is set apart in a main clause of its own? *Blushed for shame* is also set apart, so the two main statements of the sentence become those because they are the only two set apart. How is being called loose by "some old Rebecca" made less important? Try this out loud a few times, and you will soon see. What happens when *And then you burned my ignorance away* is joined to what precedes it, as I have amended it?

9/10. This is easy, but it is meant to remind you of the vital exercise every actor should go through when looking at any script. (If you need help with this, reread the pages on *Who's Afraid of Virginia Woolf?* in this chapter.) How is it that in my "bad" version Abigail is the bare one and not the other women?

11. Think carefully about this one. How is Abigail's character changed by putting *And hypocrites in their hearts!* after a dash rather than as part of the flow of her sentence as it is in the original?

12/13. What are the differences between Abigail's saying all this without the separate minisentences the semicolons produce?

14/15. What is the subtle change in the omission of the comma between *Oh* and *John*? Then, the way I have it is with emphasis on her eventually being a wife, separated from the idea of the world being white again. Why do you think the "real" play *combines* being a wife with the world being white?

17/18. "A light of heaven in your house" (Miller) and "A light of heaven, in your house" are two entirely different statements. How?

Riders to the Sea, J. M. Synge

MAURYA (*In a low voice, but clearly*) It's little the like of him knows of the sea . . . Bartley will be lost now, and let you call in Eamon and make me a good coffin out of the white boards, for I won't live after them. I've had a husband, and a husband's father, and six sons in this house—
5 six fine men, though it was a hard birth I had with every one of them and they coming to the world—and some of them were found, and some of them were not found, but they're gone now, the lot of them . . . There were Stephen, and Shawn, were lost in the great wind, and found after in the Bay of Gregory of the Golden Mouth, and
10 carried up the two of them on the one plank, and in by that door. (*She pauses for a moment. The GIRLS start as if they heard something through the door that is half open behind them*)

CATHLEEN (*In a whisper*) There's someone after crying out by the seashore.

NORA   (*In a whisper*) Did you hear that, Cathleen? Did you hear a noise in the north-east?

MAURYA   (*Continues without hearing anything*) There was Sheamus and his father, and his own father again, were lost in a dark night, and not a stick or sign was seen of them when the sun went up. There was Patch after was drowned out of a curagh that turned over. I was sitting here with Bartley, and he a baby, lying on my two knees, and I seen two women, and three women, and four women coming in, and they crossing themselves, and not saying a word. I looked out then, and there were men coming after them, and they holding a thing in the half of a red sail, and water dripping out of it—it was a dry day, Nora—and leaving a track to the door.

Questions and Discussion

By now, Irish actors and critics, even Irish audiences, find Synge's lyrical cadences "too much" and even "cute"; but there they are. In their day the cadences were fresh and amazing, recreated from the Aran Islands off the southwest coast of Ireland with meticulous care by a playwright with a raincoat, old cloth cap, notebook, and pencil. They are still magical and were never intended to be "true-to-life" in the trite sense. These women in the isolated fishing cottage on the craggy island cliffs speak in a heightened and strange prose. Many famous actresses have played the part of Maurya because it offers such rare opportunities to express intense grief and resignation in an almost preternaturally condensed form. (The play runs for about forty minutes, with two deaths in it and the recounting of six from the past.)

The questions that follow are not intended to be a guide to the acting of Maurya as much as a means of opening up the performer's sensitivity to patterns and rhythms and repetitions. The two speeches are also very useful for exercising the ability to sustain breath, although it would probably be quite wrong to *play* the longer sentences of the speeches on one inhalation since the very sound of breath-intake can recreate some of the necessary texture of the role.

1. Listen to somebody's southern Irish accent. You might like to try the recording of Siobhann McKenna's *These Are Ladies* or any of her poetry records on the Caedmon label—perhaps Michael Maclli-ammhor; or Jack Macgowran's wonderful Beckett record of *Malone Dies*; don't try these speeches until, with the presence of a critical friend or coach, you can successfully imitate the particular rises and falls. You will discover that there is a tendency to rush softly all monosyllabic phrases toward the main noun and verb.

"It's little the like of him knows of the sea." What makes the voice fall downward onto *him* and *knows*? Study the effect forced on the voice by the tongued consonants *l* in *little* and *like* coming before the nasal consonants *m* and *n* in *him* and *knows*. You'll notice as you proceed through her lines that Maurya is prone to spondees (see definition in glossary if you have difficulty with recognizing this): little the like of *him knows* of the sea.

I'll list some of the spondees for you. See if you can find more, and you'll have a good inkling of the character's rhythm: *good coffin; white boards; won't live after; six fine men* . . .

2. What do you think is the reason for the concreteness of *lying on my two knees* after *and he a baby?* The same physicality is evident in *carried up the two of them on the one plank,* and in *by that door.* The playwright could (though not as interestingly) have said *lying on my knees* and *in by the door* or *in by the front door.* What is the effect of that *door?* and of *my two knees?*

3. Why are the women *counted* rather than simply described? *And I seen two women, and three women, and four women crossing themselves* . . . Do you think that the audience (who, after all, is the most important element in any play) is put more in Maurya's shoes by this technique? You're right, of course. First of all, the audience is made to see—*with* Maurya, and what a gift this is to the alert actress!—two women, and for a second, that is all they see; the connective *and* that follows could be getting them ready for anything; but then it's three women, and then . . . four . . . and they're all crossing themselves. The audience is made to experience the arrival of the mourning women with Maurya in her mind's eye, and surely that is what we as performers most earnestly desire: that the viewers feel with us rather than sit there passively watching us pretend to feel or even really feel.

4. Again, a shock is given the viewers as they realize with Maurya (pronounced *Moira,* from the Greek word meaning "Fate") that it "was a dry day." Why does Maurya address this memory to Nora? Why does she address Nora at all?

5. Why does the speech end yet again with the word *door?* Maurya is what you may like to call a very physical person. After all, she has given birth to "six fine sons."

Come Back, Little Sheba, William Inge

LOLA   Marie, would you help me move the table? It'd be nice now if we had a dining room, wouldn't it? But if we had a dining room, I guess we wouldn't have you, Marie. It was my idea to turn the dining room into a bedroom and rent it. I thought of lots of things to do for extra money—a few years ago—when Doc was so . . . so sick. (*They set up table. LOLA gets cloth from cabinet up left*)

MARIE This is a lovely tablecloth.

LOLA Irish linen. Doc's mother gave it to us when we got married. She gave us all our silver and china, too. The china's Havelin. I'm so proud of it. It's the most valuable possession we own. I just washed it—will you help me bring it in? (*Getting china from kitchen*) Doc was sortuva Mama's boy. He was an only child and his mother thought the sun rose and set in him. Didn't she, Docky? She brought Doc up like a real gentleman.

MARIE Where are the napkins?

LOLA Oh, I forgot them. They're so nice I keep them in my bureau drawer with my handkerchiefs. Come upstairs and we'll get them.

Questions and Discussion

In 1950 *Come Back, Little Sheba* starred Shirley Booth as Lola, the alcoholic's wife. "A woman's love almost buried under tragic neurosis" is possibly the standard key to Lola. Although Inge's dialogue in this play is "simple" and what critics of the time called "straightforward, and without submerging dialogue under technicalities" (whatever that means), it is not uncrafted. Unfortunately, by now the theme of the alcoholic restored by love, and youth saved from the damnation of influence has had many treatments in possibly superior plays and screen plays (*Days of Wine and Roses, The Subject Was Roses, My Favourite Year* are just a few); the problem facing the actress, therefore, is to avoid soap-opera delivery of lines that can indeed sound simple-minded and even cloyingly noble and suffering. The best way of doing this is to play the straight values of the lines and look for the physical references—and there are, happily, many.

1. What could be the purpose of mentioning "dining room" three times?

2. Why does Lola speak in such short sentences? For instance, there are *seven* sentences where she talks about Irish linen. Other characters with other ways of thinking and feeling could well have said something like this instead: "It's Irish linen that Doc's mother gave us when we got married, along with all our china and silver too. The china—I'm so proud of it—is Havelin, the most valuable possession we own: I've just washed it—will you help me bring it in?"

The first, obvious answer to this question is that, of course, Lola does not think that way, especially in her excitement about setting the table for Marie, the bright young lodger. Work out from these two speeches—and perhaps look up the play and work on the character some more—how she talks. You will find, naturally, that she *is* what she *says*.

3. Why *real gentleman* rather than just *gentleman*? What does this tell you about Lola?

4. Why *we had a dining room* rather than *I*? What does this say about Lola?

Look Homeward, Angel, Ketti Frings

BEN   Oh, I know you're pleased, but you don't know how it feels to be the weakling. All the other members of this family—they're steers, mountain goats, eagles. Except father, lately—unless he's drunk. Do you know, though, I still think of him as a little boy—a Titan! The house on Woodson Street that he built for Mama with his own hands, the great armloads of food he carried home . . . the giant fires he used to build. The women he loved at Madame Elizabeth's. Two and three a night, I heard.

Questions and Discussion

Ketti Frings, who adapted this novel by Thomas Wolfe for the stage twenty years after Wolfe's death, won the Pulitzer and Dramatic Critics' Circle awards in 1958 for, among other things noted, "the selection of dramatically apt phrasing." The play is set in the Dixieland Boardinghouse in Altamont, North Carolina (Ketti Frings lives in that state) in 1916. Ben, aged thirty, is "delicate and sensitive;" here he is speaking to a Mrs. Pert who is knitting socks for him.

1. How can you begin to estimate the intelligence of the character from his vocabulary and sentence structure? First by comparing his speech with the other person in the scene, Mrs. Pert:

MRS. PERT   I know you talked to the doctor today. What did he say? Tell Fatty. It's nice for parents to have their children think of them as they were young. (*As BEN chuckles*) I mean, that's the way I'd like my children to think of me. Oh, you know what I mean.

How does his speech differ from hers?

2. What does his imagery (*steers, mountain goats, eagles*) tell the audience and the rehearsing actor about Ben?

3. How about his construction and vocabulary as in "Except father, lately"?

4. What about the phrasing of "The house on Woodson Street that he built for Mama with his own hands, the great armloads of food he carried home"? Compare this with this lesser version, which makes him a different character altogether: "He built the house—the one on Woodson Street—himself. With his own hands. He carried home great armloads of food." Ben is a man who while speaking can think ahead far enough to form complete sentences with the points in a certain order. His *mind* is capable of speech, you could say. Mrs. Pert's mind is capable of *thought*, which she has to *translate*, as many of us have to, *into speech*. In this, the characters are quite apart.

5. Discuss the difference between "The women he loved at Madame Elizabeth's" and "The whores at Madame Elizabeth's" or "He loved lots of women, at Madame Elizabeth's."

The Time of Your Life, William Saroyan

JOE Well—no. To tell you the truth, I'm not sure. I guess I am [still in love with Margie Longworthy—ed.]. I didn't even know she was engaged until a couple of days before they got married. I thought *I* was going to marry her. I kept thinking all the time about the kind of kids we would be likely to have. My favourite was the third one. The first two were fine. Handsome and fine and intelligent, but that third one was different. Dumb and goofy-looking. I liked *him* a lot. When she told me she was going to be married, I didn't feel so bad about the first two, it was that dumb one.

Discussion

This is good exercise for the phrasing and economy of breath. Although the speech is notable for its very short sentences, this is not to say that a breath is properly taken between each of them. I suggest that you work through the lines and mark where the logical and emotional breaks are and use exhalation between nonbroken sentences. Let me explain more fully.

A wonderful feeling of control—one of the actor's greatest pleasures—can be got from continued exhalation in pauses, waiting for the telling moment to inhale before a culminating phrase—a technique soon learned. But I need to emphasize that I am not advocating the use of such technique before some familiarity has come about with the feeling of the art. However, one of the most fruitful ways of arriving at a character in whom the playwright's lines and the actors' own emotional experience and sensitivity merge into a creative whole is this sort of methodical search for truth in the *lines* and not only in yourself. It would be easy for me to draw for you a chart showing several sensible places to put your breaks in this speech—as I do with scansion and stress in other parts of this book—but by now I think it would be wrong to appear to impose where I had only meant to suggest. Let me, nevertheless, give you only one idea about the first few short sentences of the speech and tell you why, playing this part, I might breathe where I indicate.

Well—no. To tell you the truth, I'm not sure.(*breath*)I guess I am. I didn't even know she was engaged until a couple of days before they got married. I thought *I* was going to marry her.(*breath*)I kept thinking, etc.

Why would I do it that way? I repeat that this is only one way of many, but it does have its own truth and it nowhere contravenes the script.

Now you're on your own again. Have fun with this exercise, but always ask yourself (or someone listening to it for you and with you) this question of every choice you make: *What do I mean?*

Dream Girl, Elmer Rice

CLARK They really do a beautiful minestrone here, don't they? (*GEORGINA eats her soup without replying*) You'd think I owned the joint, wouldn't you, the way I go on? You ought to eat here three or four times a week and build yourself up. You're too damned skinny. (*She throws him a look*
5 *but doesn't reply*) Personally, I find the natural curves of the female body quite appealing. (*As LUIGI approaches with the wine bottle*) Ah, here we are! Luigi did you know that the ancient Romans drank this wine?

LUIGI No, I didn' know. I come from Napoli. (*He fills the glasses and goes*)

10 CLARK (*Sniffing the wine*) I want you to taste this. But finish your soup first. I'm glad to see you concentrating on your dinner. I can't stand girls who are so busy gabbing that they just pick at their food.

Questions
1. Clark Redfield (played by Wendell Corey in the 1945 first production of *Dream Girl*) is worth studying for pace and tempo as well as speech pattern. How would you play the part? Without further

help from me, or from Elmer Rice, use the clues in these two restaurant speeches from the second act.

2. It's worthwhile to ask yourself why Luigi's reply to Clark's joke has a comma after the initial *No*.

Harvey, Mary Chase

VETA   I know—but they'll just have to invite you out and it won't hurt them one bit. Oh, Myrtle—you've got so much to offer. I don't care what anyone says, there's something sweet about every girl. And a man takes that sweetness, and look what he does with it! (*Crosses to mantel with flowers*) But you've got to meet somebody, Myrtle. That's all there is to it.

MYRTLE   If I do they say, That's Myrtle Mae Simmons! Her uncle is Elwood P. Dowd—the biggest screwball in town. Elwood P. Dowd and his pal . . .

VETA   (*Puts hand on her mouth*) You promised. (*They exit*) (*Through door U.L. enters* ELWOOD P. DOWD. *He is a man about 47 years old with a dignified bearing, and yet a dreamy expression in his eyes. His expression is benign, yet serious to the point of gravity. He wears an overcoat and a battered old hat. This hat, reminiscent of the Joe College era, sits on the top of his head. Over his arm he carries another hat and coat. As he enters, although he is alone, he seems to be ushering and bowing someone else in with him. He bows the invisible person over to a chair. His step is light, his movements quiet and his voice low-pitched*)

ELWOOD   (*To invisible person*) Excuse me a moment. I have to answer the phone. Make yourself comfortable, Harvey. (*Phone rings*) Hello. Oh, you've got the wrong number. But how are you, anyway? This is Elwood P. Dowd speaking. I'll do? Well, thank you. And what is your name, my dear? Miss Elsie Greenawalt? (*To chair*) Harvey, it's a Miss Elsie Greenawalt. How are you today, Miss Greenawalt? That's fine. Yes, my dear. I would be happy to join your club. I belong to several clubs now—the University Club, the Country Club and the Pinochle Club at the Fourth Avenue Firehouse. I spend a good deal of my time there, or at Charlie's Place, or over at Eddie's Bar. And what is your club, Miss Greenawalt? (*He listens, then turns to empty chair*) Harvey, I get the Ladies Home Journal, Good Housekeeping and the Open Road for Boys for two years for six twenty five. (*Back to phone*) It sounds fine to me. I'll join it. (*To chair*) How does it sound to you,

Harvey? (*Back to phone*) Harvey says it sounds fine to him also, Miss Greenawalt. He says he will join too. Yes—two subscriptions. Mail everything to this address . . . I hope I will have the pleasure of meeting you sometime, my dear. Harvey, she says she would like to meet me. When? When would you like to meet me, Miss Greenawalt? Why not right now? My sister seems to be having a few friends in and we would consider it an honor if you would come and join us. My sister will be delighted. 343 Temple Drive—I hope to see you in a very few minutes. Goodbye, my dear. (*Hangs up*) Harvey, don't you think we'd better freshen up? Yes, so do I. (*He takes up hats and coats and exits L.*)

Questions

1. The part of Elwood P. Dowd was first played in 1944, by the vaudevillian Frank Fay when the play opened on Broadway, and James Stewart played the role in the popular film, both enterprises netting authors, investors, and players highly satisfactory critical and financial results; rightly so. *Harvey* is very funny and very good. The lead's first appearance, quoted here, is practically a-laugh-a-line. The situation is thoroughly set up for him, of course, as well as the distinctly different speech patterns of his sister Veta and her socially rising daughter Myrtle Mae. Although Elwood is speaking mainly on the telephone, we find that his speech patterns are being established and that he generally talks in short sentences. This style belonged to the comic artists of the forties, as we know from memory and recordings and radio of the period. The American style then was rapid, and many an actor sounded like a sportscaster, particularly comedians. We hear the same influence today in the transference to the stage, of television and film style, although fortunately the spell of musical comedy remains felt in straight theatrical acting, and it is still possible in the legitimate theatre for the public in the cheaper seats to see facial work and hear the nuances of the vocal delivery.

Motivate the character according to the brief falling cadences of this phone speech. How do you know that Elwood is not in the habit of rising at the end of a line?

2. How do you know that Elwood is a confident person?

3. Decide on some points at which to breathe and then rationalize them.

Now take these kinds of questions to all scenes you study.

PACES AND PAUSES—HOW THEY SET CHARACTER AND MOOD IN *HAMLET*

What is a Verse Play?

Verse is not prose. The following is an example of prose:

> Although the memory of the death of our dear brother Hamlet is still green, and it befitted us to bear our hearts in grief and our whole kingdom to be contracted in one brow of woe, human nature has fought so much with discretion that we must now think of him with wisest sorrow, together with remembrance of ourselves.

The following is an example of verse:

> Though yet of Hamlet our dear brother's death
> The memory be green, and that it us befitted
> To bear our hearts in grief and our whole kingdom
> To be contracted in one brow of woe,
> Yet so far hath discretion fought with nature
> That we with wisest sorrow think on him
> Together with remembrance of ourselves.

Those lines (spoken by Claudius in the second scene of *Hamlet* and discussed thoroughly on pages 216–222) are written in iambic pentameter. John Hollander, who wrote a superb, short, readily comprehensible introduction to a book on English verse called *Rhyme's Reason* (Yale, 1981), describes the form and function of iambic pentameter as follows:

> *Iambic pentameter*, a line pattern made up of five syllable pairs with the first syllable unstressed, can be illustrated by a line which most perfectly conforms to the pattern itself:

> $$/ \quad / \quad / \quad / \quad /$$
> About about about about about

> or this:

> $$/ \quad / \quad / \quad / \quad /$$
> A boat, a boat, a boat, a boat, a boat

(for a monosyllable, with its preceding article, is accented like a word of two syllables). But actual lines of iambic pentameter, because they can't simply repeat identical pairs of syllables, have individual and particular rhythms which depart from the metrical pattern slightly. It is in this variation that poetry lives.

Hollander goes on to give an example of such variety:

> Iambic meter runs along like this:
> Pentameters will have five syllables
> More strongly stressed and other ones nearby—
> Ten syllables all told, perhaps eleven.

But:

> Trochees simply tumble on and on
> Start with downbeats just like this one
> (Sorry, "iamb" is trochaic.)

Many playwrights are their own "directors" in several interesting ways. First, they are sensitive to the shadings of the human voice to the extent that, as we have already seen with Ayckbourn, the actor's delivery is almost described in the lines he says. The *pace* of what an actor says is often given in a stage direction at the beginning of a line but more often in the consonant and vowel combinations of the lines—what is known as their texture. And in verse plays there is the convenient presence of a constant meter from which to deviate in rhythm.

Shakespeare perfected the iambic pentameter form, and its potential for subtlety of expression is discussed and explained more fully later in this book; however, in this chapter on comprehending the script, it will be useful to rehearse a Shakespeare scene in detail to determine the ways in which the playwright helps the actor embody the character and mood. For this purpose we shall study all four parts—Bernardo, Francisco, Marcellus, and Horatio.

ACT I—SCENE 1

(Elsinore. A Platform before the Castle)
Enter two Sentinels—(first,) FRANCISCO, *(who paces up and down at his post; then)* BERNARDO *(who approaches him).*

BERNARDO   Who's there?

FRANCISCO   Nay, answer me. Stand and unfold yourself.

BERNARDO   Long live the King!

FRANCISCO   Bernardo?

5   BERNARDO   He.

FRANCISCO   You come most carefully upon your hour.

BERNARDO   'Tis now struck twelve. Get thee to bed, Francisco.

FRANCISCO   For this relief much thanks. 'Tis bitter cold,
And I am sick at heart.

10   BERNARDO   Have you had quiet guard?

FRANCISCO   Not a mouse stirring.

BERNARDO   Well, good night.
If you do meet Horatio and Marcellus,
The rivals of my watch, bid them make haste.

Enter HORATIO *and* MARCELLUS

15   FRANCISCO   I think I hear them. Stand, ho! Who is there?

HORATIO   Friends to this ground.

MARCELLUS   And liegeman to the Dane.

FRANCISCO   Give you good night.

MARCELLUS   O, farewell, honest soldier.
20   Who hath reliev'd you?

FRANCISCO   Bernardo hath my place.
Give you good night.

Exit.

MARCELLUS   Holla, Bernardo!

BERNARDO   Say—
25   What, is Horatio there?

HORATIO   A piece of him.

BERNARDO   Welcome, Horatio. Welcome, good Marcellus.

HORATIO   What, has this thing appear'd again tonight?

BERNARDO   I have seen nothing.

30 MARCELLUS   Horatio says 'tis but our fantasy,
                And will not let belief take hold of him
                Touching this dreaded sight, twice seen of us.
                Therefore I have entreated him along,
                With us to watch the minutes of this night,
35   That, if again this apparition come,
                He may approve our eyes and speak to it.

HORATIO   Tush, tush, 'twill not appear.

BERNARDO   Sit down awhile,
                And let us once again assail your ears,
40   That are so fortified against our story,
                What we have two nights seen.

HORATIO   Well, sit we down,
                And let us hear Bernardo speak of this.

BERNARDO   Last night of all,
45   When yond same star that's westward from the pole
                Had made his course t'illume that part of heaven
                Where now it burns, Marcellus and myself,
                The bell then beating one—

Enter GHOST

MARCELLUS   Peace! Break thee off! Look where it comes again!

50 BERNARDO   In the same figure, like the King that's dead.

MARCELLUS   Thou art a scholar; speak to it, Horatio.

BERNARDO   Looks'a not like the King? Mark it, Horatio.

HORATIO   Most like. It harrows me with fear and wonder.

BERNARDO   It would be spoke to.

55	MARCELLUS	Speak to it, Horatio.

HORATIO   What art thou that usurp'st this time of night
Together with that fair and warlike form
In which the majesty of buried Denmark
Did sometimes march? By heaven I charge thee speak!

60   MARCELLUS   It is offended.

BERNARDO   See, it stalks away!

HORATIO   Stay! Speak, speak! I charge thee speak!

Exit GHOST

MARCELLUS   'Tis gone and will not answer.

BERNARDO   How now, Horatio? You tremble and look pale.
65   Is not this something more than fantasy?
What think you on't?

HORATIO   Before my God, I might not this believe
Without the sensible and true avouch
Of mine own eyes.

70   MARCELLUS   Is it not like the King?

HORATIO   As thou art to thyself.
Such was the very armour he had on
When he th'ambitious Norway combated.
So frown'd he once when, in an angry parle,
75   He smote the sledded Polacks on the ice.
'Tis strange.

MARCELLUS   Thus twice before, and jump at this dead hour,
With martial stalk hath he gone by our watch.

HORATIO   In what particular thought to work I know not;
80   But, in the gross and scope of mine opinion,
This bodes some strange eruption to our state.

MARCELLUS   Good now, sit down, and tell me he that knows,
Why this same strict and most observant watch
So nightly toils the subject of the land,
85   And why such daily cast of brazen cannon

And foreign mart for implements of war;
Why such impress of shipwrights, whose sore task
Does not divide the Sunday from the week.
What might be toward, that this sweaty haste
90 Doth make the night joint-labourer with the day?
Who is't that can inform me?

HORATIO   That can I.
At least, the whisper goes so. Our last king,
Whose image even but now appear'd to us,
95 Was, as you know, by Fortinbras of Norway,
Thereto prick'd on by a most emulate pride,
Dar'd to the combat; in which our valiant Hamlet
(For so this side of our known world esteem'd him)
Did slay this Fortinbras; who, by a seal'd compact
100 Well ratified by law and heraldry,
Did forfeit, with his life, all those his lands
Which he stood seiz'd of, to the conqueror;
Against the which a moiety competent
Was gaged by our king; which had return'd
105 To the inheritance of Fortinbras,
Had he been vanquisher, as, by the same comart
And carriage of the article design'd,
His fell to Hamlet. Now, sir, young Fortinbras,
Of unimproved mettle hot and full,
110 Hath in the skirts of Norway, here and there,
Shark'd up a list of lawless resolutes,
For food and diet, to some enterprise
That hath a stomach in't; which is no other,
As it doth well appear unto our state,
115 But to recover of us, by strong hand
And terms compulsatory, those foresaid lands
So by his father lost; and this, I take it,
Is the main motive of our preparations,
The source of this our watch, and the chief head
120 Of this post-haste and romage in the land.

BERNARDO   I think it be no other but e'en so.
Well may it sort that this portentous figure
Comes armed through our watch, so like the King
That was and is the question of these wars.

125 HORATIO   A mote it is to trouble the mind's eye.
In the most high and palmy state of Rome,
A little ere the mightiest Julius fell,

The graves stood tenantless, and the sheeted dead
Did squeak and gibber in the Roman streets;
130 As stars with trains of fire, and dews of blood,
Disasters in the sun; and the moist star
Upon whose influence Neptune's empire stands
Was sick almost to doomsday with eclipse.
And even the like precurse of fear'd events,
135 As harbingers preceding still the fates
And prologue to the omen coming on,
Have heaven and earth together demonstrated
Unto our climatures and countrymen.

Enter GHOST *again.*

But soft! behold! Lo, where it comes again!
140 I'll cross it, though it blast me.—Stay illusion!

GHOST *spreads his arms*

If thou hast any sound, or use of voice,
Speak to me.
If there be any good thing to be done,
That may to thee do ease, and grace to me,
145 Speak to me.
If thou art privy to thy country's fate,
Which happily foreknowing may avoid,
O, speak!
Or if thou has uphoarded in thy life,
150 Extorted treasure in the womb of earth
(For which, they say, you spirits oft walk in death),

The cock crows

Speak of it! Stay, and speak!—Stop it, Marcellus!

MARCELLUS Shall I strike at it with my partisan?

155 HORATIO Do, if it will not stand.

BERNARDO 'Tis here!

HORATIO 'Tis here!

Exit GHOST

MARCELLUS   'Tis gone!
            We do it wrong, being so majestical,
160   To offer it the show of violence;
            For it is as the air, invulnerable,
            And our vain blows malicious mockery.

BERNARDO   It was about to speak, when the cock crew.

HORATIO   And then it started, like a guilty thing
165   Upon a fearful summons. I have heard
            The cock, that is the trumpet to the morn,
            Doth with his lofty and shrill-sounding throat
            Awake the god of day; and at his warning,
            Whether in sea or fire, in earth or air,
170   Th'extravagant and erring spirit hies
            To his confine; and of the truth herein
            This present object make probation.

MARCELLUS   It faded on the crowing of the cock.
            Some say that ever 'gainst that season comes
175   Wherein our Saviour's birth is celebrated,
            This bird of dawning singeth all night long;
            And then, they say, no spirit dare stir abroad,
            The nights are wholesome, then no planets strike,
            No fairy takes, nor witch hath power to charm,
180   So hallow'd and so gracious is the time.

HORATIO   So have I heard and do in part believe it.
            But look, the morn, in russet mantle clad,
            Walks o'er the dew of yon high eastward hill.
            Break we our watch up; and by my advice
185   Let us impart what we have seen tonight
            Unto young Hamlet; for, upon my life,
            This spirit, dumb to us, will speak to him.
            Do you consent we shall acquaint him with it,
            As needful in our loves, fitting our duty?

190 MARCELLUS   Let's do't, I pray; and I this morning know
            Where we shall find him most conveniently.

Exeunt.

BERNARDO   Who's there?

Since the play is written in iambic pentameter, to which the

Elizabethan audience was fully accustomed, and all of this scene is in that meter, it is obvious that the opening lines are not prose but verse, and that there is a pause of three beats or even four, at any rate the equivalent of however many stresses there would be if the line were to continue, which it does not. An iambic pentameter line of the strictest kind runs:

$$\smile \, / \smile \, / \smile \, / \smile \, / \smile \, /$$

(as in

$$\smile \quad / \smile \quad / \smile \, / \quad \smile \quad / \smile \quad /$$
        Though yet of Hamlet our dear brother's death)

Bernardo's opening line can be scanned in two ways, the first with a three-stress pause, the second with a four-stress pause:

$$/ \qquad / \;\; (///)$$
    Who's there?
$$\smile \qquad / \;\; (////)\cdot$$
    Who's there?

I favor the latter for more than one reason. The spondees of // make for too strong a beginning for what we learn of Bernardo later in the scene. Reading his line iambically, with one stress, on *there*, at once makes Bernardo more tentative and allows a beat longer for him to approach Francisco in the real or imagined darkness. Reading the line this way also makes it more a question than a mere habit, and it is generally noted that the play opens with a question.

FRANCISCO Nay, answer me. Stand and unfold yourself.

It is improbable that Shakespeare (or any poetic dramatist) would give six stresses in the second iambic pentameter line of a play, resulting in:

$$/ \;\; / \qquad / \;\; / \qquad / \qquad /$$
    Nay, answer me. Stand and unfold yourself.

The line more correctly reads:

$$\smile \, / \;\; \smile \, / \;\; / \smile \;\; \smile \, / \;\; \smile \, /$$
    Nay, answer me. Stand and unfold yourself

creating an assertion of the sentinel already on duty; his *Nay* is very short, like the *er* of *answer*, and helps to put greater weight on *answer* and *me*, preparatory to the strong beat that follows, pauseless, on *Stand*. How do we *know* there is no pause: None is written, apart from the brief caesura or natural break in the middle of the line caused by the period after *me*. We shall discuss this matter of the caesura later. *Unfold* means to disclose; just as the play concerns itself a great deal with disclosure, it is appropriate that *unfold* occurs so early in the opening scene.

BERNARDO Long live the King!

FRANCISCO Bernardo?

BERNARDO He.

FRANCISCO You come most carefully upon your hour.

Bernardo probably has three stresses, allowing a silence of two beats while the two soldiers step closer to each other.

The soldiers are not walking very quickly. There are four beats in the pause after *Bernardo?* and four-and-a-half after Bernardo's reply, *He*. The actors are not close until after *He*.

Shakespeare could have written this exchange in any number of different ways, of course. Line 5, for example, could have had a much shorter pause after it, and Bernardo's reply could have been longer. Study the difference in mood and character the following plain alternative would create:

BERNARDO Long live the King!

FRANCISCO Is that Bernardo there?

BERNARDO Ay, indeed it is.

FRANCISCO You come most carefully upon your hour.

For one thing, the alternative has Bernardo echoing the rhythm of Francisco's /// of suspense, and has much harmony—quite unlike what Shakespeare gives us.

FRANCISCO ˘ / ˘ / ˘ /˘ / ˘ /
FRANCISCO You come most carefully upon your hour.

FRANCISCO ˘ / / / ˘˘˘ / ˘ /
FRANCISCO You come most carefully upon your hour.

FRANCISCO ˘ / ˘ / ˘˘˘ / ˘ /
FRANCISCO You come most carefully upon your hour.

In the first version above, I have scanned Francisco's line strictly, according to the base rhythm of iambic pentameter. Obviously, the line cannot be said with the stresses like this. My second version is "natural" but, in order to make it have five stresses, I have had to stress *most*, resulting in a spondaic beat and very deliberate delivery. My third version is more speakable still but has only four stresses. Since Bernard's next line has five stresses no matter how one says it, I believe that Francisco's line also has the same number of stresses and that by the time it is said the two sentinels are close enough to see each other properly in the darkness (Bernardo does say Francisco's name for the first time, after all) and feel comfortable in a regular meter now, pauseless, after the hesitancies of their opening interchange. *The fact, then, of regularity after incompleteness is both psychological and metrical: The state of persons resembles the state of their speech.* Therefore, I think that the two lines do in fact "scan" as near the following version as naturally possible (brackets around a stress indicate that it is "felt" more than "stressed"):

FRANCISCO ˘ / ˘ / ˘(/)˘ / ˘ /
FRANCISCO You come most carefully upon your hour.

BERNARDO ˘ / ˘ / ˘ / ˘ / ˘ / ˘
BERNARDO 'Tis now struck twelve; get thee to bed, Francisco.

FRANCISCO ˘ / ˘ / ˘ / ˘ /˘ /
FRANCISCO For this relief much thanks: 'tis bitter cold,
˘ /˘ / ˘ /
And I am sick at heart.

This entire three-and-a-half line dialogue is regular, the human and comradely chat of two soldiers in an upset country. Note the interesting stress on *thee* suggested by this regular reading. Note especially the two-stress pause after *sick at heart*, giving Bernardo about a second to absorb Francisco's description of his mental state and giving the audience the same opportunity. The moment is brilliantly "directed," true to character and clear in exposition.

```
           ◡    ◡    ◡    /    /
BERNARDO  Have you had quiet guard?
```

```
                                    /  ◡  /    /◡
FRANCISCO                          Not a mouse stirring.
```

This is the first example in the scene of an incomplete line completed by the next speaker. In poetic drama this device is most useful in indicating the absence of tension between speakers, however tense may be the situation in which they find themselves.

It should be clear by now that there are often at least two ways of scanning iambic pentameter lines, just as there are many variations written in. In this split line, for instance, I have given Bernardo two stresses and Francisco three; it could, *with the same effect*, be reversed:

```
           ◡    /   ◡    /    /
BERNARDO  Have you had quiet guard?
```

```
                                   ◡  ◡   /    /◡
FRANCISCO                          Not a mouse stirring.
```

In fact, this reading gives a hushed yet emphatic tone to Francisco's considered but nonetheless nervous description of the hours he has just spent.

```
          /    ◡    /   (/ ◡ / ◡ /)
BERNARDO  Well, good night
```

```
          ◡  /  ◡  /   ◡ / ◡ /   ◡  / ◡
          If you do meet Horatio and Marcellus,
```

```
          ◡ /◡  /  ◡  /    /   ◡   ◡   /
          The rivals of my watch, bid them make haste.
```

After *good night* there is a pause of three stresses, sufficient time for Francisco to start moving away (as he has been more or less bid) and be interrupted in his departure by Bernardo's understated nervousness. Line 13 is the first example of a phrase that deliberately and effectively breaks the regularity of the meter, mildly jolting the audience by giving beats that are not at all expected and plainly conveying the jumpiness of the character. Starting with *If you do meet* after the pause, there are five regular stresses followed by what sounds like what is going to be five more—*The rivals of my watch* begins normally enough; after the caesura at the comma, however, the meter becomes trochaic. We—character, actor, and audience—all are expecting a regular unstressed syllable after *watch*; instead, there is a stress on *bid*. Trochaic, indeed anapestic, the final phrase is the most rapid utterance so far in *Hamlet*. TiddilyTUM goes the rhythm. Bernardo's speech is as urgent as his wish.

I must make it clear that my remarks so far in this section are not intended to encourage the actor, after being sensitized to the lines, to use them *as a basis for characterization*; my remarks rather are intended to help the actor *characterize accordingly*. There is no need to exaggerate the delivery of haste, for instance: most of the haste is there in the lines waiting for the actor aware of their rhythm variations to utter them. As I said at the beginning of this treatment of *Hamlet*, I i, "the actor's delivery is almost described."

<blockquote>
ᵕ / ᵕ / ᵕ / ᵕ / ᵕ /

FRANCISCO   I think I hear them. Stand, ho! Who is there?
</blockquote>

Even this, which looks and can sound like prose, is formed verse written so that when spoken its emphases and pace are clear. For one thing, it should be noted that this line has no breaks. There is punctuation, surely; there is a period and an exclamation mark before the line is over. However, generally when Shakespeare wishes a pause he writes it in by breaking the line in the ways we have just discussed. Francisco's challenge to Horatio and Marcellus has been infected with the urgency of Bernardo's previous line. It is important to know that the puncutation marks are *merely grammatical propriety and not guides to tempo or mood*. Francisco's line is, therefore, *giving the effect of great speed without asking the actor to rush. This effect is simply created by passing quickly from the first thought to the second, and then again at a speed from the second to the third. The thoughts are not rushed. The transitions are*. That is the vital point.

<blockquote>
HORATIO   Friends to this ground.

MARCELLUS   And liegemen to the Dane.

FRANCISCO   Give you good night.
</blockquote>

MARCELLUS   O, farewell, honest soldier!

5   Who hath relieved you?

FRANCISCO   Bernardo hath my place.

                  Give you good night.

(Exit)

MARCELLUS Holla! Bernardo!

BERNARDO   Say,

10   What, is Horatio there?

HORATIO   A piece of him.

BERNARDO Welcome, Horatio: welcome, good Marcellus.

All this transition from watch to watch is regular; the meter is uninterrupted. The feeling of comradeship and understanding this gives is satisfying. No sooner has Francisco said good night than Marcellus, with no break and no waiting to watch Francisco leave (by the illusion established he could not see him anyway), hails Bernardo. This interchange is very busy, delivered while getting into place, and the pace is as rapid as the pauselessness would indicate. Note that Horatio's *A piece of him* is not especially focused on, the famous line is given as an understated part of general introductory conversation. Much of the scene's tone, as we can judge from its pacing and rhythm, is one of formality and friendliness flavored with apprehension and general jumpiness.

MARCELLUS What, has this thing appeared again tonight?

BERNARDO I have seen nothing. (∪/∪/∪/)

Only after the mention of Hamlet's father's ghost is the iambic pentameter broken again, and that with a pause of at least two and possibly three stresses. Coming as it does after almost half a minute of regularity, this sudden silence is quite chilling. The actor playing Marcellus will notice that his character is not given to interruption of rhythm: after Bernardo's pause, he delivers a seven-line speech of uninterrupted, smooth normality.

HORATIO   Tush, tush, 'twill not appear.

BERNARDO   Sit down awhile;
And let us once again assail your ears,
That are so fortified against our story,
That we have two nights seen.

HORATIO   Well, sit we down,
And let us hear Bernardo speak of this.

BERNARDO   Last night of all, $(\cup\,/\,\cup\,/\,\cup\,/\,)$

How is the actor to know that Bernardo wastes no time in asking Horatio to sit down and listen again to the story of the apparition? By realizing that his *Sit down awhile* completes Horatio's line of doubt. Does Horatio hesitate in the sitting? No. Persuaded by the emphatically uncomplex syntax of Bernardo's three lines, Horatio picks up Bernardo's rhythm, indicating "agreement" with him. This agreement of rhythm has already been used in this scene, and it is a standard technique in poetic drama. As we can see, the technique is in fact one of the ways of comprehending the script. Another standard technique is at play in Bernardo's next line, the one that introduces his story: *Last night of all* is followed by a pause of at least two stresses, allowing time for the "once-upon-a-time" tone to establish itself in the other characters and in the audience, and also, of course, allowing time for Horatio and Marcellus to be seated.

BERNARDO   Last night of all,
When yond same star that's westward from the pole
Had made his course to illumine that part of heaven
Where now it burns, Marcellus and myself,
The bell then beating one,—

As we noted in Chapter 3 where we dealt with *The Fall of the House of Usher,* the periodic sentence is an excellent means to the end of suspense. Here, Bernardo utters an incomplete sentence with a periodic structure: There are no less than six qualifying phrases and clauses in this sentence without a subject—and the subject (the Ghost) enters physically in a wonderful coup de théâtre.

   The actor will note now that there are no further pauses in the scene until fourteen lines have been said and the Ghost has made his exit. Marcellus's *Question it, Horatio* are the three completing stresses of the two in Bernardo's *It would be spoke to,* and Marcellus's *It is offended* is completed by Bernardo's *See, it stalks away!*

```
                  ˘  /   ˘  /  ˘
BERNARDO    It would be spoke to.


                                     /  ˘    ˘ /˘
MARCELLUS                    Question it, Horatio.
            ˘ / ˘ / ˘
            It is offended.


                                     /  ˘  /  ˘  /
BERNARDO                     See, it stalks away.
```

The ghost is no sooner onstage than it has gone again. The effect of this brief appearance was well appreciated by Garrick in his eighteenth-century *Hamlet* and his audience nicely frightened. The lines spoken during the appearance do slow down from those preceding them, however. How does the actor know this? The main key is the texture of Horatio's address to the ghost.

HORATIO   What art thou, that usurp'st this time of night,
          Together with that fair and warlike form
          In which the majesty of buried Denmark
          Did sometimes march? By heaven I charge thee, speak!

This writing is discernibly the thickest of the scene so far, and when it is spoken we can feel that the words do not come with ease; they are neither tortured nor wrenched but are far from fluid. *Usurp'st* takes longer to say than at first sight. *Together with that* is slowed by the double *th*'s of *which with that.* If the actor had any doubt that his enunciation was weighted down by the sounds of his words, such doubt would disappear on the third line of the speech, where *which* and *majesty* are extremely difficult to rush and the double dentals of *buried Denmark* easy to lose. *March* and *charge* in the fourth line continue the pattern established by *which* and *majesty*. The actor will find, then, that Horatio is courageous and strong of utterance but inwardly not unaffected by the strangeness of the sight.

Let us mark the speech in those parts:

          What art thou, that u*surp'st* this time of night,
          Toge*ther with that* fair and warlike form
          In wh*ich* the *maj*esty of bur*ied Den*mark
          Did sometimes mar*ch*? By heaven I *charge* thee, speak!

I am not saying, of course, that any special attention is required by these sounds at all but simply that they are responsible for the pace of these lines. The pace quickens the moment Bernardo says "See, it stalks away!" and slows again because of the spondees of Horatio's final appeal:

HORATIO   Stay! Speak, speak! I charge thee, speak!

which, it must be noted, is not a line split up in any way, but one iambic pentameter verse line. When I say it is slowed by the spondees, we must understand that it is a slowed *line*; like a musical phrase, it is unbroken and therefore a good deal faster than the eye might, because of the exclamation marks, be tempted to think it.

MARCELLUS   'Tis gone, and will not answer.
    How now, Horatio, you tremble and look pale:
    Is not this something more than fantasy?
    What think you on't?

HORATIO   Before my God, I might not this believe . . .

The actor who has followed me closely in this chapter will now know that there is a two-stress pause after *will not answer* and be able to see in what ways it helps motivation, provides a subtext, and focuses the attention of the other characters and the audience. For one thing, the pause allows sufficient time to look at Horatio. There is another pause, of three stresses this time, before Horatio is able to gather his wits and speak, after Bernardo's *What think you on't?*

HORATIO   Before my God, I might not this believe
    Without the sensible and true avouch
    Of mine own eyes.

BERNARDO   Is it not like the king?

These are very considered words, their meter is regular, as befit thoughts uttered by a man after a shocked silence. Bernardo, eager to have the apparition confirmed by the sceptic Horatio, comes right in with his *Is it not like the king?* This is neither smug nor really self-satisfied but certainly quick and even slightly triumphant.

ᵕ / ᵕ / ᵕ / (ᵕ/ᵕ/)

HORATIO   As thou are to thyself:
           Such was the very armour he had on
           When he the ambitious Norway combated;
           So frown'd he once, when, in an angry parle,
           He smote the dreaded Polacks on the ice.
           'Tis strange. (FOUR SILENT BEATS)

MARCELLUS Thus twice before, and jump at this dead hour,
           With martial stalk hath he gone by our watch.

Horatio is not fully ready for speech yet. The two-beat silence after *As thou art to thyself* is excellently contrived to give the actor opportunity to confirm, in spite of his previous scepticism, that what he has seen indeed resembles old King Hamlet as he remembers him in victories born of revenge. When the actor finishes his brief remembrance and says *'Tis strange*, the assembled trio of soldiers and friends fall silent for what could have been four stresses of speech. The effect is "conversational," natural, and uneasy. Marcellus's lines about precedent appearances are "normal" and regular, as Marcellus always is.

The pace of Horatio's next contribution to the exchange of views and histories is influenced by *particular*, of course. If the actor were to deliver the word to its fullest possible value, the ordinary five-stress line it is in would become far too long and not work:

HORATIO   In what particular thought to work I know not;
           But, in the gross and scope of mine opinion,
           This bodes some strange eruption to our state.

With its monosyllables, Horatio's second line is obviously more ponderous and considered and is a key to that side of his nature and character, continued as it is in the last line of the speech with *bodes* and *strange. Eruption, particular,* and *opinion* are the only multisyllabic words in these three lines. This matter of multisyllabic words is worth our attention since it can be seen from the next speech, by Marcellus, that the character is not in the habit of using words of more than two syllables. This is not to say that Marcellus should be any more direct than Horatio or Bernardo, but simply that he does begin with monosyllables as if Shakespeare were indicating that he speaks as a good soldier should. The actor can use this fact in whatever ways that bring out the most sense and interest but ought most certainly to be aware of such a fact.

MARCELLUS   Good now, sit down, and tell me he that knows,
Why this same strict and most observant watch
So nightly toils the subject of the land . . .

Horatio's expository speech about the conflicts between Denmark and Norway is a real problem for the actor in much the same way as are many expository lines in the plays; the facts must be conveyed to the audience, and it is difficult for the actor to feel very strongly about them without appearing either too eager or boring—or obvious, which is probably worse for an audience accustomed to some degree of verisimilitude. The art is to not sound as if information is being conveyed, of course, and that is easier said than done. Miss Tesman in *Hedda Gabler* is burdened with this sort of thing; so is another Ibsen character, Renate, in *Ghosts,* and so is every actor in the first ten minutes of most films. (I played the cameo part of Mr. Pruett in the Bernadette Peters film *Tulips;* toward the end of that scene in the Unemployment Insurance office, Miss Peters says to me, "Go tell Carl." "Who's Carl?" I ask. "My psychiatrist," replies Miss Peters; it is essential information; the audience must know there is a psychiatrist and that his name is Carl. Motivating a moment of this kind is a crafty business.) That Shakespeare knew he was writing fairly complex exposition in lines 79–107 is clear in the *as you know* he gives to Horatio.

If Alfred Harbage's *Shakespeare's Audience* is to be relied upon, it is possibly true that the Elizabethan audience relished well-spoken passages of exposition if they were decorated in rich, in this case military, fashion. How is today's actor to behave? The actor cannot stride Down Centre, take position, and "sing" the lines but must find a motive for uttering them. As this book intends to show, that motive must be found in the script. It has been established that Horatio is "a scholar," proud of the character and accomplishments of old King Hamlet's "fair and warlike form," courageous in that although the Ghost "harrows him with fear and wonder" he addresses it bluntly with "What art thou . . . ?," honest and straightforward ("I might not this believe/Without the sensible and true avouch/Of mine own eyes"), and patriotically condescending about other nations ("the ambitious Norway"). That is about all we know of him before he embarks on his concentrated recent history of Denmark's late king. The actor approaching this role (and in this section I would remind readers that we are playing all the parts) has that knowledge to bear in mind; they do help the following lines, to use a phrase of Gerard Manley Hopkins, to "explode into meaning."

HORATIO   That can I;
         Or least the whisper goes so.

Of course, Horatio can answer Marcellus's question. Who better, from what we have heard of Horatio so far? But all is rumor; Horatio can only repeat what he has heard and make deductions from his knowledge of recent affairs. Horatio is, interestingly, removed enough from the affairs of state—despite being a friend of Hamlet—that he was not at all on intimate terms with the king. In fact, there is no indication of Horatio ever having met the king. To play Horatio as a noble is to play another part. But the tone is that of one who knows whereof he speaks and also of one who desires to be friendly to all who ask honest questions and who have given evidence of wishing no harm. The list of historical facts is punctuated by these phrases, *That can I; for so this side of our know world esteem'd him; Nor, Sir;* and *I take it,* interjections of a thinking, balanced, and friendly personality; the speech is spoken vividly (*of unimproved metal hot and full, some enterprise/That hath a stomach in't*) and forcefully (*Shark'd up a list of lawless resolutes*). The speech is logical, full of careful qualifying phrases helping Marcellus and Bernardo follow the points (e.g., *Against the which*).

However, the line-by-line analysis of the speech would take up too many pages in this chapter. We are speaking more of pauses and pacing indicated by the script in our attempt to arrive at a good way of comprehending it. Let us leap over two minutes' worth of dialogue and look at the second appearance of the Ghost.

HORATIO   But soft, behold! lo, where it comes again!
          I'll cross it, though it blast me. Stay, illusion!
          If thou hast any sound, or use of voice,
          Speak to me: (/ ∪ / ∪ / ∪ /)

It is interesting that in strict scansion *illusion* carries a strong final stress. The effect of *Stay, illusion!* is not /, ∪ ∪ ∪, but rather /, ∪ / ∪. *Horatio is not describing the ghost as an illusion; he is accusing it of being one.* There is, of course, a pause of at least three stresses after *Speak to me* while he waits for a response.

          If there be any good thing to be done
          That may to thee do ease and grace to me,
          Speak to me:

The noticeable repetition of the vowel sound *ee* in *thee, ease,* and *me,* and of *ay* in *may* and *grace* is so redolent of an imploring attitude that the actor need hardly stress it; as is the case with many of the lines we have been discussing, the words need only be said with care, and the character, mood, pace, and motivation are produced.

> If thou art privy to thy country's fate,
> Which happily foreknowing may avoid,
> O, speak!

It is not only in Shakespeare that the actor is confronted with misprints, confusing punctuation, editors' meddling and occasional meaninglessness. The moment a play is printed and becomes public property and the author is not at rehearsals, problems, usually small ones, arise. *The Folger Library General Readers' Shakespeare,* for instance, adds commas around *happily* in line 134 to produce *Which, happily, foreknowing may avoid.* Most other editions following the 2nd Quarto and the 1st Folio of *Hamlet* allow *happily* either to mean *haply* or be an adjectival qualification of *foreknowing.* The actor of such instances must arrive at a decision.

> Or if thou has uphoarded in thy life
> Extorted treasure in the womb of earth,
> For which, they say, you spirits oft walk in death,
> Speak of it: stay, and speak! Stop it, Marcellus.

Horatio's speech to the Ghost has been as logical as we know his character to be, and it is very patterned, because of the four *speak*'s. It is as if Horatio were using all the persuasiveness at his command.

MARCELLUS   Shall I strike at it with my partisan?

$\qquad\qquad / \cup \cup \ / \ \cup \ /$
HORATIO   Do, if it will not stand.

$\qquad\qquad\qquad\qquad\qquad\qquad \cup \ /$
BERNARDO   'Tis here!

$\qquad\qquad\qquad\qquad\qquad\qquad\qquad \cup \ /$
HORATIO   'Tis here!

$\qquad\qquad \cup \ /$
MARCELLUS   'Tis gone!

It will be noted that this urgent series of discoveries and command occupies the time of only one line. Marcellus's final *'Tis gone*, coming so quickly after Horatio's, is interesting for its implication that the Ghost exits very suddenly. The pause comes *after* Marcellus's line.

MARCELLUS   We do it wrong, being so majestical,
            To offer it the show of violence;
            For it is as the air, invulnerable,
            And our vain blows malicious mockery.

Marcellus is moved by the swiftness of the events to break from the habit of brevity we have noted so far and lets his mind produce vocabulary and imagery consonant with the deep effect the ghostly encounter has had on him. What he says here, and a few seconds later in the famous speech about the "bird of dawning," is indicative of a gently superstitious, romantic, and likable heart.

MARCELLUS   It faded on the crowing of the cock.
            Some say that ever 'gainst that season comes
            Wherein our Saviour's birth is celebrated
            The bird of dawning singeth all night long;
            And then, they say, no spirit dare stir abroad,
            The nights are wholesome, then no planets strike,
            No fairy takes nor witch hath power to charm,
            So hallow'd and so gracious is the time.

The most obvious thing to say about these lines is that they are quiet, even, and subtly sibilant. Indeed, if they are delivered quietly enough, the many s sounds create a mood of reverence and simplicity. Another sensible thing to say is that the actor can try these lines in a whisper for the first few times in order to discover the phonetic values; he will, this way, initially avoid the temptation to provide a vocal music extraneous to the lines, the mood, and the character. The simpler the delivery of such beautiful descriptive passages, the better their essence is delivered to the audience. It would be salutary to remember that these lines are not so much a description of Christmas in any case as a verbalization of the kind of concerns that make up the soul of Marcellus; in them, we see inside them.

HORATIO   So have I heard and do in part believe it.
          But look, the morn in russet mantle clad
          Walks o'er the dew of yon high eastward hill:

The actor playing Horatio is faced with "poetry" here. Horatio has been affected (as who could not be?) by what Marcellus has just said, and it is entirely appropriate for him to have his speech affected by it too. *So have I heard* begins with an *s* and continues the *h* of Marcellus's *hallow'd*. Although Horatio believes it only "in part," there is no opposition here. The apparition, the exchange of beliefs about the crowing of the cock, the unease in Denmark, all have combined to join these three characters with a common feeling and a common decision to "impart what we have seen tonight/Unto young Hamlet."

MARCELLUS Let's do't. I pray; and I this morning know
Where we shall find him most conveniently.

We have seen with Graham Baker, Eben, Abbie, Simeon, Peter, Aston, Davies, Nick, George, Francisco, Bernardo, Marcellus, and Horatio how the shape of the lines and the sound of the word help the actor to comprehend the script. In the next chapter we will be looking more closely at the physical feeling of the lines and how the actor absorbs them.

Absorbing the Lines: Scene Study and Exercises

Using all the techniques shown in Chapters 1–4, this chapter reinforces what you have learned. The chapter begins with a poem, proceeds through two relatively advanced scene studies and some exercises, then ends with a final checklist of points to watch for when preparing a scene.

ABSORBING THE LINES

Words in Their Right Order

The right word in the right place is as good as having the sun in the sky at the right moment.

Wordsworth's Sonnet Not Composed Upon Westminster Bridge

In the July 12, 1827, entry in *Table Talk,* Coleridge said perhaps a mite snobbishly:

> I wish our clever young poets would remember my homely definitions of prose and poetry; that is, prose words in their best order;—poetry the *best* words in the best order.

Of course, there has been much argument about what he meant by *best* in his last phrase. Does it mean "the most appropriate"?; "the most telling"?; "the finest"?; "the grandest"?; or "the simplest"? *Best* has as many connotations as does *good*. By my process of exegesis and analysis, you will soon learn in this exercise that the right word in the right place is as good as having the sun in the sky at the right moment.

In the following poem, only the last line has been left as Wordsworth wrote it. The lines are in their original sequence, but the order of the words within each has been slightly changed. There are no contractions or substitutions except in lines 1 and 5.

> Earth has nothing to show more fair;
> He would be dull of soul who could pass by
> So touching a sight in its majesty.
> Now this city doth like a garment wear
> 5 The morning's beauty; bare, silent,
> Ships, theaters, temples, towers and domes lie
> Open to the fields and unto the sky,
> All glittering and bright in the smokeless air.
> Sun did never more beautifully steep
> 10 In his first splendour rock, valley, or hill;
> Never felt I, ne'er saw, so deep a calm.
> At his own sweet will the river glideth.
> The very houses seem asleep, dear God!
> And all the mighty heart is lying still.

Our task is to put the words back in the order that Wordsworth thought "best." We can begin mathematically and simply, by finding out which words rhyme or could. Once you have done that, consult the key at the end of this section to be sure we all are in agreement with Wordsworth.

Now you know at least the endings of lines 5, 11, 12 and 13, and that the rhyme scheme is *abba abba cdcdcd*. Such information is of the barest use, however. Wordsworth imposed a form on his emotional expression: the form of the sonnet, with that particular rhyme scheme. The appropriateness of that rhyme scheme is not our business in this book. Let us have a good look at some of the lines.[1] Remember you are studying acting and must be very conscious of words.

In fact, rather than having a good look at them, we should listen very closely to them. Try line 1 aloud: It sounds rather good as it stands. That word *nothing*, you will agree, is quite strong. There is nothing more fair on earth than the sight before the writer at that moment. I hope you will be as surprised as many students have been to learn that Wordsworth wrote the line thus:

Earth has not anything to show more fair

Try this line aloud. Do you notice any difference? Please take the line slowly; it will take you a while. This exercise cannot work if it is skimmed through; comb it through or brush it off! Open yourself physically to the line. Feel where your tongue goes and how the inside of your mouth moves with the statement. Notice what happens right at the back of your throat when you say *anything*. Compare this to the physical sensation of saying *nothing*. Say the line both ways a few times. With *anything* your glottis is in action, and the vocal cords inside your neck have a feeling of surprise and awe that in this line at least, *nothing* does not provide. Poetry of a certain type, the carefully constructed kind or the product of almost indefinable genius, is a physical act as well as an intellectual and emotional explosion. When you experience an emotion, your body is affected, isn't it? The strain and pleasure of love is actually felt, isn't it? Envy and jealousy both arrive complete with a set of physical symptoms to accompany their green and gloomy thoughts. Dancing in a properly organized discothèque—where the lights are as hallucinogenic as you want and the music as loud as you wish, and where friends and acquaintances share their individualities—is a physical joy accompanying or sometimes replacing an emotional joy. Just as thought of someone for whom you feel affection or love can produce a leap of the heart or a tingle of the spine, so can great art—in the interests of reminding us that we are not utterly alone—recreate by creating pleasures of the mind that frequently border on physical sensation. I would suggest that you

---

[1]Note that, in prose, it is weak to rhyme as I have done with *book* and *look* unless one intends a very particular effect, which I certainly did not, and what results is carelessness. In scripts watch for this kind of rhyming, which makes a script inferior unless a good reason can be found for it.

now read the revised line 1 again, to be the more ready for our discussion of some other lines of this sonnet about a moment in a morning in 1802.

Now, Wordsworth wrote the next two lines of his sonnet thus:

> Dull would he be of soul who pass by
> A sight so touching in its majesty.

One hardly knows where to begin. What is the effect of putting *dull* at the beginning of this line? Apart from the fact that nobody ever did or would "speak" that way and that Wordsworth is driving with his poetic license, the line is not beautiful to hear and is not meant to be. Say the two lines aloud; say them again. Now read the "bad" version twice. Is anything happening to your throat and voice as they physically experience the complete statement? Is anything happening to your teeth? There must be a dental noise when *dull* is uttered. With that *d* so close is the tip of the tongue to the teeth that the very *ll* formed by the tongue's tip between or just behind the teeth is a flat and quite unliquid noise. *Prove this to yourself* by trying line 2 in the "bad" version. The word following *dull* there is *of.* The mouth is getting ready to open, and the *ll* is farther back, formed by the tip of the tongue meeting the upper front of the palate—a much more pleasant oral and aural sensation. But at this point Wordsworth is not trying to produce pleasure; he is recreating what it feels like to be— and what it feels like to consider—somebody untouched by the sight he is seeing. *Dull* followed by *would* is pressing the lips forward, and the *ll* is dull.

Dull, then, is dull. The first word in the sentence, *dull* is a used arrow winging its way to the target, a word about *soul,* which occupies the center of the line; the person untouched by the view of London in the morning is not dull of wit or unintelligent: The *soul* is dull. Reading the line aloud, it is impossible to inflect the voice upward on *soul.* The voice of our body is made to sink (and the monosyllables also thump us down). The same principle is operating with *touching* in line 3, but for quite a different reason. As we have seen, the order of the words is:

> A sight so touching in its majesty

Touching, in the center, drops from the lips with a gentle surprise after the repeated *s* of soul, pass, sight, and so; however, its vowel raises our lips momentarily before the pursing forward into the kiss of touching, which is enriched by the similar but more authoritative *j* of *majesty*. By no means read on. I have been saying complex things quite quickly. Please reread this whole paragraph, and test the truth of my comments with your own teeth, lips, tongue, palate, and vocal cords.

I insert this paragraph to urge you to do what I just said. Before you read on, be sure to hear and feel the dullness, the emphasis on *soul*, the passing of the sibilants (*s*) into the dental sounds of *t*, *ch*, and *j*. You might like to consult a book on phonetics or the International Phonetic Alphabet (IPA) to consolidate your interest in this kind of discussion, but my remarks should be understood by anyone without a knowledge of phonetics or linguistics. Do not take lightly my assertion that writing is felt physically as well as intellectually; until one realizes this, conversation is likely to be dull of soul, and attempts at argument merely touching.

To continue . . . Let's look at lines 4 and 5.

a.   This city doth like a garment now wear
      The beauty of the morning; silent, bare

b.   This city now doth like a garment wear
      The beauty of the morning; silent bare

c.   Now doth this city like a garment wear
      The beauty of the morning; silent, bare

d.   This city like a garment now doth wear
      The beauty of the morning; silent bare

Did the writer write a, b, c, or d? To answer this question we should engage the meaning and focus rather than the sound alone, a practice that helped us arrive at satisfying conclusions about lines 1 to 3. We should also consider rhythm elementarily, briefly, and intensely—as important a technique to have in acting as in understanding poetry.

a. Does anything strike you as awkward or unpleasing about this when you read it aloud? Does the *now* seem sudden? As if the garment had been thrust on the city without notice? That may have been what the writer meant. If he did, why should he speak of beauty in an unpleasant way? Might he have a reason?

b. *This city now* seems to be some kind of unit. Can the writer mean "This city is here and it is now, and the moment I am experiencing is in the present, has not been in the past, and is unlikely to occur again in quite the same way"? Can he also be saying that the moment has come suddenly? The line is undeniably regular, with a beat that goes *ti-tum-ti-tum ti-tum-ti-tum-ti-tum*. Can this regularity and this harmoniousness have anything to do with what he is feeling and seeing?

c. *Now doth this city* (read it aloud) thrusts us into the present. *Now* is strongly at the beginning of the line. Can it mean that the city was not like this five minutes ago but only now? Do you read it "*now* doth this *city*" or "*now doth* this *city*?" In the latter case, does *now* not mean "listen, now, I have a statement to make"? The rhythm could be either *tum-ti-ti-tum-ti* or *ti-tum-ti-tum-ti* (like the version before this one). This version makes *now* the most important idea.

d. *This city like a garment:* Is the city the garment or is the city wearing the garment? It certainly seems that the city is being compared to a garment. What is the subject of the sentence?—*this city*? What is the qualifying clause?—*like a garment*? What is the verb of the sentence?—*doth wear*? What is the object of the sentence?—*the beauty of the morning*? What does *like a garment* qualify?—*the beauty of the morning*? or *this city*? Obviously, *like a garment* qualifies the former. If we take *The apples in the basket are red* and say that its subject, because of the absence of commas, is *the apples in the basket* (as we have every right to do), then we can say that *This city now* is the subject of the sentence in lines 4 and 5.

Now, it's up to you. The following exercises are for toning your sensitivity to words and their order. As an actor, you have discovered that a concern for words, sounds, and sentence structure is one of your principal pleasures and responsibilities.

Here is how the poem really goes:

> Earth has not anything to show more fair;
> Dull would he be of soul who could pass by
> A sight so touching in its majesty.
> This city now doth like a garment wear
> The beauty of the morning; silent, bare,
> Ships, domes, towers, theaters and temples lie
> Open unto the fields and to the sky,
> All bright and glittering in the smokeless air.
> Never did sun more beautifully steep
> In his first splendour valley, rock or hill;
> Ne'er saw I, never felt, a calm so deep.
> The river glideth at his own sweet will.
> Dear God! The very houses seem asleep,
> And all that mighty heart is lying still.

EXERCISES

You have been hired to perform at a poetry reading. Many actors do this, and most who do often do it much better than the poets themselves. Think carefully about the following questions, and get yourself into the habit of asking such searching things about the scripts you encounter in the theatre and in your scene study.

1. In line 8, the present participle *glittering* preceded the adjective bright in my "bad" version. But here in the original poem it functions both as a verb and an adjective. How does it not do that in my version?

2. *Bright,* in my version, stops the line in the middle with its final dental. Why is this not as effective as the original way?

3. Look at line 11. Compare the two versions. Why is it better to have *felt* after *saw* as Wordsworth has it? Don't think only about the sound. Think also about the processes of seeing and thinking.

4. Remember that as an actor you are a creator—not the author, but a creator nonetheless. In line 13, the *Dear God* belongs at the beginning. Why? How does the meaning change by putting it at the end as I did in the bad version?

CHARACTER VOICES

This subject is very difficult. There are many teachers of voice and diction in theatre departments and schools—as well as some actors—who believe the subject should not be taught at all. True, the inexperienced voice could possibly be harmed by certain special "effects" if it has not been already trained in breath control and alignment. There are, therefore, certain "tricks" that I shall omit for this section for fear they might endanger the unpracticed voice.

But the subject cannot be ignored, if only to put those young actors in the right direction who may be trying some effects on their own with either unsatisfactory or harmful results—that is, tricks that could become a habit inhibiting the expansion of the voice into the realm of its full potential. In this book's introduction you will remember Morris Carnovsky's anecdote about the actor of the twenties with the "sostenuto *but.*"

How can an actor apply makeup to the voice? Many actors do: Among many others, Rod Steiger, Geraldine Page, Marlon Brando,

Stacey Keach, Ellis Rabb, Alec Guinness, Laurence Olivier, and Henry Winkler spring immediately to mind. It is a sad fact of life in the world of television situation comedy that many actors are contracted simply because they have "a funny voice" and an even sadder fact that in both the male and female artist that funny voice sounds the same, as if variety would terrify a marshmallow audience out of its comfortable complacency. Strangely enough, in soap operas, which have become such a pervasive art form in the past fifteen years, and which deal with life in a more interesting way than do many television serials, we do not find this reliance on the new high, scratchy, insistent vocal delivery that is the staple aural diet in many other shows. This is not the kind of vocal makeup I will speak about.

Quite simply, "vocal makeup," is changing the voice so that you don't sound as you normally do; that's all. And we all change our voice anyway every day of our lives, in baby talk, "sweet nothings," coded messages to close friends, jokes, and anytime we "act a part" of any kind. Some of us even change the quality of our voices, depending on what kind of business or professional public or private situation we find ourselves in. At big meetings without microphones, I have even been accused of "putting on my actor's voice." Change of voice is a standard risk for performers who have to present their own ideas outside those of a character they have to act in a play.

Kristin Linklater (and some other writers and teachers) makes the valuable point that

> It takes so long for . . . deep relaxation to become familiar and for organic awareness to develop as a result, that it is wise to postpone work that increases breathing capacity and strengthens the breathing musculature until it can be done with awareness and sensitivity to ensure that breath stays in touch with inner impulse whatever the demand.

As I have said a few times, this book will not help you free your natural voice. I also agree with Kristin Linklater, however. So, as you read the following advice particularly, please bear in mind that you will not be likely to get very far with your voice until you have developed a "free voice." Having said that, let me proceed to tell you "how to do" certain things that can produce sounds of different character. The oldest technique, in my recollection at any rate, for altering the texture of the voice is very easily learned and involves breathing out and losing quite a lot of breath before actually beginning to speak. Some actors have used this technique so often that it became their normal mode of delivery after a while—the late Dame Edith Evans, for instance, who many times practically left herself breathless before even beginning a line or a phrase; with her, it was especially useful for expressing indignation, affronted dignity, and other moods and emotions connected with pride or *hauteur*. Her infamous line from *The Importance of Being Earnest*—"A hannnnnnnnndbaaagg!"—takes its eccentricity and character precisely from this technique. The following extract from a letter written to Geraldine Page by a professor of fine arts at Georgetown University in Washington, D.C., is an indication of how certain members of the public can become attracted to such eccentricities of delivery. The extract is reprinted with the permission of Professor Donn Murphy and Miss Page.

> I would just like students to hear what a really fine sense of variety in volume, pitch, and timing can be:
>
> DOC-TOR! May I *please* POINT OUT toyou, that *AT* this time SISter AGnes IS—UNDER—*MY* charge? NowIdonotintheslightest want to disPARage the suPPOSED achieeeeeevements of DOC-*TOR* Freud ... But-I-think-that-as-her *MOTHER* SUPERIORRRRRRRRRR, I know *BET*ter than anyoneincluding *you* what is BEST for *SisterAgnessss.*

It is possible that Professor Murphy's interest in speech pattern is as extreme as his extremely sensitive response, but readers of my book—who intend to enter the profession—must surely take note of such careful listening on the part of the public. I mean to go so far as to say, too, that there is *nothing wrong whatever with imitation if it is understood to be only an exercise and not a habit.* The great twentieth-century poet W. H. Auden (1907–1975) tells a story about the Austrian lyric poet Rainer Maria Rilke (1875–1926), to whom, as a young man, Auden had sent several poems for critical comment. The poems were sent back with the statement that, while Rilke knew there was strong feeling in them, that's about all there was *and the feeling was left unfelt by the reader*; Rilke advised Auden to throw away the poems for the time being and concentrate on imitating other poets and their forms of expression (as opposed to their feelings). Only after Auden had done imitation for some time, said Rilke, would he be able to "find his own voice." And, of course, as people attracted to acting as a career, you all know perfectly well that you started out imitating what you saw and what you heard. You all imitate radio, television, film, and stage performers. Imitation is the most natural thing to do—and actors have traditionally been pretty good mimics too. "It comes with the territory," as is said of Willy Loman in *Death of a Salesman*. How do you think Shakespeare could write plays? By seeing and reading and copying them. Good artists have very seldom, if ever, been capable of spontaneous combustion or working out of a vacuum. Part of the experience of artists has almost always been other artists and their work.

So, knowing about the necessity of imitation, try the following speech Tennessee Williams gives Mrs. Venable in the strange and affecting *Suddenly Last Summer*. There is no harm either in knowing that in the movie the part was played by Katherine Hepburn and on stage by Hortense Alden. Note, please, that I am *not* saying "here is how to play Mrs. Venable"; nothing could be further from my intention. If by chance you are rehearsing that part for production, you might indeed do well to ignore the next page or two and go on to exercises of another kind altogether. I assume, you see, that the actors reading this book have the *time and leisure* to devote attention to this exercise *merely as an exercise.* That understood, let me proceed.

Let the breath out almost completely. You will feel the muscles of the diaphragm pushing upward. You are in a position of slight strain, in fact, unless you have reached the stage of being able to do without much oxygen in the system! Now start the first line and ask yourself or someone who is with you what meaning is attached to the sound you have produced.

SUDDENLY LAST SUMMER

MRS. VENABLE Without me he died last summer, that was his last summer's poem. (*She staggers; he assists her toward a chair. She catches her breath with difficulty*) One long-ago summer—now, why am I thinking of this?—my son, Sebastian, said, "Mother?—Listen to this!"—He read me Herman Melville's description of the Encan-
5 tadas, the Galapagos Islands. Quote—take five and twenty heaps of cinders dumped here and there in an outside city lot. Imagine some of them magnified into mountains, and the vacant lot, the sea. And you'll have a fit idea of the general aspect of the En-cantadas, the Enchanted Isles—extinct volcanos, looking much
10 as the world at large might look—after a last conflagration—end quote. He read me that description and said that we had to go there. And so we did go there that summer on a chartered boat, a four-masted schooner, as close as possible to the sort of a boat that Melville must have sailed on ... We saw the Encan-
15 tadas, but on the Encantadas we saw something Melville *hadn't* written about. We saw the great sea-turtles crawl up out of the sea for their annual egg-laying ... Once a year the female of

the sea-turtle crawls up out of the equatorial sea onto the blazing sand-beach of a volcanic island to dig a pit in the sand and deposit her eggs there. It's a long and dreadful thing, the depositing of the eggs in the sand-pits, and when it's finished the exhausted female turtle crawls back to the sea half-dead. She never sees her offspring, but we did. Sebastian knew exactly when the sea-turtle eggs would be hatched out and we returned in time for it . . .

DOCTOR You went back to the—?

MRS. VENABLE Terrible Encantadas, those heaps of extinct volcanos, in time to witness the hatching of the sea-turtles and their desperate flight to the sea! (*There is a sound of harsh bird-cries in the air. She looks up*)
—The narrow beach, the color of caviar, was all in motion! But the sky was in motion, too . . .

DOCTOR The sky was in motion, too?

MRS. VENABLE —Full of flesh-eating birds and the noise of the birds, the horrible savage cries of the—

DOCTOR Carnivorous birds?

MRS. VENABLE Over the narrow black beach of the Encantadas as the just hatched sea-turtles scrambled out of the sand-pits and started their race to the sea . . .

DOCTOR Race to the sea?

MRS. VENABLE To escape the flesh-eating birds that made the sky almost as black as the beach!
(*She gazes up again: we hear the wild, ravenous, harsh cries of the birds. The sound comes in rhythmic waves like a savage chant*)
And the sand all alive, all alive, as the hatched sea-turtles made their dash for the sea, while the birds hovered and swooped to attack and hovered and—swooped to attack! They were diving down on the hatched sea-turtles, turning them over to expose their soft undersides, tearing the undersides open and rending and eating their flesh. Sebastian guessed that possibly only a hundredth of one percent of their number would escape to the sea . . .

DOCTOR	What was it about this that fascinated your son?
MRS. VENABLE	My son was looking for—(*She stops short with a slight gasp*)— Let's just say he was interested in sea-turtles!
DOCTOR	That isn't what you started to say.
MRS. VENABLE	I stopped myself just in time.

55

The first most obvious thing to note is the playwright's stage direction that Mrs. Venable "catches her breath with difficulty." She "has light orange or pink hair and wears a lavender lace dress, and over her withered bosom is pinned a starfish of diamonds." Mrs. Venable is old, she is frail, she is excited, and it all tells on her heart, which in turn tells in her voice. Remember, she is also a woman of great will, and she is determined to have her niece Catherine locked up and lobotomized for having seen the true horror of her son Sebastian's death on a Spanish beach, where he was cannibalized by pre-adolescent boys from whom he had been buying sexual favors. Physically, dizziness and difficulty in breathing characterize this strange mixture of a woman.

I think it would be weak and unhelpful to breathe in places other than where there are punctuation marks because Tennessee Williams has heard the voice he has created in his head, has often heard such voices in and around the southern towns he has lived in and visited, and he has provided sentences of remarkable brevity. Where the sentences are longer, they are generally broken up by dashes and qualifying clauses. The sentences start with her "now, why am I thinking of this?" and become more and more interesting when she quotes from Melville's description of the Encantadas, which in itself has a peculiar sentence formation with the sentence beginning with *And*. I would use only one breath up to "Isles," breathe again after "look" and again after "conflagration" and again after "quote." Quite a few breaths help to structure the speech at the same time as indicate character. Let me list breathing points for the whole speech and then discuss them more fully. Remember these are only my suggestions, and there must be other equally productive ways of dealing with the breaths of the speech.

summer/now	Islands/Quote
this?/my	Quote/take

this!/He	there/And
lot/Imagine	on . . ./We*
sea/And	about/We
Isles/extinct	egg-laying/Once*
look/after	there/It's*
conflagration/end	half-dead/She*
quote/He	did/Sebastian

Let us discuss the ones marked with asterisks; first, the *on . . ./ We.* Since its subject is all Melville's boat, the sentence preceding this breath can well be delivered on one exhalation; try it, and you will see what character it creates and how all the energy is put on the major point—which is, after all, what the character is doing. Mrs. Venable doesn't *have* much vocal energy at all. The next very long utterance on one inhalation I would recommend for this speech is the sentence that begins "Once a year" and ends "deposit her eggs there." There is no reason I can see for splitting up this sentence; indeed, it gathers force toward its weak ending; further, it is very difficult to breathe with any meaning anywhere within it. The more "exhausted" the actress makes her voice (remember the connection between the words *exhaust* and *exhausted*), the more she will appear like an old female sea-turtle who has laid eggs that others eat after hatching. If the actress splits the sentence into breaths, I think she will miss much of its point.

EXERCISES

1. Rehearse the scene, playing Mrs. Venable, and experiment with breathing places. Justify everything you do, and have a teacher or fellow student comment on the different moods and meanings created by your various phrasings.

2. Pick a scene involving an older person and apply the ideas you have heard.

The "Old" Voice

What about the following standard question young, high school, or amateur actors ask in a production where old people are not available to play old parts: How does a young man go about playing the voice of an old one?

Acting an old voice is a lot easier than acting a middle-aged one, and much easier still than acting the voice of someone only a few years older. I shall start this long section by telling you what happened to me when I had to play a part seven years *younger* than I was.

At the Citadel Theatre in Edmonton, Alberta, in 1968, when I was twenty-eight, I auditioned successfully for the title role in a play about desertion in World War I, *Hamp*. When I went for the audition, I was playing Falstaff on a far-flung school tour with the Vancouver Holiday Playhouse's adaptation of the *Henry IV* and *Henry V* plays of Shakespeare, and was sporting a belly and a beard—both real and both full. I looked nearer thirty-eight. Anyway, by speaking *quietly* and quite quickly at the audition and by understanding the rhythms of the character through his speech—now fluent, now disjointed, I obviously persuaded the director (Robert Glenn of Texas) that I could play the part. I was thrilled and frightened. To lose a great deal of weight in ten weeks while touring was possible, of course, because there were only six of us in the Holiday Playhouse Company, and in between eating and sleeping and performing, we ourselves moved, set, and struck lights and scenery and even our stage (a large, cumbersome, heavy, and unnecessarily complicated structure). Losing the weight would be easy. Shaving off the beard would also be easy. But how was "youthening" to be done? I was to play opposite the Welshman Powys Thomas, one of the greatest Canadian actors and founder of the National Theatre School (he died in 1975). Thomas had just scored a hit with his performance of the terrifying Russian monk Rasputin in the play of the same name at the Stratford Festival in Ontario. I *had* to be believable.

As things turned out, we both were so believable that Act I (which consisted totally of a long dialogue between us) shocked and moved every audience. A contrast between the two voices was essential, of course, and (unfortunately for me) Powys Thomas had what many would consider a "soft" or "beautiful" voice, so a mere softening on my part was not enough to sound younger. By *raising the pitch half-an-octave* and *bypassing the strongest lips of the vocal cords*, I took all "edge" off my voice, moving from baritone to alto. To do this, I had to open my mouth wider to make sure that the *mouth cavity was the main resonating chamber.* Of course, I started the process from the diaphragm but tried to put very little strength on the larynx, forcing the glottis into a state of *unusually small vibration.* From this type of voice production came some of the character I was playing; a voice certainly entirely different from mine. I have a large voice, with much edge to it.

More usually, young actors are required to age. Let me now turn to this. There are simple rules for aging, after which I shall offer a few suggestions.

First of all, the old do not often speak slowly so much as *deliberately,* in an effort to be understood. At least, one kind of old person does this. Merely to slow down your speech could very well wreak havoc on the pace and tempo of the play and is to be avoided. By "deliberately" I mean that you should try to speak as carefully as you can, as if speech itself were a bit of a strain. I can't give you exercises on this except in person, but you are likely to succeed by careful observation of others, good mimicry, and by remembering this rule of thumb—to cry on stage, one effective way is to *try not to;* to be drunk on stage the best way is to try *not* to seem drunk and make obvious efforts in that virtuous direction. Deliberateness of speech is such a strong signal that the character needs to be careful, that in general it is the first most obvious thing to do in reproducing age.

Unfortunately, drunken speech and aged speech share the same technique, and often young actors confuse the two effects by arriving at them in the same way. Of course you don't want this to happen. Therefore, *a change in vocal quality* is also needed if you are to distinguish the influence of aging from that of alcohol. I would be shot if I were to tell you how I've always done this myself because it is a potentially harmful method involving "cracking" the vocal cords. Your coach or teacher will be able to tell you what I mean; enough said. As you have seen from chapters 3 and 4, there are more honorable methods of arriving at "character" than by the mere application of vocal makeup. The next section is also about these methods: three women whose voices are characterized by their lines.

KING LEAR, I. i—52–106; 270–312

Let us look thoroughly at the speech of three Shakespearean women, Goneril, Regan, and Cordelia, the three daughters of King Lear. At the beginning of the play they have been assembled to be given equal parts of the kingdom as dowries for their three impending marriages and they are called upon by their father—who is giving up a large part of his kingship to their new husbands while he "Unburdened crawl[s] towards death"—to announce publicly their love for him. The sisters are to be characterized by what they say in this first scene, and the alert actress will notice how obviously they are distinguished from each other by the textures of their speech.

King Lear, who speaks in resounding cadences with vowels as wide-skirted as the meads he has prepared to give to his eldest daughter, Goneril, says:

> Tell me my daughters
> Which of you shall we say doth love us most,
> That we our largest bounty may extend
> Where nature doth with merit challenge. Goneril,
> Our eldest born, speak first.

I noted fully in the discussion of *Hamlet*, Act 1, scene 1, that frequently when a line of iambic pentameter falls short of five full stresses, it may be assumed that if the next speaker does not begin the line by completing the previous short one, there is most likely a directed pause roughly equal to the missing stresses. Goneril can have about two stresses, then, to ready herself for her proclamation of filial love. In other words, Goneril does not rush in where she fears to tread; she may move toward the king, she may take a deep breath, she may arrange her clothing, and she may make all sorts of preparations, but the plain fact is that as an indication of part of her character, the playwright gives her the opportunity to *prepare*. Having done so, Goneril speaks, and it is rather amazing what she does:

> 56 Sir, I love you more than word can wield the matter,
> Dearer than eyesight, space, and liberty,
> Beyond what can be valued, rich or rare,
> 59 No less than life, with grace, health, beauty, honour,
> As much as child e'er loved, or father found;
> A love that makes breath poor, and speech unable—
> Beyond all manner of so much I love you.

This begins as very clever stuff indeed: Goneril's main point is to say that she loves her father more than life itself. You can see that, if you follow her logical connection between lines 56 and 62. "No less than life" in line 59 is logically the end of her statement, but, being a talker (like her sister Regan also, as we shall see), she is not content with stopping there but feels the need to prove (in words only, be it said) that she isn't making it all up—which, of course, she is. Goneril is not a nice lady at all. Look at the measured way she talks, with truly overdone alliteration and the same wide vowels as her father:

> **w**ords can **w**ield the matter
> **r**ich or **r**are
> **l**ess than **l**ife
> **f**ather **f**ound, **m**anner of so **m**uch

This is highly patterned speech, betokening a character of similar nature. Count the long vowels she utters: m**o**re, w**o**rd, w**ie**ld, d**ea**rer, **eye**sight, sp**a**ce, bey**o**nd, v**a**lued, r**a**re, l**i**fe, gr**a**ce, h**ea**lth, b**eau**ty, hon**ou**r, ch**i**ld, **e'e**r, f**a**ther, f**ou**nd, m**a**kes, br**ea**th, p**oo**r, bey**o**nd, **a**ll. Here are twenty-four very long or wide vowels in the space of seven lines! It is obvious to the actress, then, that Goneril is at the very least an expansive person, certainly an expansive speaker, and in fact, it is not improbable to say that she has a big mouth. Try those lines and you will find how much jaw movement you have to produce to say them at all. The pathetic part of Goneril's attempt at flattery is that she is unable to complete it; she cannot even summon up a rhythmical last line. Goneril's proclamation peters out and dribbles away in rhetorical if not emotional confusion—in embarrassment, at least:

> ᴗ / ᴗ / ᴗ / ᴗ / ᴗ /
> As much as child e'er loved, or father found
> ᴗ / ᴗ / / / ᴗ / ᴗ /
> A love that makes breath poor, and speech unable—

Her speech has indeed already become "unable"; the feminine ending of this line is weak, and she is continuing to speak in near hexameters (six-stress lines), messing up, as it were, the standard line spoken by others in the scene. What can Goneril make of her next one, her last line for a while? Nothing. The line has no discernible meter; it tries to begin loudly, expansively, logically, but produces no effect. In this moment, we see into her cold and ineffectual heart. Try saying line 62 in such a way as to make it powerful. See? Try as you might, the "I love you" takes away some of the strength the line might have started with. Why? *Because the preceding lines have been so much* more *regular, so much more formed.* After the exaggerations of her verse, this line is really more like prose. In spite of the alliteration of "all manner of so much," in spite of the power of the hypocritical *thought* in the line, what the thought *sounds like* is next to nothing. But her father likes the line a lot.

The youngest daughter Cordelia has an aside just before King Lear takes up Goneril's assertion of love by giving her what he had already planned to give in any case, and it is clear from this aside that she already *sounds* totally different from Goneril:

> What shall Cordelia speak? Love, and be silent.

The *s* of *speak* and *silent* could help the actress be soft in delivery of the line, but let's wait until other characters have said more before making any conclusive suggestions about Cordelia.

LEAR   Of all these bounds, even from this line to this,
      With shadowy forests and with champains riched,
      With plenteous rivers, and wide-skirted meads,
      We make thee lady. To thine and Albany's issue
      Be this perpetual. What says our second daughter?
      Our dearest Regan, wife of Cornwall? Speak.

Regan needs little preparation. She has heard her sister Goneril and knows what she has received from her father for loudly and widely saying she loves him as much as she loves life, as much as any child ever has, as much as any father has ever experienced. Regan has to top that. And, in her pert, quick, self-contained way, she does. She opens her pursed lips the moment her father tells her to:

REGAN   I am made of that self metal as my sister,
      And prize me at her worth. In my true heart,
      I find she names my very deed of love.
      Only she comes too short, that I profess
      Myself an enemy to all other joys,
  76 Which the most precious square of sense possesses,
      And find I am alone felicitate
      In your dear Highness' love.

This speech is one line longer than Goneril's but probably takes less time because it is so full of sibilants and short vowels that it is quickly said.

Based on an examination of the two hymns of filial love, how does Regan differ from Goneril? For one thing, Regan does not alliterate beyond a mild example in line 70. She utters appreciably more monosyllables than does Goneril. Regan is also a much "neater" speaker, as I shall now illustrate. Count her monosyllables. Don't be ashamed about doing something like this, which may strike you as a mindless kindergarten game or academic nitpicking; the exercise I am encouraging you to do is neither of those things but an opening up of the performer's sensibility to the guides in the script that are there to create character. Regan's monosyllables are (and I am counting only the stressed ones on the assumption that there are generally five stresses to a line, as I have said before): *I, made, that, prize, at, worth, my, heart, find, names, deed, love, comes, short, joys, square, sense, find, your, love.* Now let us compare these with Goneril's stresses:

Sir, love, more word, wield, matter	I made, that, self, metal, sister
Dearer, eyesight, space, liberty	prize, at, worth, my, heart
Beyond, can, valued, rich, rare	find, names, very, deed, love
less, life, grace, health, beauty,	Only, comes, short, I, profess
honour, Much, child loved, father	Myself, enemy, to, other, joys
found, love, makes, poor, speech	precious, square, sense, possesses
unable beyond all manner, much, love	find, am alone, felicitate your, Highness', love

Now, a long glance at these two lists will tell you that Regan is sibilant and Goneril is not. The glance will also tell you that Regan's vowels are preponderantly shorter than Goneril's. When Regan's vowels look as if they are about to be long or wide, there is often a consonant of a type that will shorten the effect; that is, when she opens her mouth on a word like *prize*, for instance, *she has to close it again* quickly to say the z after the i. Anyone would have to agree that *metal* contains a wide vowel in its first syllable. But the mouth is forced to close on itself again to say the unstressed second syllable and its concluding *l*. Regan is consonants where Goneril is vowels. Goneril has a big mouth, and Regan a small one (or behavior has made it small). Goneril expands her delivery to enlarge her heart; Regan, her intellectual superior, is almost smug and most certainly self-contained. Had these women no servants, Goneril would sweep the house with a broom, and Regan with a wire and feather whisk. The actress faced with the part of Regan will learn a great deal from saying line 76 several times until it comes "naturally" because there is so much of the character in those six words:

And find I am alone felicitate . . .

The way the d stops the i of find, the agility needed to proceed to the f of felicitate after the n of alone, and, above all, the calm primness of that neat, shipshape, well-scrubbed[2] word felic-i-tate itself, these things tell us much about the woman's physical self and—since she is a creature in a play—something about the workings of her mind and her heart.

Once again—because plays like this are symmetrical in construction—Cordelia, the youngest daughter, has an aside before her father doles out the bounty to her second sister. We can tell a fraction more about this young woman this time because she says more. And as we shall see, she says it in quite a different way from Regan and Goneril. First of all, notice that Cordelia continues the line left incomplete by Regan. Later in our discussion of these three people we will be able to come to some useful conclusion about that.

CORDELIA   Then poor Cordelia—
(Aside)   And yet not so, since I am sure my love's
      More ponderous than my tongue.

You can see that in these lines there is nothing at all similar to what her sisters have said or even to how they have said it. In fact, about all we can tell from the lines is perhaps that Cordelia is undistinguished of speech. Her language has nothing special to recommend it and nothing to damn her—at least, not in the eyes of the audience. However, there is something in her language to damn her in her father's eyes, as will shortly transpire in the first great explosion of the play when she is banished for plain speaking—not only for speaking straightforwardly, but also in the other sense of unprepared and unembellished talk coming from the heart rather than the mouth, as she will soon herself say.

Meanwhile, back on the throne: Regan has just finished saying that she's probably made of gold like Goneril and worth the same,

[2]In Lewis Galentière's translation of Jean Anouilh's Antigone, Creon uses this phrase to describe how he likes a state to be. I think the phrase is quite appropriate for Regan.

that Goneril has said just what Regan was going to say but not sufficiently. Regan (and it is easy to note that she uses "I," "me," "myself" and "my" rather often) finds no happiness and no joy in anything but her love for her father, who, of course, finds this appropriate and gives her her due in land:

LEAR   To thee, and thine hereditary ever,
        Remain this ample third of our fair kingdom,
        No less in space, validity, and pleasure,
        Than that conferred on Goneril. Now, our joy . . .

Lear has preserved the best third of the newly divided and apportioned kingdom for his youngest and favorite daughter Cordelia and is so eager to give it out, so eager to declare his greatest love in public to warm his heart and the hearts of the assembled court and family, that he hardly takes a breath after giving Regan her gift before turning to Cordelia with that tender salutation:

> Now, our joy,
> Although our last and least, to whose young love
> The vines of France and milk of Burgundy
> Strive to be interested. What can you say, to draw
> A third more opulent than your sisters? Speak.

Cordelia does speak—right away, but she says the wrong thing.

CORDELIA   Nothing my lord. [Pause of three stresses]

LEAR   Nothing? [Pause of four stresses]

CORDELIA   Nothing. [Pause of four stresses]

This celebrated interchange, the crux of the beginning of the play and the motivator of all the subsequent action and inaction, the "chief setter forth of all the mischief," falls outside my concern in this chapter.

LEAR   Nothing will come of nothing. Speak again.

CORDELIA   Unhappy that I am, I cannot heave
            My heart into my mouth. I love your Majesty
            According to my bond, no more nor less.

LEAR   How now, Cordelia? Mend your speech a little,
        Lest you may mar your fortunes.

CORDELIA   Good my liege
     99 You have begot me, bred me, loved me. I
    100 Return those duties back as are right fit,
        Obey you, love you, and most honour you.
        Why have my sisters husbands, if they say
        They love you all? Haply when I shall wed,
        That lord whose hand must take my plight shall carry
        Half my love with him, half my care, and duty.
        Sure I shall never marry like my sisters,
        To love my father all.

Arguments and speculations about the wisdom of Cordelia saying this are irrelevant for the actress playing the part. The fact is that Cordelia says it, and it is her father's undoing. She can no more help saying it than she can help breathing. The actress can see from this speech that she is not playing the role of someone stupid but that of somebody who asks honest questions; whether this quality—in public and on an occasion like this—is commendable is not a question that concerns me here. You can see from lines 99 and 100 that Cordelia has a full sense of order; she even *sounds* ordered. The problem is that it is forward of her to ask questions when she has been commanded, albeit whimsically, to answer. You can see that she thinks in numbers, as she has been brought up to do, especially with a father like Lear. What she says is natural, and she says it naturally.

Cordelia says her speech in accordance with her nature. So, too, do her older sisters make their statements. Look at the ease and speed with which she completes and reflects Lear's short lines, as much as he has refused to be metrically harmonious in any way by doing the same to her:

        To love my father all. [Two-stress pause]

LEAR   But goes thy heart with this?

CORDELIA   Ay my good lord. [She continues his line]

LEAR   So young, and so untender? [He establishes a new and different rhythm]

CORDELIA   So young my lord, and true. [She uses his rhythm exactly and repeats his sentence construction exactly too]

Again, I must say that the wisdom of Cordelia's utterances is not under discussion. The utterances are wise but are not appropriate to the situation; that is the most that need be said.

What of the texture of Cordelia's voice and speech, then? It is ordered, not ornamented, has in fact no distinguishing characteristics. She is known, simply, by the company she does not keep.

CLAUDIUS' OPENING SPEECH IN *HAMLET*

An Advanced Scene Study

Claudius is as consummate an actor as Hamlet, and the performer who betrays his villainy too early in the play is doing the text, character, and drama a disservice. To argue that we all know about Claudius because we all have read the play before is patently stupid, but this argument is often implicitly used as an excuse for enriching the portrayal with undertones of rasping nastiness as early as his first appearance in council when, in balanced cadences, he urges that Denmark shed its sable suits and mourning tears in the interests of a balanced and happy political state. This opening speech must smile and smile and appear villainous only to Hamlet. Furthermore, this necessity is dictated not by me, by any director or actor, but by the rhythmic structure of the speech, which, in its parallelisms, contains in fluidity and deliberate formality, an inner fear that an actor might wish to exaggerate but not add. That fear already lies within the noise the words make and the shapes they make in the theatre's air. Approach the role in an auditory way, and its secrets will explode into meaning. The facial muscles of the actor can be controlled by the music and the texture of the verse. Add no smiles or grimaces; they are there and will emerge. I use such words as *structure, texture, rhythm*. These words will be meaningless until the speech is heard and gone through thoroughly—ideally in a darkened room, without a candle or a sneak of light, and particularly in sequence; that is, following on the battlement scene and its nervous erratic foreboding. *A Flourish. Enter Claudius, Gertrude, Polonius, Laertes, Voltimand, Cornelius, etc., etc.* And Hamlet is focused by his blackness and separateness. There is color, music, ceremony, warmth, even jollity, and there is the contrast with what has immediately preceded. The contrast probably lasts less than ten seconds; the mere setting into place of dignitaries, king and queen, in its orderliness, is a potent visual symbol of the Order over which the new king wants to reign. And out of this careful courtly hierarchical bustle comes what? What is the tone of the opening announcement? Its first sentence opens with a qualifying clause. The way the stresses lie, the clause doesn't sound qualifying, but it is. Uncertainty and qualification expressed in strong downbeats is the basic music of the speech. The effect is opposite to that of Lear's opening declaration of relinquished though desired power: Lear's pronouncement has the effect of *My Country 'tis of Thee* played on a battered piano rather than by the Vienna Philharmonic. Claudius' speech is as though *Rock of Ages* had as its instrument an expensively rented and brilliant brass band rather than a newly-bought harmonium. In its rhetoric, the speech is very much open-air and in fact, should have that effect. The speech is an open-air one spoken indoors. And in some instances the speech's rhythms go against its sense, and that is part of its point.

As you go through the speech, remember that the King's Men delivery was presumably so formal as to include the stop at the end of almost every line. We should be wary of enjambements and indeed try to refuse them entry into our delivery of this—and any other mature Shakespearean—speech. There is an echo at the end of each line that must be heard before proceeding to the next. We can assume that this method belongs to the seventeenth century because of how the stuff is written and how it can be spoken. This stuff is dramatic poetry, which means that unlike prose the effect is totally cumulative. So, remembering all this (do not force belief until you've tried it), hear the speech.

> Though yet of Hamlet our dear brother's death
> The memory be green; and that it us befitted
> To bear our hearts in grief, and our whole kingdom
> To be contracted in one brow of woe . . .

The speech is very slow, and in the first line the accents fall on *yet, Hamlet, brother's,* and *death. Our* and *dear* can actually share an accent. In the strict iambic the accent falls on *our,* and it can even be inverted and forced onto *dear,* which some actors would do, overstressing the false sincerity of the speaker; but (in rehearsal) it is safer, richer, and truer to begin by counting the iambic feet wherever they fall, even to the apparent distortion of any sense. Then the sense can appear more obviously. When *our dear* is given the value of one word, neither word will take precedence over the other, and the result is a kind of precise chaos, reflecting precisely what lives in Claudius' head. Claudius *cannot* fawn and overstress the *dear*. His court does not consist of dimwits, and such sickly sweetness would not pass unnoticed by those assembled. It is essential for Claudius to use the word and not to stress it. The total effect is thus clear and foggy as far as it reveals the inner truth of the character and supremely balanced in what it reveals of its surface to the assembly. The line-ending, *death*, hangs in the air a second and is the principal content of the line. At least several milliseconds pass before the studied freshness of *The memory be green*. Resounding as it does just before the caesura, *green* echoes and contrasts with *death*, politely reinforcing to Denmark's political elite the essence of the present situation: We have been sincerely mourning the loss of a fine leader. But behind it all is that subtly slipped-in *Though* that began the statement. So, the statement is major in a minor key whose signature has been established by its opening chord. Claudius is carefully describing the situation and carefully setting the mood for change; his whole declaration has to be careful, it has to work, it has to be *liked* as well as accepted. Claudius is trying for a great political maneuver.

This speech sounds well-rehearsed. No sooner has Claudius obviously won sympathy with his first twelve words than the concept of protocol is introduced ("and that it us *befitted*," with the double burden of that word). For the court, it was right and good to mourn; for Claudius it was necessary and therefore right. The actor who wants the audience to catch the conscience of the king this early has opportunity enough in the mere utterance of that word since it falls at the end of the line and so is gifted with the hanging pause before the voice returns to momentary rest on *To bear our hearts in grief*. *Death* has been most sympathetically and palpably contrasted with *green* but is now augmented by *befitted* and further qualified by *bear*. (The word is not *hang* nor *feel*; it is objective.) Consider, too, the sheer balance of this half-line with its very steady beats—*bear our hearts in grief*—that is continued in a widening and falling cadence with *and our whole kingdom*. Here the stresses are shared as in the first line of the speech; it opens a metaphor:

To be contracted in one brow of woe

This metaphor shares the gift of Richard III's imagination (*Grim visag'd war hath smooth'd his wrinkled front*) and rings as true as when spoken by the crookback. In fact, the metaphor is true to Claudius' truth and to that of the court. The metaphor is fine and all-embracing but, in the deep open vowel of *woe,* obviously far from final and is followed by the qualification that the speech's first line set up.

> 5 Yet so far hath discretion fought with nature,
> 6 That we with wisest sorrow think on him
> 7 Together with remembrance of ourselves.

Supremely reasonable, the very process of choosing the words cannot help being felt as we hear their public utterance and the irrefutable logic of their balance. The words do not have to be inflected by the actor—once more, they inflect themselves almost no matter what an actor may do to them. For instance, the feminine ending of line 5 dictates the voice's fall. This line is quiet; that fact is insured by the *th* of *hath,* which avoids any scratchiness that could possibly emerge from *discretion,* and the *sh* in that word is (to be simple) naturally hushed. As many people have said, this part of the speech is "bland, respectable commonplace"; that is, however, the hardest kind of thing to act in a situation as precarious as this. In its care and symmetry, the speech is as insecure as it is ruthless. Note how the following two lines (6 and 7) flow to rest in absolutely perfect and uninterrupted iambics, which call for no subjective accents from the actor. In fact, to "go up" on *ourselves* is to overinterpret considerably and even to go against one's own voice. Even to lay extra stress on the word is to contravene the meter. To let the word merely speak—simply to issue it, in which case it will be bland—is to be true to it and to Claudius the politician.

    Therefore (the speech is model rhetoric—*Though; Yet; Therefore*) starts the infamous periodic sentence, Miltonic in its length, that frightens many an actor, gives a sore challenge in "listening" to the actress burdened with the role of Gertrude, contains little but a reinforcement of the ordered balance Claudius has been conveying, and eventually comes to rest on *Taken to wife:*

> Therefore our sometime sister, now our queen,
> The imperial jointress to this warlike state,
> Have we, as 'twere with a defeated joy,
> With an auspicious and a dropping eye
> With mirth in funeral and with dirge in marriage,
> In equal scale weighing delight and dole,
> Taken to wife.

Most actors have turned to Gertrude at this point in the speech, given her a proper loving glance until *state*, and turned back to the assembly for the rest. This procedure can hardly be faulted. Gertrude is best left to cast a glance at Claudius, perhaps, or stare ahead unmoved as would befit the public nature of the occasion. This problem is only the first of many that face the actress throughout the play, and it tends to support T. S. Eliot's complaint of the general lack of objective correlatives in *Hamlet*. Anyway, Claudius' job is easy at this point: his characterization is handed him. Lines 8 to 14 are the epitome of order and well-rehearsed politics. Nothing is left unsaid, though little is said but said well. Further, the texture of the verse constitutes much of the character of the man: Its alliterations and its sometimes luxurious richness (*discretion, remembrance, imperial jointness, auspicious, mirth, dirge*) are the two poles that really make up luxurious, politically active, cool Claudius. Luxurious, bland, and blunt. How coolly *taken to wife* lands on the ear after the long preparation for it. And how soon after the phrase has been spoken (it occupies two pretty weak stresses at the beginning of a line) does Claudius proceed to include the gathered court with:

> nor have we herein barred
> Your better wisdoms, which have freely gone
> With this affair along, For all, our thanks.

Claudius quickly reminds advisers, friends, and enemies—after a very early caesura following what is basically only one stress of the line—that he did not act, as it were, alone. The alliteration of *barr'd* and *better* is Claudius' "harmonious" way of buttering up these people. But Claudius is not merely a wily man; he is also rich of spirit. "For all, our thanks." Not content with thanking everybody for advice, Claudius thanks them for the fruitful, sensual, long-desired results of that advice.

The periodic sentences that are the hallmark of Claudius (you may note that Polonius tries them but cannot carry them off nearly as well as can Claudius) continue with the recent engagements between Denmark and Norway. The actor can learn a great deal from a close examination of the phonetic effects of this expository speech, a speech that—although intended to give the audience sufficient historical information to enable them to proceed with their understanding of the rest of the play and some of its subsidiary characters—

provides a quickly discernible basis for the characterization of the man who says it.

> Now follows, that you know, young Fortinbras,
> Holding a weak supposal of our worth,
> 19 Or thinking by our late dear brother's death
> 20 Our state to be disjoint and out of frame

Worth comes at the end of the line. Preceded as it is by *our*, Claudius is clearly talking chauvinistically and with some cool fervor. Note too how sophisticatedly Claudius constructs his sentences as far as their internal balance is concerned: How *weak* and *worth* are monosyllabic alliterations at once mocking and challenging the king of Norway (or at least young Fortinbras) and strengthening the intellectual position of Claudius and Denmark. The repetition of our *dear brother's death* from line 1 is interesting. There are, indeed, quite a few ways of interpreting this phrase. Merely repeating the phrase as written is bound to make any audience note it and conclude that it most likely slips easily from the man's lips. But this easiness does not imply villainy—nor should it, as I said at the beginning of this actor's interpretation. It is surely much more satisfying for the people in the audience to conclude things for themselves than have an actor signal them with vocal underlinings and purple pointing. Anyway, Claudius carries on his established habit of alliteration and formality with *dear, death,* and *disjoint*. You have learned from the agility exercises in Chapter 2 that a line like 20 would require considerable poise just to utter. Try the line and you will feel what I mean precisely. Well, this is what it feels like to be Claudius. In *state to be disjoint* and *out*, when you feel those patterns of *d* and *t* against your upper palate and discover the very small movements made by the lips in moving from word to word, you will have some of Claudius's vocal measure.

> 21 Colleagued with this dream of his advantage,
> 22 He hath not fail'd to pester us with message
> 23 Importing the surrender of those lands
> 24 Lost by his father, with all bands of law,
> 25 To our most valiant brother. So much for him.

There are more *d*'s in line 21 and then they more or less stop. Before you begin to think that I'm obsessed with consonantal matters like this, I would like you to notice that the *d*'s *all concern the character and intents of Fortinbras,* beginning with the lead word *thinking* in line 19. The consonants change once Claudius starts to say what *he* thinks of Fortinbras. This change happens in line 22 and is particularly strong because of the plosive of the medial *pester*, which stands out all the more because it is preceded by relatively urbane and quiet aspirates of *He* and *hath* and the fricative of *fail'd.* Claudius can "change his tune" to suit his subject, but he is no ham actor; he is very subtle about it, and it comes naturally to him. Look, for instance, at yet another proof of his supreme balance: the middle points of these four lines 22–25:

> pester
> surrender
> father
> brother

What does this suggest to the actor and—through him—to an audience? *Pester/surrender* are what Fortinbras does and wants; his *father* (old Fortinbras) and our *brother* (old Hamlet) are the historical essence of the present international conflict. Shakespeare the playwright and Claudius the clear-spoken politician are making exposition and strength of balance of character as clear as crystal.

The *So much for him* is beautifully dismissive, as has frequently been noted in analyses of this scene. The fact that the phrase is the completion of a line of iambic pentameter is of course a straightforward indication that not much of a pause before or after it is called for. Claudius is businesslike and swift of purpose if not exactly of speech.

26 Thus much the business is: we have here writ
27 To Norway, uncle of young Fortinbras,
28 Who, impotent and bedrid, scarcely hears
29 Of this his nephew's purpose . . .

Although he cannot end his speech on a resounding note because of the inconclusiveness of the outcome of the Norway-Denmark disagreement, Claudius nonetheless does his level best to end conclusively. Claudius has sent Fortinbras' uncle a memo; but he makes it sound strong: *Writ* is at the end of the line and therefore gets a fine prominence. With its final *t*, the word no doubt echoes around the assembly, or it certainly did in an older school of declamatory acting of which the Shakespearean tradition was a beginning. Claudius' sheer poise is quickly and suavely apparent again in the agile lip and tongue changes of *impotent and bedrid* (p, t, t, n, d, d).

The pace of the speech does not quicken toward its kingly, commanding, and easy conclusion but becomes phonetically more expansive and therefore very evenly paced or even slow: in music, *andante* ("walking pace"). Let me explain. The lines we have looked at from 16 on have dealt only with the war and not with personal matters as the previous lines had. Observe how Claudius slows down after delivering the mechanics of international squabbles to address (in front of quite an assembled court, remember) two members of his own staff who are to act as messengers.

> . . . and we here dispatch
> You, good Cornelius, and you, Voltimand

After the reasonably brief word *dispatch*, whose vertical vowel *a* is crispened by the final *tch*, two assonantal *oo*'s occur that can only slow down any actor who says them: *You, good.* (I am well aware that the pronunciation of the 1980s, especially in the U.S. and Canada, differs from sixteenth-century English and that *good* is now shorter. But I'm not trying to tell you how to act a part; instead, I'm showing you how the words in your roles can be approached and loved so that they form a character appreciable to an audience and true to a script. In any case, my point still stands because of the following *you* in the same lines, as you will see.) *You* is repeated, putting the brakes on further. Cornelius and Voltimand are names hardly easy to skip over, particularly if they are to be heard at all. Look at what happens next, caused by the following vowels: *ea, ee, o, aw, ay, oo, ur, eh, ow, o, o, ee, ay, ar, ow, eh, el, eh, ay, eh, oo.*

> For bearers of this greeting to old Norway,
> Giving to **you** no further personal power
> To business with the King, more than the scope
> Of these dilated articles allow.
> Farewell, and let your haste commend your duty.

CORNELIUS AND VOLTIMAND   In that, and all things, will we show our duty.

KING   We doubt it nothing. Heartily farewell.

We have seen, then, that the *balance* of a speech, its *sentence construction*, its *pattern of vowels* and *consonants*, if noticeable to an actor who has learnt how to look for them, all serve to create the character.

A REMINDER CHECKLIST FOR SCENE STUDY

Complete Short Physical and Vocal Warm-up

raise eyebrows, tense, release
scrunch eyes and nose, tense, release
purse lips, tense, release
turn head left, tense, release
turn head right, tense, release
raise head, tense, release
lower head, tense, release
raise arms, clench fists, tense, release
pull stomach in, tense, release (repeat)
push stomach out, tense, release (repeat)
tighten buttocks, push out pelvis, tense, release
press knees together, tense, release
raise toes, tense, release
yawn
stressing the *h*, repeat *me-hay, me-hay, me-hay*
stressing the *m*, repeat *a-hum-a, a-hum-a, a-hum-a*
loosen your jaws with *ah-eh-ee-oo-o-aw-ah* ten times
maintain your range by doing *ah*, starting high, ending low, slowly
    getting higher and lower
for your lips and tongue and jaw, do:
Planning to plop in the public pool?
Blame Blake's bulbs.
Damned disinheriting countenance!
. . . and finally, for the relaxation that only agility and concentration
    can produce:
The sixth sick sheik's sixth sheep's sick,
concluding with:
She stood on the balcony, inexplicably mimicking him hiccuping,
    amicably welcoming him in.

Checklist for Everything

Ask yourself these questions of your part in the scene:

    1. *Falling cadence:* Am I ever going down when going up might
be better?
    2. Do any *d* sounds need emphasizing or unfocusing?
    3. Are there any *m* or *n* or *mn* sounds that aren't coming over
as strongly as the vowels around them?

4. Are my ng sounds being heard. Should I focus on them?

5. Any sibilants sounding hissy? What can I do?

6. Am I giving a glottal stop where it isn't needed? Are there places where one might mean something to my character?

7. Are my plosives clear? Are there any that signal something about my character and the character's mood or feeling?

8. Any polysyllabic words that the character uses for an interesting reason? (Remember, *all* reasons for speech in good plays are interesting!)

9. Any sentences that keep the main point back until the end (periodic sentences)? How can I use them to create my character through my voice?

10. Any repeated patterns of rhythm in my character's lines? What do they say about my character?

11. Any rapid changes of thought or rhythm? Should I change the pace? Is a change of pace perhaps unavoidable?

12. Any sounds in my lines that might be intended to sound like the experience my character has lived or is living through?

13. Are there any phrases the value of which I cannot see? (Omit them and discover the reason for their presence!)

CHECKLIST FOR TEACHER OR COACH

This checklist might be useful for rehearsal scenes or comments on the vocal components of performances in a theatre school or university.

Breath and Projection
Is the actor:

—breathing from the diaphragm?

—providing closeness of effect by projection? (Which sounds are not satisfactorily projected?)

—straining? Where? On what sounds? Because of bad breathing?

—enlarging without exaggerating?

Quality of Sounds and Dexterity
Is the actor:

—sounding vowels appropriately? Note deviations and difficulties.

—sounding plosives effectively? Too much? Too little?

—slowing to pronounce, or agile? Where? What on?

Inflection and Comprehension

Is the actor aware of the following? Is the actor perhaps too aware and therefore signaling? Of which of the following elements is the actor obviously not aware?

Quality of polysyllabic words.
Structure of periodic sentences.
Glottal stops.
Patterns of rhythm.
Alliteration.
The use of patterns of sibilants.
Rapid voice changes.
Pattern of inflection monotonous?
Masculine and feminine endings.
Punctuation.
Repetition as a character trait.
Rhythmic similarities between characters.
Personal pronouns. (Does the actor emphasize them only when really necessary?)
Does facial expression ever go against the sound produced?
Is there vocal give-and-take with other characters?
Use of pauses.

What Actors Say About Vocal Craft

While I was writing this book, I was fortunate to have the opportunity of speaking to working performers who had seldom been asked the kinds of questions I asked them. The actors were pleased to be able to articulate some of the problems they had encountered in their own careers and to share their experience with others. As you read through the interviews that follow, you will find the expression of a common task—acting the truth. Every one of the actors mentions the word at least once.

PROJECTION AND SOME OTHER ASPECTS OF THE CRAFT: AN INTERVIEW WITH GERALDINE PAGE

(Miss Page spoke to me at the Music Box Theatre, W. 44th Street, New York, after a performance of *Agnes of God* on Wednesday, November 23, 1982. She had just returned from Europe from a week's vacation with her husband, the actor Rip Torn, and this was her first night back on stage.)

HILL: I see your shopping bag from Paris beside your chair, and tonight's show was your first night back with *Agnes of God* after returning from France this very afternoon. You look well, but you must be tired. What is it like? How do you do it? How was it tonight?

PAGE: I was frightened. I hadn't spoken for ten days! I was in Tunisia, in Spain, in France, relaxing hectically. So I was frightened I'd go *mi-mi-mi-mi* in a tiny voice; after all, it's a bunch of feathers I've got to work with, you know—it goes up. Well, I just have to yank it down into place.

HILL: How?

PAGE: Well, nine-tenths of it is willpower with me, and I've worked on it slowly over the years. I know now that I should have spent much more time working on it at the beginning of my career but, you see, I was hired so much—I wasn't working as assiduously as I should have.

HILL: Do you think your lack of work on the "voice of feathers" did you harm?

PAGE: I should have worked harder. When Elia Kazan and Tennessee Williams (who thought at first that I was far far too young for the part) hired me as the Princess on *Sweet Bird of Youth*,[1] I had been told to "do it as big as you can." So I just went bonkers with my voice and had a wonderful time! "Just talk loud," I was told. Well, I couldn't, really. Tennessee still thought I was too young, and they offered the part to everybody else, but no one would do it or could do it, so finally they asked me to. Well, I worked. I worked very hard. On the voice. On projecting. I came out one day and boomed. What did my coach do? *He kept making me be heard.* He'd go into the other room and insist on hearing me from there. I realized the most important thing of all was clarity.

[1] At the Martin Beck Theatre, New York, in 1959, directed by Elia Kazan and with Paul Newman, Geraldine Page, and Rip Torn.

HILL: What about breath control in a part like that? Projecting and breathing, being clear, being heard, being the part too?

PAGE: Hm, yes. There was a line I was running out of breath on: "I flew, and I flew. I flew as fast and fast as I could." My coach said, "Stay on the vowels rather than losing all your breath on the consonants." The trouble in this line was, you see, the fricatives. All those f's take up a lot of your breath, you know. So, from then on, I concentrated on the vowels.

HILL: You mean that everything was all right from then on?

PAGE: No. Then there was another line, naturally, for which this didn't work at all. So I asked what was wrong this time, and he said I had to hum on the m's and stress the consonants and not the vowels.

HILL: To be heard at all?

PAGE: To be heard at all. That is, after all, necessary, isn't it? Eric Portman had a beautiful remark on this subject, not necessarily to his credit: "Oh," he once said, "if it's *important*, I make sure they hear it!"

HILL: Getting back to what you said earlier about projection—which is what being heard is—and your nine-tenths willpower, how hard is it to get back into form after time off?

PAGE: Well, during all those days off that I've just had I was really like a racehorse that had held back, or been held back. To put it another way, because I was so happy to get back here to this stage and this show and this dressing room I . . . well, I shot out of a cannon.

HILL: Some actors experience a particular and special physical state of being when they are projecting . . .

PAGE: Oh, yes! I feel the *ease* when it goes out.

HILL: And when it's not?

PAGE: And when it's not, I have to pick everything up off the floor and it weighs ten times as much. I keep a journal of how performances go, and I know that it's nice when it flows out, when it really goes and there's no strain. That's wonderful.

HILL: And with breathing you find the same thing?

PAGE: There's the challenge to find the *spot*, the breathing place, the *caesura*, where you take the initiative to pick things up again if they are getting a bit low, and then it's now flowing out easily.

HILL: Have you ever been conscious of a particular vocal effect, loved it, and been determined to repeat it? I'm talking about the fact that audiences often need to find pleasure in the actor's voice as well as his character and the unfolding of the plot.

PAGE: I know exactly what you're talking about. But I want to get them involved in what I'm saying rather than with the technique—they shouldn't notice just the technique. It's the difference between listening (in music) to someone play with great technique in order to display that technique and someone letting themselves be creative. I'm speaking, remember, about artists who *have* technique. Before this century, orchestras' main purpose was to play the music, to make music. Now, however, quite a few seem to be so preoccupied with technique that they don't realize the beauty of the music.

HILL: They sometimes play as fast as they can?

PAGE: Sometimes, yes. Actors too. You need to be able to play both fast and slow and you don't learn one first.

HILL: What *do* you learn first? Feeling or technique?

PAGE: Well, that's the great controversy right now in the theatre and in the theatre schools, isn't it? If you learn to be truthful first but not to be heard, it's terribly hard to learn later to be heard. And if you learn to be heard first of all but don't pay attention to speaking truthfully it's terribly hard to lose that way of speaking later and to learn to speak truthfully. Now in some schools they are working on developing both at the same time, so it won't be such a case of the chicken or the egg and which comes first.

HILL: Rapid change of subject now. Do you do any relaxation exercises before performances?

PAGE: Let me tell a story. A few years ago, Ethel Merman was in a show where they had to replace the Stage Manager for a week. This young and nervous S.M. goes to her dressing room to give the thirty minute call and says (because he'd been used to this way of doing things somewhere), "Miss Merman, would you like to warm up?" Her reply was loud and nearly blew him away: "*What f-o-r?????*" For this play, *Agnes of God*, I did have to do some relaxation exercises up to two months into the run before going on, and also when I went offstage, because of the tension of not having things decided. Some of these scenes come high and fast, you know. But now I don't have to do that anymore.

HILL: When you do do them (and when you still need to), what sort of relaxation exercises are they?

PAGE: Oh, the usual thing: head down between the knees and breathing very deeply. Loosening up.

HILL: And for the voice?

PAGE: Ah. For the voice. I listen to *Manon Lescaut*. I've listened to it every day for four years. People get irritated by it, I'm sure, but I sing along, I hum along. When I started doing this, I couldn't keep up with Monserat Caballe, only with Placido Domingo. But slowly it gets better. When there comes a part in one of Caballe's arias where I simply can't get it right—I'm not a singer anyway—I hum along.

HILL: What does it do for you?

PAGE: Warms up the pipes. Makes the voice more elastic. That's what it does.

HILL: I'd like to refer back to an earlier question. Do you ever get so much pleasure from a vocal effect, a certain sound, say, that you know night after night is going to produce a thrill in the house?

PAGE: Oh yes, Oh, yes. Unfortunately if I get to enjoy it too much, it disappears. If I get proud of it, it can go away. It's the old *hubris* thing. Once I had something—it was a gesture, not a vocal effect in this case—which I *loved*. But then I told somebody about it and it went away.

HILL: You must be *in the play* as well as technically skillful.

PAGE: In the beginning of doing *Agnes of God* we had trouble with the fact that the audience *enjoyed* it! "How can they laugh?" we asked ourselves, "it's so sad." What they were really enjoying, of course, was the fact that we were doing it and the fact that they were being moved by it at the same time.

HILL: You mean the audience in an ideal state knows that you are actresses, enjoys your effects, appreciates your acting, and at the same time thinks it's really happening? That there's an identification and distance existing together?

PAGE: Quite. The main perception of the audience must be of the concept and their appreciation of my skill must be less than their appreciation of the content that skill is being used to deliver.

HILL: Is there any advice you feel you could give to young actors?

PAGE: I think those last things we've been talking about are probably the most important of all, and I'm glad to be saying them. When I graduated from the Goodman School in Chicago I was asked to teach a class in rehearsal at DePaul University in the same city. I didn't like that. I didn't really feel I could teach. But now, as I say, I'm happy to mumble on to you with feathers in my voice. There are things you can say that are helpful to other people, to young actors. For instance, I listen a great deal to classical music. It gives me a sense of form and pattern. It helps me a lot. Let's see . . . the first best piece of advice that comes to my mind here and now is that if you really want to be able to express the maximum variety of things, then the more technical mastery you can achieve the more fun you're going to have.

HILL: Anything else?

PAGE: Oh, there's so much that I do, really. All those mini sit-ups I do at home to strengthen my abdominal muscles and the singing lessons I take that do the same thing. Just before going onstage I'll do the vowels *a e i o u* on a descending scale to get the lower register warmed up. I do the exercise of whispering in short phrases—that's something I can do in the wings before an entrance. There are, of course, tongue exercises that I ought to do a lot more.

HILL: What's the most important thing of all when an audience is there?

PAGE: Ha! Not to bore them.

AN INTERVIEW WITH CANADIAN ACTRESS FIONA REID ON ASPECTS OF VOCAL TECHNIQUE

(I spoke to Fiona Reid during the run of *Duet for One* at the Centaur Theatre in Montreal. She had recently taken voice-work with Kristin Linklater at the Stratford Shakespeare Festival in Ontario.)

HILL: Projection is nine-tenths willpower, many actors say. For you, is it any more than that? Is there anything that you especially do? Apart from shout? Is there any . . .

REID: For me, projection has always been a psychological thing. I have a mental image in my mind of who I want to communicate to and the size of the space in which I have to communicate.

HILL: You mean one member of the audience?

REID: No, the physical space that I inhabit as an actor gives me an idea and it's instinctual after that. There have been a couple of times when, after playing in a 2200-seat house like Stratford, I've come to a smaller place like the Toronto Free Theatre that (maybe once) I've been made aware that I didn't have to use as much, but that was simply because I hadn't made the mental adjustment.

HILL: Use as much what?

REID: Use as much vocal energy, I would call it.

HILL: Is there anything extra you have to do and, if so, where does it come from?

REID: It's certainly nothing I think about when I'm doing it. If the demands of the play are indeed quite heavy, I make sure that my abdomen is free, that my ribs are free to expand and that I've got them used to expanding . . . because you see we've all been through bad training, good training, and then finding out what works for us, and the dangerous thing is that I did all this rib-reserve stuff and what it did was build more tension, so I was producing a tense voice and what I've now come to is that I'm allowing my instrument to do what it was created to do.

HILL: Is that the result of your Linklater session?

REID: Much of it is, yes. I think it's fair to say that very few actors produce their voices freely. And projection is often got at by some means of straining in the chest, straining in the abdomen, or just pushing the vocal cords together. Projection is not a problem for me as a result of Kristin's work because I'm producing my voice from lower down. I'm not going from here [*touches abdomen*]; I'm now going from here [*touches groin area*]. And I'm involving more of my body in the production of the sound. You'll find that most actors are using only one part of their body.

HILL: Can I ask you if there's at all a special physical state to the point where the audience notices a different kind of person?

REID: Well, I think that's just if you don't do it properly. I think that the work that I did with Kristin is only going to make sense to me in the ensuing years because, initially, I didn't incorporate this training to the benefit of the role. There's the danger that you are so overcome by having a free voice that you don't necessarily adapt it to the demands of the play and the production. If you don't use this stuff, well you are producing . . . let me see if I can describe it . . . It's so resonant . . . I don't know how to describe it. All I know is that it's not enough. It's only one part of the acting process, and the danger is in taking it all for its own sake and ... A little learning is a dangerous thing. It depends on how good an actor you are: you can have the freest voice in the world but finally somebody's going to sit there and say, "Who cares?" unless you've got something else to give.

HILL: Suppose you were lying on your back on the stage. If you were in that position, would there be anything special you would have to do?

REID: I can't see why. If anything it would be easier on your back because your body doesn't assume any of the ridiculous position we assume when standing up.

HILL: Quite. Because it's completely supported.

REID: You see the reason I'm talking more about this is, in the summer, I involved myself in this training session in Stratford which is now paying off for me because it is there in me and I am not thinking about it. And this summer it didn't necessarily pay off because I had just learned it and it was foreign. And then I forgot about it. And now it's actually serving up to my work. And that's why I think it's so important for an actor to keep filing information. I was at a point in my career where my instrument was limiting the emotions that I wanted to convey. I had a lot more power emotionally than I had vocally, and now there is more of a match between my vocal power and my emotional substance.

HILL: And obviously that means a lot less frustration.

REID: Yes. And I'm not straining my voice. I used to do two shows of *Automatic Pilot*[2] a day, and I had to smoke in the show, which didn't help, and I'd find that after two days of two shows a day I had a tired voice. Kristin has taught me that *there's no such thing as losing your voice*. It actually doesn't happen. Once I went in to her and said I had lost my voice; she sent everybody out of the room and worked with me for

[2] a play by Erica Ritter

fifteen minutes and I had an amazing range and absolute clarity. The danger is in actors who are very conscious of their voices and how nice they sound ... Unfortunately a lot of people like this confuse this with good acting ... and in many ways it has been coincidental to good acting, but finally the veteran theatre-goer is looking for something more, because ultimately you can see through the actor who is using this or listening to himself at the expense of something else.

HILL: You said that there are some actors who like special vocal effects; you must nevertheless know, the freeing of your voice notwithstanding, that there's an effect you can create within the role that you as an actress know is good and you are determined to make successful.

REID: Actors work two different ways. An actress like Susan Wright comes up with the sound first ...

HILL: ... of the emotion, you mean?

REID: Yes; and the core second. She has a real director's instinct. She knows the result. I work less in that order. For me the vocal expression really is the tip of the iceberg. And I may have in the recesses of my mind an idea of how that sounds, but I am very wary of becoming conscious of that.

HILL: Why?

REID: Well, it's exactly parallel to this: knowing how something sounds to get a laugh (granted I may be able to say to somebody, "You've got to go up at the end of the line and not fake the pause," blah, blah, blah ... because my technique is fairly good, I know that that's what's required to get the laugh). That's fine. But if I don't ally that to the truth of the moment and the truth of the situation, it won't get the laugh. So just the same thing happens vocally: I may know that a certain vocal tenor works for a certain moment, and I know where to pitch something, say—but I don't ever think I must do that every time, I don't obligate myself to that, because the danger is that this will become the effect and I'll lose the core that brought the effect. So, if one night I don't do it, I don't kill myself.

HILL: What if it's a comedy and it's a laugh line?

REID: You won't get the laugh just because you do it a certain way. Well, some people will. It's just that the kind of actor I am, I can't do that. It's just my mental approach because, if I don't obligate myself to it, chances are that four times out of four I'll do it that way anyway. But again to me those things come from the truth of the moment. I ask myself to be the kind of actress that does everything truthfully, but I have to be . . . I *ask myself* to be so replete with a technique and a system of approach to my work that I can exploit that moment to its technical height.

HILL: What happens on nights when you're not feeling well and you really don't want to be in the theatre?

REID: Well it's different with every play as to how you tackle that problem, because some plays you can coast through more than others. The one I'm doing now is absolutely impossible to do that with. I have learned that, if I find at the half hour that I'm elsewhere, I make sure that my instrument is ready. I maybe do more than I would normally. I'll make sure that I've got a nice stretch between the abdomen and the shoulder, and that my abdomen is free and then I'll pant on the diaphragm just to make sure it's free and will respond to any emotions that may come. I try to work at a point of departure because the danger is that you'll do what I call "trying to digest the whole meal." You think, "How am I ever going to get through this?" You're trying to digest the whole play and so just giving yourself zero. So the best thing to do is be like a conductor and not think about the whole symphony, just think about the first note. Because if the first note goes wrong, chances are the rest will go wrong too. So, what I do is try to concentrate on the other person. And what I find works as a trick for this show is that I focus on the other character. That frees me more than thinking, "God, how can I get myself going?" It's like sex. If you're continually focusing on yourself and getting yourself going, nothing's going to happen. You focus on the other person and ultimately something is going to work.

HILL: Of course, because all acting is reacting, isn't it?

REID: I think acting gets simpler and simpler. As Uta Hagen said, "Unfortunately, good acting looks so simple that you'll never get the response from your audience that you'd hoped for." So there's the frustration.

HILL: Did you read the interview with Paul Newman in *Time* magazine? He said, "People think it's so simple. All I have to do is be Paul Newman, but they have no idea what I have to go through to be that."

REID: Well, it's a facetious statement when I say it's simple. Sometimes I wish I could go out and buy a new me like a violinist can go out and buy a new violin. But we can't do that. I think one gets long periods of stupidity and occasional moments of brilliance. That's how it feels. Now I feel that I have some clarity in my performance. If you had spoken to me a week ago it was altogether different. Sometimes it's like wading through mud with snowshoes on. But the simpleness of it is this: The better you concentrate, the better actor you'll be. I think the best actors have extraordinary concentration. That is a simple truth, but to have that is quite extraordinary. You get more technique as you get older, but you still need that sharpness.

HILL: What you're saying about simplicity, getting rid of ornament and excess and focusing and concentrating . . . Sir Alec Guinness said, "Give emphasis firstly to the verb, secondly to the noun and lastly (if at all) to adverb and adjective, and *never* emphasize a personal pronoun, except for a particularly good reason." What do you think?

REID: The director with whom I did my second Shakespeare, that was his cardinal rule—*always the verb*. Two years ago I asked him what to do with my work on Shakespeare and that's exactly what he told me. Concentrate on the verb. The man I did my first Shakespeare with, who shall remain nameless, really enjoyed the personal pronoun. And that to me is the easy, bad way. That is really Shakespeare for the bozos. Because it's like "This is who I'm talking about" and "That's who I'm talking to." So, if you're only worried about the audience understanding the broad chunks, at least you know who is being referred to. It's just too easy. "I go" or "I go"? You wouldn't believe how many choose the latter! And what they do is set in the audience's mind, "As opposed to whom?" Well, I mean, who else was there? And then you start thinking about all sorts of other things which you needn't. But with Shakespeare, there is so much *action* in the poetry that you are making a mistake if you use the adjectives, and you become static. It's in the verb. "Oh you *leaden messengers* that *ride* upon the *speed* of *fire*." Those leaden messengers are those bullets that are going to kill my husband, my love. You get so much closer to the rhythm that Shakespeare intended if you look at what the verb gives you. The danger is that you get a very ponderous type of speech in Shakespeare if you don't appreciate the verb. The verb will give you the tempo, it will give you so much.

HILL: What about other kinds of plays?

REID: I'd say that with any well-written play, you can use what you learn in Shakespeare. In this play, *Duet for One*, which is a well-written play, I find . . . You've probably read Bertram Joseph's book *Acting Shakespeare* . . . well, there is a device called something, where you set up one premise and then he says the opposite. For example he says, "My father, etcetera, etcetera, *but I* . . . ," etcetera. In long speeches, if you don't use this ability to be clear about what your important words are, your audience will never follow you.

HILL: That's just like what Eric Portman said—"If it's important, I make sure they hear it."

REID: Oh yes. Because you have to choose what they hear. I can bet you they're not listening to everything. And you should realize they're not listening to *everything*. This is why modulation is very important. But you see the thing that I'm finding now is that I'm getting comments from my peers about my vocal expression and clarity that I never thought of, so it shows you that—well it's like World War II in the final invasion. You attack on all fronts. You go at the acting, at the voice, and you just file all these things in. Because if I took a vocal approach to my acting or a visceral approach to my voice, neither would be right.

HILL: But you have a charming or distinctive quality in your voice.

REID: But some people play that.

HILL: I know. Do you?

REID: I don't. I pitch certain characters intentionally . . . There's a dangerous point you reach as an actor when you realize you have certain identifiable characteristics, a very dangerous point where you either start to play that, or you use it and always keep it slightly out of reach. I'm becoming aware of my voice replicating the emotional depth I'm achieving as an actress. I want to keep it out here, because if it becomes something I contain, well I've seen it happen to other actors . . . It really gets quite boring. And when you see someone like Maggie Smith get tired of it in herself and make a bold attempt and with extraordinary success, I think, overcome things she became tired of in herself, I find it a most inspiring example.

HILL: You mentioned earlier that you pitch certain characters. Where would you say you pitch for the character you're now playing?

REID: At first I didn't have a solidity; I wasn't centered enough; I wasn't giving an air of confidence; I wasn't occupying my space. And I realized that when I started my performance with a kind of "Bah Bah!! I am here, I know what I'm doing," etcetera, it helped me. And when I was angry I really had to come from very deep down. I've watched actresses get shrill and there's a danger of that (especially for a woman) if you get too much up in the chest. I think anger is a tough one. Because for women it represents something . . . In society we have many adjectives to describe a woman in anger. She's bitchy or petulant. Those, to me, are attempts to short-circuit the anger. But if a man does it, it has more social acceptance.

I feel the audience shake when I get angry with a bass tone. They're not used to hearing a woman's voice that low.

HILL: What do you think of the idea that an evening of an all-woman play would be unbearable unless there were at least two or three actresses who could represent bass or baritone?

REID: Well, it's my contention that women really *are* like that. You're seeing a new kind of actress come out now. When you're put in touch with what's going on inside you, you start to do that.

It's a part of the socializing process that limits the voice, in a man as well: socially we think of a man having a lower voice and a woman having a higher voice. But the danger is that some actresses try to go too far too fast and they try to get a strength and they get nodules instead; men do too, because there's this vogue now for having a deep voice. But it's *your* voice you have to find. It's as bad to affect a deep voice. Whatever your voice is, you can modulate it. I think it's the voice that's *stuck* that becomes boring. In casting any play, whether it's women or men, you've got to find different tenors of voices. I guess I've seen enough actresses getting angry on stage with a certain shrillness. That's a particular bone I have to pick.

HILL: Do you have bones to pick about your own voice?

REID: I did have nodules!

HILL: From nature?

REID: Oh no. From trying and pushing and trying to sound like a man and trying to be strong. Doing all this and having the most extraordinary tension.

HILL: Often nodules are caused by characters assuming thick, heavy voices and wearing too much vocal makeup.

REID: Usually it's from trying to reach notes you're not trained to reach properly so you're tightening. I was singing in a register I wasn't ready to sing in, but also I was carrying around a lot of physical tension that I was totally unaware of. And I didn't have a very good forward resonance.

HILL: What are your warm-up exercises?

REID: Again that's changed since Kristin. I do *hohuma ha-hum-a* just to get the sound coming out. A lot of loosening of the tongue and the jaw, because that tends to get in the way. I don't do enough for forward resonance. I should do more just to get the cheeks and around the nasal cavities resonating because that's the dead part of me.

HILL: Do you do this every show?

REID: Most shows. It depends what I've done in the day. And then making sure that I'm breathing quite low—not shallow breathing.

HILL: When you shift from the theater to film or TV, what do you find yourself having to do?

REID: No problem. Because it's communication. And when it's a camera, I know it's a camera I have to communicate to and I adjust. It's absolutely natural.

HILL: Did you find this from the beginning?

REID: Yes. It was never a problem. And, if it is, it's because you're being an actor as opposed to playing the situation. Once or twice I've been reminded to give more projection in a scene. If I'm having problems with a scene, then I may have a problem being heard because I'm working on something else and I'm retreating maybe. But if I'm clear about what I'm doing and what I want to communicate there's never a problem now. Projection can be blown out of proportion. Being heard has a lot to do with clarity.

HILL: Do you mean clarity of intent, clarity of consonants . . . ?

REID: I mean the tongue. A tongue that is not lazy. Most of us have lazy tongues. There is a tendency to project and not to have a tongue that functions very efficiently, so it's just flapping in the breeze and it's just stopping a lot of *emotion* from coming out and it's stopping a lot of the *language* from coming out. More than anything, many actors eat their words whether they talk loud or soft. Most of us can shout, but to be heard is far different. And this is where the mainstage at Stratford is so interesting. You can yell all you want and not be heard.

See, very often people have quite literally a stiff upper lip. Or they use their jaw, or they work their jaw on every word. You just have to hold your jaw still and practice speaking, and learn not to use your jaw every time you say something, so it's coming from the right place.

HILL: Are you saying in a way that freedom comes from control?

REID: You won't do what you want to unless all your articulators are in shape. You're limiting yourself if you have emotional freedom and a lazy tongue, or a stiff jaw or a stiff upper lip. You can have all the emotional freedom in the world, but if you have a stiff upper lip, who *cares*? It's just not going to come out.

HILL: Have you ever seen this one?

REID: [*Reading*] "She stood on the balcony inexplicably mimicking him hicupping, amicably welcoming him in." The secret is to think of what it means because, if I think of how it sounds, it will mess me up. I have a picture of her "inexplicably mimicking him"; that helps; and then the progression, she was "inexplicably mimicking him hiccupping . . . amicably welcoming him in." Now that's two separate thoughts. I would get the thought first, to do it.

HILL: In the voice and in the emotion, try whatever way of acting you're approaching it with, everything has to be split up into little separate units of meaning. It really has, or else it's not going to make any sense to anyone at all. Young actors often do not read much. What do *you* most often want to say to young actors and actresses about their flaws and what they're doing wrong?

REID: When you serve one theory or concept, you're short-circuiting what a difficult process acting is. And the best thing to do when you're learning something as an actor is to take all kinds of things in and then see how they serve you. I've learned so much from method-type workshops, but then that's only become interesting when I've gone into a stringently disciplined program or rehearsal period when none of that was asked for, and it's served me. But I wasn't allowed to serve it up, I had to work in another framework.

HILL: It wasn't an obsession?

REID: I guess that's my reservation about an actor learning about his craft—that an actor may become too messianic about what he does. The danger is that you lose the joy of serving something higher than yourself. You start to project an earnestness that's very boring. I'm learning how important it is to continue your growth as an actor. But the question of degree is so important I guess I've learned not to try *too* hard. You become self-centered if you try too hard. If you *believe* in your feeling, or if you *believe* in your voice, or if you *believe* in your "star" quality, you lose the essence of what you do, which is that you are there serving a playwright in order to communicate something to an audience. And I think the truth of that is sometimes lost in the b.s. of the business.

PACING YOURSELF—AN INTERVIEW WITH KAREN VALENTINE

Many performers have such command of their technique—which could also be expressed as confidence in themselves and their art—that they have little advice to offer beyond "Go ahead and do it . . . if you can do it, you can do it." But most would agree with a Ziegfield Follies star of the twenties in her statement "The whole secret about this Follies business is to be cool but act hot." (Kenneth Tynan, *Show People*)

Karen Valentine, familiar to North America for her character in *Room 222* as well as for numerous successful stage appearances and her CBS movies, spoke to me during breaks in the shooting of *Illusions* in October 1982. I reprint the interview in its entirety because she is an especially relaxed performer, and this interview was conducted in cramped corners of a car showroom between takes on a cold Sunday morning.

HILL: You said last week when we were shooting the tearoom scene that you'd had a cold. What happens in a film [*where actors often have to shoot the end of a scene days or even weeks before they shoot its beginning, because of location and other problems*] when you have a cold? Is there anything you do, any vocal technique you call up to reduce the appearance of the fact?

VALENTINE: When I have a cold, then the character has a cold. I can't change that. There's nothing you can do. A while ago, I was touring with a play and, of course, had to be on stage. Well, I played the character as if she had one too. I had to. But when the camera is rolling and director shounts "Action!" you feel better and many of the symptoms vanish. Once I had to cry on stage, my nose was running: I was crying because of my cold and it fit perfectly. But this was just lucky, of course. It depends on what part you're playing. If the part requires a smooth, perfect voice then you have to take especially good care of your health, as singers have to do. If the character has a whiskey voice then it might be OK to go out every night and have a party and enjoy yourself that way. But usually you just have to take very good care of your health.

HILL: Do you use any special techniques to reproduce the master-take, in filming? When you've done a particu- larly good first master-shot and have to repeat that in various takes, close-ups, and other shots, do you have a way of repeating vocally what you've already done so well?

VALENTINE: No. Here's why. I try to bring the reality of the moment to whatever take is being shot.

HILL: Do you do any physical or vocal relaxation exercises before a stage performance or before filming?

VALENTINE: No. I do exercises normally; I keep in shape. I'm a strong person naturally. I work more on my own energy than on a lot of preparation suddenly before a performance. Now, of course, everybody is tense at the beginning of shooting, at the beginning of making a movie ... but there's no one pat thing I do to prepare. You've just got to be flexible. If it's a highly emotional scene, the ten- sion will help me, of course. You've got to use the life of the moment in this way and hope you can draw on what's happening around you. I'm a spontaneous rather than a planned performer, you see. Years ago I met an actor who did a *lot* of preparation; he'd got a *Gunsmoke* script and wrote out careful notes as a "subtext" for his character and the scene in which he was to be playing. I saw his script, and asked him what all those notes were about, what they were for. The pages were crammed with them. Well . . . I saw the show he did and when his scenes came he was off in his own world completely, there was absolutely no connection with the other people there. I need the connection. I want the interaction with the other people there. That's what acting is all about.

HILL: Acting is reacting.

VALENTINE: Yes.

HILL: "You gotta be cool and act hot." Isn't this rather like "the art that conceals art?"

VALENTINE: I think if you're hot you're hot. But yes. Although everybody has tricks, the ultimate trick is not to let the audience see the tricks. Some people in the audience may think that actors who sweat away are very good but it is so much better when you don't see the tricks, when you *don't see us working*. One of my favorite actors— Kenneth Macmillan—who played the Firechief in *Ragtime*, makes everything look so easy. That's great. That's the best kind of acting. I don't see his process. I think that's what acting is about. If you do all the crying for the audience they won't cry.

HILL: And often that's what they've paid for: to enter a theatre so that some actors can make them cry.

VALENTINE: Oh yes. I'm not interested in an actress who can cry. I'm interested in one who can have that effect on *me*.

HILL: You don't use "vocal tricks," then?

VALENTINE   I have them, yes. But I don't think I *use* them. I use myself, rather. The trick is to be a sponge, to be open. Of course, it depends on the role, again. There's no one trick because if you go on with a preconceived idea you might very well stunt everything. You've got to try to be in the moment of *what's going on*. If you're playing a bastard you never think you really *are* the meanest bastard in the world. You've got to convince *them* that you are. That's the point. Here's an interesting thing.

Yesterday, I was all day doing scenes about Larry [the character's husband in *Illusions*] being dead. In one I break down and cry; in another I'm strong about it, and in this particular scene "Cliff" came in, posing as Larry's brother, with bits of information. Well . . . two days ago my Uncle George died in California, and it didn't hit me until that scene last night, then it really hit me suddenly and personally. And I had to be strong. I was. You never know what's going to trigger your emotions. You must use the moment.

    If you think out what you're going to do in a scene and intend to stick to it, then you don't react to what's happening. Of course, it's much easier to work like this with a good actor; that makes it more fun to work rather than just make you nervous.

HILL: Is there anything you've wanted to tell young actors by way of advice or admonition perhaps?

VALENTINE: I've wanted to tell some older actors some things, I can tell you . . . The main thing in film acting, anyway, is not to allow the camera or script to inhibit you technically. I don't think people should beat themselves for making mistakes. We can't blame the light bulb that blows out, can we? Don't get nervous. That may sound easy to say, but just get your concentration back to square one and on what you're doing, the job you've to do and that you know you can do.

HILL: That's a delightfully positive answer to a negative question. Is there anything else you feel like saying to younger actors?

VALENTINE: Well, there is something that bugs me. Sometimes actors off-camera who are nonetheless in the scene give a lot less than they did when they were on-camera. That's no help at all. If I don't do the action for the other person when *I'm* off-camera, then I can see that it doesn't come properly for him or her on camera. You simply have got to keep up the energy of the master shot.

HILL: I noticed you were doing some leg exercises a while ago.

VALENTINE: Of course I was. This is a hard floor, these are high-heeled shoes, we've stood around a long time and I'm tired and my legs are sore. Aren't yours?

HILL: Yes. I'm glad you said that. You are doing the exercises to keep warm and happy.

VALENTINE: Right! I'm pacing myself. We've got quite a bit to go yet.

HILL: How do you pace yourself when takes can be so far apart? They're shifting the camera's position now to get a different shot from in front of the red Ferrari, and I'm finding it hard to keep my character and speak to you at the same time.

VALENTINE: You have to do what you feel to an extent, or you'll get nervous.

HILL: When takes are so far apart, how do you summon up the same pace, the same tempo? It's much harder than on stage, where the action is pretty well continuous.

VALENTINE: Much harder. You have to do what you feel and let the director be the outside eye. In a film, you can't be the judge of that yourself.

HILL: Do you watch your rushes, perhaps? Might that not help?

VALENTINE: No, I don't watch dailies. You might see something you don't like and start putting shackles on yourself. It's best not to see them.

HILL: What do you like least about filming?

VALENTINE: The lack of continuity . . . the things we've touched on, really . . . Having to wait emotionally because of technical problems.

HILL: What do you think is the hardest thing for a young actor hired for a movie part?

VALENTINE: The hardest thing is to come in cold, come in to a situation where all the others have been working perhaps for weeks and do a small scene. Rather than working all day and having the energy rolling.

THE ACTOR, ACCENT, TRADITION, AND ART— AN INTERVIEW WITH DOUGLAS CAMPBELL

Douglas Campbell is a great classical actor now living and working mainly in Canada. I saw him first when he was doubling Cassandra with other roles in Tyrone Guthrie's production of *The House of Atreus* at the Guthrie Theatre in Minneapolis in 1969, in which the range and pitch of his voice thrilled spectators with awe and pleasure. Campbell acts frequently at the Stratford Shakespeare Festival in Ontario, for which he has played Falstaff and many other difficult parts. He was born in Scotland.

HILL: Were you ever aware, or were other people ever aware of a Scottish accent in you?

CAMPBELL: Oh yes, I don't think you ever really lose your native tongue; you control it a bit when you're speaking naturally, but of course when I'm speaking to you it will return even more strongly . . .

HILL: Aye, a wee bit.

CAMPBELL: Yes, because one responds to the sort of native sound in the voice. I would say, generally speaking, that anyone with a good ear would know I was a Scot, yes.

HILL: On what vowels especially? Is it the *oo*—ü one?

CAMPBELL: I think the *oo* one and probably on the r's and the general attack on consonants. I think that the good Scots speaker uses a much more strong and definitive consonant attack. I wouldn't say that the vowels—yes, the o's I would say probably. Of course if you go right to the back of your throat, you know, like "binocular" or "Glasgow" or something like that, a glottal stop, I suppose that some . . . I don't think I ever was guilty of the glottal stop because my father, who was a Glasgow man but a Highlander in tradition, would have none of that in the house. We were constantly being stopped by him for that: "That is a hideous soünd," he would say, "and I don't wish to hear it anymore."

HILL: Have you found, coming from a place like Scotland, ever, an advantage in your own voice? Has it sharpened your ear in that you had to grow up with two languages?

CAMPBELL: Yes, I would say probably it has sharpened one's ear. I remember when I went into the theatre first in England, of course, everybody said, "You'll have to do something about your accent because it won't be acceptable. You'll never be able to get any decent parts." I would then draw myself up to my full height as many Canadians do and say, "I am not going to change the pattern of my speech; some Scotsmen have made it, you know." However, it was all pointed out to me very ably by Tyrone Guthrie that I didn't have a Scots accent, I had a Glasgow accent—something rather different.

HILL: Have you ever caught yourself on stage, in the middle of a performance, coming up with an ü rather than an *oo* and wondering what to do about it?

CAMPBELL: I really don't consciously think about accent unless I'm playing an accented part. Not now.

HILL: Do you ever do any exercise of the voice before going on?

CAMPBELL: I physically warm up, rather more than vocally warm up. Well, I do scales. Right now I'm doing the Nicholas Pennell warm-up classes—he always warms up, so he's running warm-ups for *The Dresser*. But if I'm doing it myself I just go up and down the scales and do triads, you know, and extend—the breathing actually gets it all warmed up so that it does go out there correctly.

I use any kind of technique that's around. I think there's rather a lot of vocal exercises done that don't seem to me to improve the quality of the voice much. They keep it in the same place but they don't give it much *range*. I would like to see a good deal more good *singing* taught; good singing teachers brought into the business so that people develop a sense of range, you know. Much training is off in the psychical research direction: "finding your center," all that sort of stuff. Which I suppose is very good, up to a point—it's important that people have a consciousness of the apparatus that relates to the erotic and all that kind of thing, but I think they ought to know about singing a song just as well.

I find the psychic searching to be silly and trivial and I find the protection of the spirit of the soul of the actor again runs against my traditions.

HILL: It's the audience's soul . . .

CAMPBELL: *That's* the one we want to get to, not mine! It's my job to stimulate and keep myself sharpened and perceptive, but not to protect *myself*. I find these sorts of platitudes like "finding your center" are very self-conscious making, you know.

HILL: When you're speaking quietly on stage and you are using extra energy to project, where do you find the energy is coming from?

CAMPBELL: Well, from as far down as I can push. That's like sustaining in singing; you're lifting the whole apparatus from down here.

HILL: Now if you're doing that lying on your back? Say, you're in a death-bed scene.

CAMPBELL: Yes. Well, I suppose from the back of the ribs then, really. I don't know, I haven't really analyzed that one particularly. When you're practiced in the business of speaking you don't really think about that that much; you try to fill the space with the sound you have to make. It's an imaginative process as well as a physical one. I think that really would be the most important element of all to be remembered, that speaking is part of the imagination and unless you really have some sense of where you're speaking and who you're speaking to, you are not going to be heard, no matter how you produce your voice.

HILL: Do you ever consciously think about vocal effect when you're on the stage?

CAMPBELL: No—I sometimes think I'm making a vocal effect and I immediately change it, because it means that I'm beginning to fall in love with something, some kind of aspect of what one's making as an effect. And I think once you've made the effect, if you lose touch with the sense of where it came from and it becomes an effect to you then obviously it's not true.

HILL: You think that the audience always notices that sort of thing?

CAMPBELL: I think they'll notice that you're not being true.

HILL: Of course.

CAMPBELL: Obviously there are differences. A naturalistic play such as the one I'm doing now—*The Dresser*—is naturalistic in terms of its characters being observable as human beings; self-conscious effects will argue against your own presentation, you know, your own feeling for the part, so you must be careful not to get into them. That doesn't mean that you don't play it the same pretty well. Once you've set the tune the tune stays pretty much the same unless something any other actor does changes the proportions; but it's like singing a duet together: you don't muck around with it unless you've got very good reason. On the other hand, if you're playing something like *The House of Atreus* which is really a choral work and a big opera, then sometimes the voice effect is *exactly the same thing as what you're supposed to be feeling, so that you have to train to make these impressions every time.* It's part of the detached, vocal awareness of where you fit into the scheme as you would in a big poetic work.

HILL: Do audiences like resonance? Do they crave depth?

CAMPBELL: I don't know that they always do, actually; I sometimes have difficulty, depending on where I'm speaking, on having too much vibrancy. My voice is produced in such a way that it has enormous declamatory power, but even when I'm speaking quietly, unless I'm very careful about it, in some auditoriums the actual resonance in the jaw tends to muddle the consonants. So I have to be very careful about that. I don't think audiences necessarily demand heavy speech. I remember one occasion when I was playing *The Gentle Shepherd* at the Edinburgh Festival for Guthrie. I was playing John the Commonweal in *The Three Estates* and therefore using a sort of really attacking baritone voice. And then I was playing the sort of young, gawky shepherd in *The Gentle Shepherd*, and Guthrie said, "It just isn't working. Try placing the voice extremely high." So I really played it with a falsetto, up there, practically a falsetto, very high note. And the girl's voice was much lower than mine, and it worked very well. I think it depends entirely on the relationships that you make. I'm not sure that audiences do respond constantly to masculine voices. In the theatre, almost anything you say as an absolute can be immediately turned round the next minute. Everything varies with the variation of the play, with the audience, the response to the director, everything that goes on.

HILL: When you have a cold and you're on the stage, what do you do with your voice?

CAMPBELL: Well, a cold—a head cold—doesn't really affect the voice too much in terms of the throat. When it moves down into the chest then you have simply to find a note that is comfortable to speak on without strain and slowly build from that. And it's extremely difficult: I had to play Falstaff last year when I suddenly had a throat infection of some kind and I had to play it all in a sort of bass grumble. Well, it's a very good test of your ability to get variety in pace and inflection, because you've got no variation at all in the notes, you know. So I think it's quite a good exercise; it would be a good exercise for actors to attempt to play something on one note and to find other ways to make the variance. In terms of pace, emphasis, pause, you know—all that sort of thing.

HILL: Are there any vocal things that annoy you especially in other actors?

CAMPBELL: Not having sufficient breath, so that the phrase is chopped in the middle, so that the sense of the line is destroyed, not necessarily only for the audience but for the fellow player, and not only the sense, but then a great gasp of air and another couple of lines and then another great gasp of air so that the intention of the line is gone, so that the rhythm for the other actor is thrown completely out of gear. That's why it's so splendid playing with someone like Nicholas Pennell whose apparatus is top-rank, you know; it's like playing with another musician: He relies on me to make the right kind of responses and I rely on him. And the speed and pace of the scene is developed by us both *listening* to one another, not only just in terms of intelligence, though that's important, but *musically* as well. There is a whole other dimension of play-acting which very few people pay any attention to today and that's the musical element.

HILL: Quite a lot of actors listen to music and they sing along with it; they maintain that this has produced some of the sharpness in their own ear.

CAMPBELL: I think there is absolutely no question of that at all. Just as I think we don't read enough, really. Most players don't read enough. On the whole I would say that most young people don't read enough. They don't read enough and they don't go to art galleries and they don't have interests outside themselves. It's astonishing how the theatre has dwindled—in a way I suppose because of the cinema and the television and all these dreadful commercials that people go after, you're constantly thinking about yourself and your own image and of how to put it across. I don't really think about *myself* at all. I think about what kind of character I would like to be rather than what I look like. I think that the whole of art is important to the actor and it's astonishing how few people really know anything about anything else other than what they do. And they don't do a great deal.

HILL: It could mean of course that you grew up with . . .

CAMPBELL: . . . tradition. Yes, but here am I and I'm trying to hand that on and I'm trying to give classes on it. I say that it's important to go look at paintings. "Why?" they say—"To increase your sense of color, design, what proportion is, how you might relate to someone else on the stage . . . That *all* perceptions must be sharpened if you're going to be a really good player."

HILL: And all within some kind of form.

CAMPBELL: Oh yes. The artistic form, the art form of art, so that you're not dealing with something which is naturalism or realism; you're dealing with already synthesized stuff that's *speaking* to you, that is made so that it affects your sensitivity. There's a balance in it; there's a decision about why that picture is painted the way it is, you know.

HILL: Does the demise of radio drama perhaps account in some measure for young actors' inattention to form?

CAMPBELL: It's a disaster. Radio drama had a strong tradition and there were some splendid radio actors who had a wonderful sense of place and imagination. People like John Drainie, who really was quite remarkable. Oh, lots of them. And there are still a lot of them about, but there's not that much radio work going on. People like Sandy Webster, who worked on radio for years. Oh naming names, it doesn't make any difference really—there are a lot of people who could do it very well. And the fact that we don't do it very much now is a great pity. And I think the broadcasting companies are making a great mistake in not pushing to have a very strong radio drama team again; I think people would listen to it; I think they get very tired watching that silly box. It really is a pain in the ass, isn't it?

Glossary

alle aussteigen	German for "everybody out," as in "everybody disembark"
assonance	A partial rhyme in which the vowel sounds correspond but the consonants differ, as in *brave* and *vain*
cadence	a. A falling inflection of the voice, as at the end of a sentence b. The general inflection or modulation of the voice
choric	Of or pertaining to a singing or speaking chorus; in the style of a chorus
chorister	A choir singer
circumflex	A mark used over a vowel to indicate quality of pronunciation
dialect	A regional variety of a language, distinguished from other varieties by pronunciation, grammar, or vocabulary
diphthong	A speech sound beginning with one vowel sound and moving to another vowel or semivowel position within the same syllable, e.g., *oy* in *boy*
elocution	The art of public speaking, with gesture, vocal production, and delivery (from Latin "elocutus"—spoken out)
empathy	Understanding so intimate that the feelings, thoughts, and motives of one are readily comprehended by another

explication de texte	A detailed reading and analysis of a text in each of its linguistic, compositional, and expressive parts and aspects
feminine and masculine endings	Words and phrases ending in weak and strong stresses respectively
forte	Musical term, loud
glottal stop	A speech sound produced by a momentary complete closure of the glottis, followed by an explosive release
indenture	A deed or contract
labial	A sound formed mainly by closing or partly closing the lips, as *b, m, v, w,* or a rounded vowel
legitimate stage	a. Of or pertaining to drama performed on a stage, as opposed to other media such as motion pictures or television b. Of or pertaining to drama of high professional quality, as opposed to burlesque, vaudeville, and the like
librettist	The scriptwriter of an opera or musical comedy, as opposed to the composer of the music
modulation	a. A change in pitch or loudness of the voice; an inflection b. The use of a particular intonation or inflection to produce meaning
morpheme	A unit of meaning that cannot be divided into smaller meaningful parts, as in *al* of *almost*
phoneme	The smallest unit of speech that distinguishes one word from another, e.g., *phon* in *phoneme*
piano	Musical term, soft
plethora	Superabundance
plosive	A speech sound whose articulation requires, at some stage, the complete closure of the oral passage as in the sound of *p* in *top* or *d* in *adorn*
rhetoric	The persuasive use of language to influence the thoughts and actions of listeners
sempre poco piano	Always a little softly—from Italian
sibilant	A speech sound that suggests hissing, as *s, sh, z,* or *zh*
sostenuto	A musical term meaning "in a sustained or prolonged manner"
sotto voce	Very softly (from Italian, "under the voice")
spondaic	Adjective from spondee (*see* spondee)
spondee	A metrical foot consisting of two long or stressed syllables

Selective Bibliography
of Books on the Voice

Anderson, Virgil A. *Training the Speaking Voice*. 3rd ed. New York: Oxford
University Press, 1977.
Part I—The Voice—chapters on relaxation, breathing, tone, resonance,
and expressiveness—many exercises.
Part II—Diction—pronunciation, clarity, etc. Good exercises.
Berry, Cicely. *Voice and the Actor*. London: Harrap, 1973.
Buehler, E. Christian and Wil A. Linkugel. *Speech Communication: A First
Course*. New York: Harper & Row, Publishers, 1969.
————*Speech: A First Course*. New York: Harper & Row, Publishers, 1962.
—similar to the above book—but longer. One complete chapter on Vocal
Communication, exercises on breathing, diction, flexibility, articula-
tion, pronunciation
—bibliography at the end of each chapter
Burgess, L. K. *Something to Say! A Comprehensive Textbook on Public
Speaking*. Sydney: McGraw-Hill Book Company, 1972.
—good section on voice production, clarity, articulation, and expression,
with exercises for each. Especially written for Australians
Bryant, Donald C. and Karl R. Wallace. *Fundamentals of Public Speaking*.
4th ed. New York: Appleton-Century-Crofts, 1969.
—chapter on Delivery—quite general. Appendix B has some exercises
but not for voice, rather for posture, relaxation, and gesture.

Capp, Glen R. *How to Communicate Orally.* Englewood Cliffs, N.J.: Prentice-Hall Inc., 1961.
  —usual stuff on breathing, phonation, resonation, and articulation (one chapter)
  —9 pages on preparing a speech for radio or TV
Cass, Carl B. *A Manner of Speaking: For Effective Communication.* New York: J.P. Putnam's Sons, 1961.
  —complete text on voice production
  —chapters on:—physics of sound
          —voice mechanism
          —quality of a voice
          —phonetics
          —ear training
          —enunciation and projection (projection, he says, is gained mainly by better articulation and breathing)
          —pronunciation
          —intonation patterns
          —speech personality
          —vocal flexibility
          —tempo and rhythm
  —many good exercises after each chapter
Crandell, S. Judson, Gerald M. Phillips, and Joseph A. Wigley. *Speech: A Course in Fundamentals.* Chicago: Scott, Foresman and Company, 1963.
  —the usual chapter on voice production
  Appendix A—extensive bibliography
  Appendix B—chronological table of speech education
Curry, S. S. *Foundations of Expression.* Boston: The Expression Company, 1907.
  —an old elocutionist's textbook. Based on a mind over matter approach—problems are caused partly by psychological, not mechanical problems. Psychology a bit dated but his comments on voice production are sound
Dickens, Milton. *Speech: Dynamic Communication.* 2nd ed. New York: Harcourt, Brace & World, Inc., 1963.
  —another similar chapter on elements of voice production
  —exercise for projection
Ecroyd, Donald H. *Speech in the Classroom.* 2nd ed. Englewood Cliffs, N.J.: Prentice-Hall Inc., 1969.
  —interesting chapters on child's learning of language, voice (mechanism, breathing, problems), diction, and vocal expressiveness
  —intelligently written
Eisenson, Jon and Paul H. Boase. *Basic Speech.* 2nd ed. New York: The Macmillan Company, 1964.
  —extensive chapters on the vocal mechanism, the components of speech

(including relation of pitch, volume and states of feeling, also into-
nation), gesture, phonetics, improving vocal problems, and diction

Garner, Dwight, L. *Idea to Delivery: A Handbook of Oral Communication.*
3rd ed. Belmont, California: Wadsworth Publishing Company Inc., 1979.
—textbook for public speaking—mainly on speech writing, one chapter
on voice (brief)

Lessac, Arthur. *The Use and Training of The Human Voice: A Practical
Approach to Speech and Voice Dynamics.* 2nd ed. New York: DBS Publications, Inc., 1967.
—good text

Linklater, Kristin. *Freeing the Natural Voice.* New York: Drama Book Spe-
cialists (Publishers), 1976.
—mainly on breathing, resonators, finding one's own voice. Last chapters
on words and texts

Macklin, Evangeline. *Speech for the Stage.* New York: Theatre Arts Books,
1966.
—chapters on projection, relaxation, breathing, resonance, articulation,
etc., and Speaking Shakespeare, and Dialects
—designed as actors' handbook

McBurney, James H. and Ernest J. Wrage. *The Art of Good Speech.* New York:
Prentice-Hall Inc., 1953.
—another text for public speech-making. One chapter on voice with exercises for breathing, projection, phonation, etc. One chapter on pronunciation and articulation

Rahskopf, Horace G. *Basic Speech Improvement.* New York: Harper & Row,
1965.
—another text on public speaking
—one chapter on voice production and one on vocal expression (pitch,
volume, articulation, etc.)—the usual stuff with the usual exercises

Thompson, Wayne N. and Seth A. Fessenden. *Basic Experiences in Speech.*
2nd ed. Englewood Cliffs, N.J.: Prentice-Hall Inc., 1958.
—brief, general discussion of voice. Good sections with exercises on
articulation and pronunciation

Index

Permissions